Collins

English GCSE for AQA

English
Targeting Grade C
Student Book

Keith Brindle
and Mike Gould

Matches the new
GCSE Specification

Published by Collins Education
An imprint of HarperCollins Publishers
77-85 Fulham Palace Road
Hammersmith
London
W6 8JB

Browse the complete Collins catalogue at
www.collinseducation.com

© HarperCollins Publishers Limited 2010

10 9 8 7 6 5 4 3 2 1

ISBN 978 0 00 734219 8

Keith Brindle and Mike Gould assert their moral rights to be
identified as the authors of this work.

British Library Cataloguing in Publication Data.
A Catalogue record for this publication is available from the
British Library.

Editor: Catherine Martin
Design and typesetting by EMC Design
Cover Design by Angela English
Printed and bound by L.E.G.O. S.p.A., Italy

Mixed Sources
Product group from well-managed
forests and other controlled sources
www.fsc.org Cert no. SW-COC-001806
© 1996 Forest Stewardship Council

FSC is a non-profit international organisation established to promote the
responsible management of the world's forests. Products carrying the FSC
label are independently certified to assure consumers that they come
from forests that are managed to meet the social, economic and
ecological needs of present and future generations.

Find out more about HarperCollins and the environment at
www.harpercollins.co.uk/green

Contents

What's it all about?

Being able to analyse the different kinds of non-fiction texts that we meet every day is an important life skill. It helps you understand how writers try to influence their readers. For the exam, you need to be able to move beyond describing what a text is about into explaining how effects are achieved and analysing why particular features are effective. The ability to compare texts will also help you to cope well with the demands of the exam.

How will I be assessed?

- You will get **20% of your English marks** for your ability to deal with close-reading questions in the exam.
- You will have to answer questions based on your reading of **three** non-fiction texts. You will not have seen these texts before the exam.
- The questions will carry a total of **40 marks**.

- This forms Section A of the exam paper and you will have **one hour** to complete it.

What is being tested?

You are being examined on your ability to

- read and respond to the texts, focusing on the questions
- select facts, details and quotations from the texts to answer the questions
- interpret the texts
- use evidence from the texts to support your answers
- compare the language used in the texts
- explain and evaluate how writers use language, grammar, structure and presentational features to achieve effects and engage and influence the reader.

Above all, it's important to understand the kinds of questions you are likely to be asked in the exam. This chapter will develop your close-reading and offer you practice in the necessary skills.

Understanding Non-fiction Texts and Writers' Choices

Introduction

This section of Chapter 1 helps you to

- explore a range of non-fiction texts and their features
- prepare to analyse texts in the exam.

Why is the close reading of different texts important?

- In everyday life, we are surrounded by texts which attempt to influence us, so knowledge of how they work is vital.
- You will be tested on your understanding of non-fiction texts in the exam.

A **Grade E** candidate will

- show some understanding of the texts and use some relevant quotation to support their ideas
- attempt to interpret features of the texts and offer some explanations.

E

A **Grade D** candidate will

- show understanding of the texts and use appropriate quotations to support their ideas
- interpret features of the texts and offer explanations that show understanding.

D

A **Grade C** candidate will

- show a clear understanding of the texts and use relevant quotations to demonstrate understanding
- offer clear explanations and will make personal and analytical responses, referring to specific aspects of language, grammar, structure and presentational features to justify their views.

C

Prior learning

Before you begin this unit, think about

- the many kinds of non-fiction texts you read in a day, and how they are different

Can you list them all? What are the main features of each one?

- the different purposes of those texts

Are they informing you, persuading you, entertaining you?

- what you learnt about non-fiction texts at Key Stage 3.

How many technical terms for features can you use: headline, caption, pull-quote?

What are non-fiction texts?

Learning objectives

- To consider a range of non-fiction texts.
- To begin to identify what makes them different.

What does the term non-fiction mean?

Non-fiction texts are about reality, for example:

- **journalistic text** – an article, a report, a leader from a newspaper
- **informative text** – a leaflet, a set of instructions, rules, a guide
- **biographical writing**, when someone writes about the life of someone else, or **autobiographical writing**, when they write about their own experiences
- **travel writing**
- an extract from a **diary** or a **blog**
- a **letter**, perhaps of a personal kind or for publication
- an **advertisement**
- a **webpage**.

In the exam, you will have to respond to three short non-fiction texts of different kinds. They will not be from a novel, short story or play and there will not be any poetry.

Checklist for success

- If you read a different kind of non-fiction text every day, you will become more used to their different purposes and styles.
- You need to read texts for more than just their meaning: ask yourself what the writer wants you to think and how the words and pictures influence you.

ACTIVITY

Make a log of the different non-fiction texts you have read today. For each kind of text, say why you read it.

Continue to keep your log of non-fiction texts for the next week.

Remember to include posters, notices and web texts in your list.

Focus for development:
Analysing textual features

Each form of non-fiction text has its own typical features that help you recognise what kind of text you are reading.

The exam will ask you about the language and presentational features of texts.

— dramatic caption

exciting language: 'murder mystery', 'tested', 'exposed', 'terrifying struggle for survival'

NOBODY'S SAFE!

This glossy murder mystery follows a group of family and friends who travel to a secluded island to attend a wedding – and find their lives in danger. As the festivities begin, friendships are tested and secrets are exposed as a murderer claims victims one by one – transforming the week of celebration into a terrifying struggle for survival. Followed by the second episode.

Harper's Island, 9pm and 9.40pm, BBC3, Sunday 6 September

Friendships get tested as a murderer preys on wedding guests

'glossy' women to go with text

clearly tells you when to watch

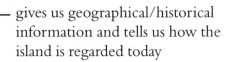
gives us geographical/historical information and tells us how the island is regarded today

Greek writing →

Mýkonos

Μύκυονος

ALTHOUGH MYKONOS IS DRY AND BARREN, its sandy beaches and dynamic nightlife make this island one of the most popular in the Cyclades. Under Venetian rule from 1207, the islanders later set up the Community of Mykonians in 1615 and flourished as a self-sufficient society. Visited by intellectuals in the early days of tourism, today Mýkonos thrives on its reputation as the glitziest island in Greece.

cute pelican →

← attractive/ colourful harbour

Petros the Pelican, the island mascot, in Mýkonos harbour in the morning.

Antarctica, 21 December 2009

5.15pm

Felix Brown:

personal comment →

Christmas is close and the temperature has rocketed by four degrees. Deep crevasses are opening in the ice and we'll be able to abseil down them soon. Mind you, we shouldn't be celebrating global warming.

story →

Because of the thaw, we can also take boat trips. It's safe, as long as you look out for icebergs! Yesterday we saw Orca whales swimming along, looking for food. Tremendous. The penguins are fabulous too, and so funny. One got confused and leapt into our boat. It shook its head, looked shocked, then dipped back into the sea. I am <u>so</u> lucky to be here …

Comment 21ˢᵗ Dec 2009 8.12 pm	SEE ALL COMMENTS (2) / ADD COMMENT
	It must be so cool to be right in amongst all that wildlife. I'd love to see an Orca in the wild!
	POSTED BY: WILL

comment by others   emotional comments →

AFTER THE RAIN, HERE COMES THE Sun

Drenched . . clear-up in Cockermouth yesterday

THE Sun joined the Cumbrian relief effort yesterday by helping people cut off by the devastating floods.

We took food to residents stranded when a raging river smashed the only bridge linking hundreds of locals with Workington.

The vulnerable and elderly like Agnes Bell have been particularly hard hit, so she was thrilled when we arrived with goodies from Asda. Great-gran Agnes, 84, said: "I am so pleased The Sun is helping us. When I heard that the bridge had gone I felt so alone.

"So many kind people have offered help. It makes you realise we have a great community."

Five hundred homes in Northside were cut off when the bridge over the Derwent collapsed on Friday, killing cop Bill Barker, 44.

It has turned a two-minute trip to town into a 20-mile detour.

Locals can collect food and toiletries from a supermarket-supported emergency aid station in the community centre.

Council officials have set up a Job Centre, GPs' surgery and a creche upstairs. Housing

BY ROBIN PERRIE

officer Estelle Kent, 44, said: "People have been cut off, so we're bringing services to them."

Engineers fear the town's sinking Calva Bridge may collapse. If it goes, 1,000 homes will lose their phoneline.

Tory leader David Cameron described the damage as "biblical" yesterday on a visit to flood-ravaged Cockermouth.

Warnings

Asked if his party would help people in the county if elected next year, he said: "Of course we will. They're going to need help."

Residents and business owners, meanwhile, continued to return. Alison Watson, 37, of Al's Toys, said: "This couldn't have come at a worse time."

Locals were hoping the floods would not return after up to **FOUR INCHES** of rain in Cumbria yesterday. Eight roads and 21 bridges remained closed.

Across Britain, there were 15 flood warnings in place last night – ten in North West England, three in Wales and one each in the Midlands and the North East.
r.perrie@the-sun.co.uk
The Sun Says – Page Eight

Visit . . . Cameron in Cockermouth

Supplies . . The Sun's Perrie with Agnes Bell

EXAM TASK

Using ideas from your discussion, write your answers to these questions:

- What is most noticeable about each text? Focus on the pictures, how the texts are laid out on the page and the kind of words and phrases chosen.
- In what ways are the texts different?
- Why has each text been written and who has it been written for? Explain your ideas by referring to the features you identify.

Remember

- **Gain a good knowledge of different kinds of non-fiction texts and their features.**
- **Think about how and why texts have been put together – it will prepare you for the type of questions in the exam.**

Focusing on purpose

Learning objectives

- *To explore writers' purposes.*
- *To read and analyse different kinds of texts.*

What does purpose mean?

Whenever anyone writes a text, they have an **aim** or **purpose**. For example, they could be writing to

- persuade the reader to buy a particular product
- entertain the reader
- inform the reader about an important issue.

Checklist for success

You need to identify

- the purpose of every text you read (why it has been written)
- which features make the text appropriate for that purpose
- why the writer includes each feature.

For all to see: Sarah laps up the glory next to her time display

Bolt 100m record is beaten by a cheetah

WORLD record 100m sprinter Usain Bolt may have thought he was pretty fast – until a cheetah lopped more than three seconds off his time. The Jamaican athlete ran 9.58sec last month but eight-year-old Sarah has managed the feat in just 6.13sec – meaning she is now officially the fastest land animal in the world. She was so quick around the track at Cincinatti Zoo in Ohio on Wednesday that she caught up with the lure encouraging her to run.

'I'm proud of Sarah every day of her life – she's a wonderful animal with a wonderful spirit,' said Cathryn Hilker, founder of the Cat Ambassador Program, which runs a cheetah exhibit at the zoo. But the record may soon fall – cheetah Zaza from South Africa is limbering up for an attempt in the next few weeks.

Blur: Usain Bolt broke his own 100m record last month

ACTIVITY

Read this short text from *The Metro News*.

Then discuss with a partner:

- which features are typically included in a newspaper report (see the example on page 9 for a reminder)
- which of these features appear in this report
- why this report has been written.

Here is part of one **Grade C** response focusing on the purpose of this text:

> The text is obviously meant to inform and interest us by using pictures of a beautiful cheetah and the fastest man on earth and telling us about the cheetah's new record. It's also supposed to make us laugh, with the cheetah sitting next to its record. We are also supposed to smile at the idea that Sarah has a rival who wants to be faster, just like a proper runner.

Notice how the student

- identifies the purpose clearly
- refers to the effect
- extends the comments
- gives evidence for each of her ideas.

Focus for development:
How adverts work

ACTIVITY

With a partner, read the advert below and decide what its purpose is. What does it want the reader to do?

Now take a closer look at each of its features. How does the advert appeal in order to achieve its purpose?

Complete a grid like this one.

Feature	Description of feature	Effect on the reader
Picture	It shows a bald man who looks like a potato!	The picture makes us laugh, and read further. The man is smiling and looks friendly so we are more likely to listen to his advice.
Layout (how it is organised)		
Fonts		
Colours		
Voice (how it speaks directly to 'you')		
Language		

POTATO LOVERS hate waste

I love spuds. So I store mine in a cool dark place to make them last longer. If they've gone sprouty, after a proper peel they're ready to mash. And I always like freezing any leftovers in bags for a quick and easy shepherd's pie topping. Lovely jubbly.

lovefoodhatewaste.com has more tips and recipes to help you waste less food and save up to £50 a month.

LOVE FOOD hate waste

EXAM TASK

Write up your points, explaining the advert's **purpose** and how it tries to achieve this.

> The purpose of this advertisement is…
>
> The advertisement makes us think of potatoes from first glance because…
>
> The man is…
>
> The whole use of colour is supposed to make us think…
>
> The heading focuses on…
>
> The main text reads as if… One sentence that is memorable is… This is good because…
>
> Overall, I think the text works well/does not work well because…

Remember

- Work out what the purpose is; it will always help you to interpret the text.
- Look closely at the language and the presentational features; these will have been chosen to support the purpose.

Audience

Learning objective

- To understand how texts are designed to attract a particular target audience.

⭐ **Examiner's tip**

Be aware of the fact that texts can have more than one specific audience. Peter Kaye's autobiography, for instance, would hope to appeal to fans, lovers of comedy or people who enjoy a 'light read' – perhaps while on holiday.

Why is it important to think about the audience?

Writers always keep their **audience** in mind, and write in an appropriate style for their readers. It could be a general readership, perhaps of a daily newspaper, or a specific readership, such as readers of *Bee-Keeper's Monthly*.

Being aware of the target audience helps you read texts more effectively.

Checklist for success

You need to

- think about how the words and the presentational features, such as pictures, have been used to appeal to the target audience.

Advertisers are particularly aware of their target audience and produce adverts specifically for that group. So, television adverts for toys might feature happy children to attract parents to buy.

ACTIVITY

The webpage below is from the Club 18–30 website.

Why do you think this might attract 18–30 year-olds to take one of these holidays?

repetition and list intended to make it sound exciting for 18–30s

adjectives to make it sound wonderful

attractive young people

nightclub colours

what 18–30s might like to do

Here are three brief extracts from student responses.

With a partner, decide why the E extract is weakest and what the others do better.

Grade E

> The picture has happy young people to make the audience interested.

Grade C

> The young adults in the picture look happy, which suggests to the reader that an 18–30 holiday might be just what they need too – it would be a good reason for going.

Grade D

> The young adults in the picture look happy, so the readers think they might be like that with 18–30.

ACTIVITY

Now look at this leaflet. It is aimed at a different tourist audience.

Working with a group, decide:

- What do the pictures tell us about the hotel? (What they suggest as well as what they show.)
- Why has the gold colour been used?
- How is the text set out and why?
- What can you say about the language used?
- What is the target audience for the text? Give your reasons.

Autumn & Winter 2009/2010

Best Western
WROXTON HOUSE HOTEL
Wroxton, Nr Banbury

Do you enjoy the finer things in life?

Excellent service
Award winning food
Cosy elegant lounges
Log burning fire
Superb location for exploring the Cotswolds

.....then visit Banbury's best kept secret!

W
H

AA
★★★
Hotel

EXAM TASK

Write your own response to this question:

> *What is the target audience for the Wroxton House Hotel leaflet and how successful will it be in attracting those visitors?*

Try to include the details from your group discussion.

Remember

- Always think about what audience the writer had in mind.
- Be prepared to write about both the presentational features and the language.

Exploring the effects of language

Learning objective

- *To learn about how language affects the reader.*

Glossary

similes: comparisons using 'like' or 'as'

metaphors: saying things which are not literally true, for example 'You get under my skin'

emotive language: language that affects our feelings or emotions

What do we mean by language?

You will be writing about the writer's **choice of words**. You might also comment on different sentence lengths or language techniques such as similes, metaphors and alliteration.

The language will be suited to the **purpose and audience**: it might be emotive or humorous or grimly factual.

In this piece of travel writing about 1920s Mexico, D H Lawrence captures the excitement as a crowd gathers to watch men dangling snakes from their mouths.

> …three thousand people had massed in the little *plaza*, secured themselves places on the roof and in the window-spaces, everywhere, till the small pueblo seemed built of people instead of stones. All sorts of people, hundreds and hundreds of white women, all in breeches like half-men, hundreds and hundreds of men who had been driving motor-cars, then many Navajos, the women in their full, long skirts and tight velvet bodices, the men rather lanky, long-waisted, real nomads. In the hot sun and the wind which blows the sand every day, every day in volumes round the corners, the three thousand tourists sat for hours, waiting for the show.

ACTIVITY

Which words give this description a flavour of Mexico?

Decide what effect is created by the long sentences. Do they make it sound slow and boring or busy and excited?

Which words or phrases emphasise how many people were there and what it was like? Select three and say what picture they paint for the reader.

Read this opening to a **Grade D** response which analyses how language is used in the extract.

> Lawrence is in a very busy place, because there are thousands of people. To give the impression, he uses words like 'hundreds and hundreds', which sounds as if there are lots. He also uses Mexican words like 'Navajos'.
>
> He gives you a picture of what is happening by giving a clear image: 'the small pueblo seemed built of people instead of stones'. There is also a simile, because the women were 'like half-men'.

For a better grade, this response would need to include more interpretation of **how** the language features are used to gain a certain reaction from the reader, thinking about

- the Mexican words
- images and metaphors
- vocabulary designed to give an impression of crushing
- repetition of 'every day'
- different sentence lengths.

EXAM TASK

Write your response to this question about the extract below.

> *How does the writer, Henry Winter, use language in this extract to affect our feelings about these football fans?*

Consider

- descriptive vocabulary
- the uses of metaphor
- emotive phrases.

As Burnley's magnificent fans made their way out of Turf Moor, muttering about how lucky Spurs had been and how proud they were of their claret-and-blue idols, a father tried to console his son. The lad's hair was damp from the rain and his face moist from the tears. 'Their legs went,' the father kept saying to the boy, 'they'd given everything.'

The lad was heart-broken, his mind too confused to take in the reasons for Burnley's late collapse…

from *The Telegraph*, 21 January 2009

ACTIVITY

Write your own answer to this question.

> *How does D H Lawrence bring to life the excitement of the event?*

Use this frame to help you.

- Start by saying briefly what happened.
- Explain the impressions created and how they were created.
- Use precise detail from the text to support your points.

For more on how to use quotations in your writing see pages 28–31.

Remember

- Interpret what the writer says to show how he/she wants the reader to react.
- Focus on the words, descriptive language and sentence lengths.
- Support what you say with close reference to the text.

Exploring presentational features

Learning objective

- To understand how to interpret and write about presentational features.

What are presentational features?

Presentational features are the visual elements of a text: colours, pictures and text boxes. Their arrangement on the page is the **layout**. When writing about them, you need to say how they are used.

Colours are usually chosen carefully to match the text and its message. For example, yellow might represent happiness or green might be used if dealing with environmental matters.

Pictures or illustrations will set a mood or appeal specifically to the audience.

The **layout** will hope to focus the reader's attention on the most important elements.

Checklist for success

When reading any media text, you need to do the following.

- Consider layout. (What do I notice first and why? Where do my eyes go next? How have these features been arranged?)
- Decide if the use of colour is significant. (Is there more of one colour? For example: Does the yellow represent sunshine? Is there red to suggest excitement?)
- Notice how pictures represent or add to what the text is saying.
- Think about how any other presentational features are intended to affect the reader.

Leaflets generally have to catch the reader's attention quickly, and be simple but effective. Design and presentation is therefore very important.

Examiner's tip

Generally, pictures support the text. They will either
- *add to what we are told*
- *or reflect what we are told.*

FREE eye test and
£50* off glasses
From Dollond & Aitchison

Book your FREE eye test and take advantage of your special offers today

It's not every day something of real value drops through the letterbox. At Dollond & Aitchison, we're committed to the highest level of eyecare and we'd like you to find out for yourself with this exclusive offer – a FREE eye test worth £27.50, as long as you visit us before 31st December 2009.

Not only that, we'd also like to offer you £30 cash back when you join our Contact Lenses By Post Scheme** and a FREE Contact Lens Assessment & Trial.

If you've never visited us before, you'll discover customer service built up over 250 years. We can offer extraordinary value on quality glasses and more, we'd also like to take this opportunity to give you £50 off a complete pair of new glasses® with the vouchers attached.

Combined with the FREE eye test, that's an incredible saving of over £100 on the health and look of your eyes.

Why have an eye test?

Looking after your eyes is our highest priority at D&A and an eye test is the best way to confirm they're in good condition.

An eye test can help pinpoint any health issues such as glaucoma and diabetes, so you'll have peace of mind.

Try contact lenses at D&A today

ACUVUE®
BRAND CONTACT LENSES
Johnson&Johnson

ACTIVITY

Read this opening to a **Grade D** response to the following question.

> *How are presentational features used in the optician's leaflet?*

> When you look at the leaflet, the first thing you notice is the woman. She looks rich and superior. Maybe that is how the glasses make you feel. The other woman is normal and must be wearing contact lenses. She is pretty though, so the lenses might be for pretty people. Every time you look at the leaflet, you notice FREE in block capitals, so it seems to be saying you won't spend any money, but then when you read the text...

Complete a table like this to evaluate the student's answer.

What has the student done well?	• looked closely at the pictures • • •
What can be improved?	• no mention yet of colour • •
What needs to be added?	• purpose and audience • mention of particular language such as... • •

EXAM TASK

Write a full analysis of how presentational features are used in the optician's leaflet.

- Decide on the purpose and audience.
- Say how each presentational feature contributes to the purpose and is designed to affect the target audience.

Remember

- **Link your comments about presentational features to the text's purpose(s).**
- **Consider the effects of layout, colour, pictures or font choices and how these appeal to the audience.**

Perspective and point of view

Learning
objective

- To learn how to
  identify and
  analyse the writer's
  perspective.

What does perspective mean?

A text will usually have a **point of view**, a perspective or 'angle' on its subject. This influences how we react to the content.

Checklist for success

- Read as many different kinds of non-fiction texts as you can.
- For each text, ask yourself what the writer thinks about the subject and how they want you to react.

The following extracts are taken from the book *Don'ts for Husbands,* published in 1913 and written by a woman.

> Don't drop, while alone with your wife, the little courtesies you would offer to other women. For instance, always get up to open a door for her, as you would for a lady guest.
>
> Don't refuse to play tennis or croquet or billiards with your wife because it is 'not worth while' to play games with a woman. If she plays badly, show her how to improve. She certainly won't play better by being left out of the game altogether.
>
> Don't insist on giving holidays to the servants during *your* holiday on the ground that your wife can 'manage' at the seaside. You are not the only person to be considered, and it's no holiday for her to be tied to the children day in and day out while you go golfing or fishing. Probably *she* would like to golf or fish as well if she got the chance.

ACTIVITY

Discuss these questions with a partner:

- What sort of life does the writer lead? How can you tell?
- What is her view of how a husband should treat his wife? Give examples from each paragraph.
- What attitudes is she arguing against?

Focus for development:
Understanding different perspectives

The perspective of the text can make the same subject seem very different. A writer can be for something, against it, or can offer a balanced viewpoint.

Read this view on smacking children, from actress Linda Robson. Then discuss the following with a partner:

- Find three points that show Linda Robson's view on smacking.
- How far do you agree with her view?

> They say you should pick on someone your own size – and smacking a child is picking on someone smaller. In fact, it's a form of bullying.
>
> I've got three kids aged 13, 17 and 26, and I've never smacked any of them. I've always found other, more effective ways of disciplining them.
>
> For younger children, I think tone of voice can be enough…

Now read another mother's response to Linda's view. Does it present a more balanced view? Why/Why not?

> I have never set out to hurt my children. I love them and would never hit them without due cause. No one should ever want to harm a child. There are times, though, when a little tap shows them something is wrong, and they won't do it again. For example, they must be stopped from running with scissors. They need that discipline. After all, it's less traumatic for them than being screamed at by a parent: that is much more violent…

A student writes…

I usually just ask myself, 'Is this written from a first person perspective?'; 'Is it biased or balanced?'; 'Am I taking the right approach?

Answer…

If you can decide what viewpoint the writer is adopting, that is a good beginning.

Write about the perspective in the mother's response about smacking.

Explain her viewpoint, supporting what you say with evidence from the text.

Remember

- **Identify the writer's point of view first. Then find evidence to support your choice. The perspective affects how the reader responds to the subject.**
- **Practise analysing perspective in texts and you will learn to spot viewpoints more easily in the exam.**

Glossary

anecdote: a short story that illustrates a point

What does analysing structure mean?

Structure is the way texts have been put together: how they start, develop and end, and how the different parts contribute to the overall purpose.

Checklist for success

You need to

- decide on the purpose of the text, then how the writing is structured to fulfil that purpose
- pay particular attention to how texts begin, develop and end
- focus on the techniques writers use to develop their points – for example, including quotations, anecdotes, facts, opinions and figures or contrasts.

Structure and purpose

Texts are structured in different ways depending on their purpose. Some writers of newspaper articles create a balanced argument, offering different viewpoints and ideas. Others might focus on just one argument or idea, as in the short report below.

gives summary of findings

summarises main argument

presents overview of problem

presents evidence to support main argument

ARCTIC GETS HOTTER

GREENHOUSE gases are being blamed for soaring Arctic temperatures – they are higher than at any time in the past 2,000 years.

US scientists examined ice cores, tree rings and lake sediments at 23 sites across the region to form a decade-by-decade picture of temperatures. And 1998 to 2008 stands out as the warmest decade in the entire series.

Darrell Kaufman of Northern Arizona University said: "The last half-century was the warmest of the 2,000-year record, and the last 10 years have been especially dramatic."

It backs up other reports, including NASA satellite measurements, which show Arctic sea ice is both shrinking in size and thinning.

The study's co-author David Schneider said: "Greenhouse gases from human activities are overwhelming the Arctic's climate system."

offers more supporting evidence

links back to the opening

ACTIVITY

Discuss these questions about the article with a partner.

- What techniques does the writer use to support his argument (look back at the checklist above)?
- How effective are the opening and ending?
- What might have been added in a more detailed text?

Focus for development:
Organising a text

Below are details from an article about Radio 1 DJ, Chris Moyles.

- Decide what description of Chris Moyles you could create from the details. Put the details into the best order to create this 'picture'.
- Be ready to explain your decisions.

1. Moyles' success is the result of professionalism for which he is rarely given credit.
2. His job appeared under threat recently but, whilst other presenters were sacked, he remained to rule the airwaves.
3. He first worked at a radio station as a schoolboy doing work experience.
4. 'I find his continued presence on Radio 1 unacceptable' said Oxford University's professor of broadcast media.
5. His programmes appear to 'just happen' but that cleverly disguises Moyles' real attention to detail.
6. He has been criticised for being racist, disliking gay people, and 'laddish'.
7. He is Radio 1's longest serving breakfast DJ.

Here is part of a formal letter to a newspaper. Write an analysis of the text explaining

- the writer's viewpoint
- how the writer uses facts and opinions in their argument
- how the structure supports that viewpoint.

You could use a writing frame like this:

- *The writer wants to...*
- *The letter starts with the writer explaining...*
- *In the second paragraph, the main point is developed by...*
- *To conclude, the writer...*

Sir,

I am tired of reading about young people running wild and terrorising their neighbourhoods. It is true that teenagers are not all angels but, similarly, they are not all bad, either.

Young people collect for charity, live as part of communities and are just as civilised as many older people. It is criminal to keep picking fault because of the behaviour of the few. Every year, British jails are filled with murderers, burglars and drug addicts: that does not make the entire adult population a set of criminals. In the same way, you should not generalise about the young.

We have our rights too: please remember that when you are reporting.

Remember

- **Always identify how the structure of the text supports its purpose.**
- **Analyse the structure stage-by-stage for the best results.**

Grade Booster

Extended Exam Task

Choose a lead story or article from a newspaper to use with this question.

> *What features can you find in the text that are typical of newspaper text's? How successfully have they been used?*

Focus on

- the headline
- any pictures or illustrations
- other presentational features
- the structure
- the story and/or argument
- the language used
- the writer's point of view.

Evaluation: what have you learned?

With a partner, use the Grade checklist list below to evaluate your work on the Extended Exam Task.

- I can say why texts have been produced and can identify the target audience.
- I can identify and explain why the language and presentational features of the text have been used.
- I can comment on the effects created.
- I can understand and explain clearly the writers viewpoints.
- I can include appropriate supporting quotations for the points I make.

- I can understand texts and am aware of their purposes.
- I can identify the text's language and presentational features and make comments on them.
- I can comment on writers' viewpoints.
- I can include some evidence for the points I make.

- I can make some points and attempt to interpret the text, using some relevant evidence.

F

- I can make a few points about the text, with limited explanation.

You may need to go back and look at the relevant pages from this section again.

Close Reading in the Exam

Introduction

This section of Chapter 1 helps you to

- focus on the reading skills you will have to show in the exam
- develop and practise these skills by analysing different non-fiction texts in detail.

What will close reading mean in the exam?

You will have to select the right material to answer the questions on the exam paper. These will require the following skills:

- Finding information in the text
- Dealing with inference – what the text is suggesting
- Analysing the language and presentational features.

A **Grade E** candidate will

- show some understanding of the texts and use some relevant quotations to support their ideas
- attempt to interpret features of the texts, offer some explanations and attempt to compare the texts when asked.

E

A **Grade D** candidate will

- show that they understand the texts and use some relevant quotations to support their ideas
- interpret features of the texts, offer explanations which show understanding and compare the texts when asked.

D

A **Grade C** candidate will

- show clearly that they understand the texts and use relevant quotations to show their understanding
- show that they engage with the content of texts and interpret them through the writer's choice of language, presentational features and structure
- offer clear explanations and make clear and appropriate comparisons when asked.

C

Prior learning

Before you begin this unit, think about

- what you have already learnt in school about language, structure and presentational features in non-fiction texts (look back at pages 14–15, 16–17 and 20–21 if you need to)
- what features you are likely to consider when comparing texts
- the different kinds of texts you read every day.

Have you thought about the use of colour or font size and why a particular picture or headline has been used?

Think about the 'story', the message, the writer's viewpoint, the purpose, audience, language and presentation.

As you read newspapers, letters, leaflets and notices, focus on **how** they have been written.

Selecting and putting together information

Learning objectives

- To understand the need to select the right information.
- To learn how to put together relevant information.

What does selecting and putting together information mean?

To respond to questions with authority, you first need to be able to **select** the details from the text that are most relevant to answering the question.

You then link these details logically as you comment. For example, you might put together three relevant related points or develop a point using more than one piece of evidence.

Checklist for success

Whenever you write about texts, you need to make sure

- the information you select answers the question
- any quotation or reference to the text actually supports the point you are making.

ACTIVITY

Look at the advertisement on the opposite page. With a partner, answer the following question.

- What do we learn from the advertisement about Herta Frankfurter sausages? List your points.

Now, look back at the information you have written down. Have you included information from

- the text at the top
- the text in red and black under the picture
- the details on the right hand side?

If necessary, add more points.

ACTIVITY

Looking back at the information you selected, write a response to this question.

- What reasons does the advertisement give for buying Herta Frankfurters? Think about how this information is presented. Consider the effect of

- images
- headlines
- colour.

Try to develop your points, putting different pieces of information together to explain them.

Focus for development: Putting ideas together

In the exam, one question is likely to ask you to write about information you find, rather than just listing points.

Notice how the annotations around this text pick out details to answer the question:

How does Shaq try to attract viewers to his television series?

Shaq tells Becks that the football's in his court

Jeered by ungrateful LA Galaxy fans, David Beckham has now fallen foul of a true American sporting icon.

Shaquille O'Neal, the NBA basketball legend, has challenged Beckham to a game of "soccerball" in a new all-star reality TV series, *Shaq Vs*, in which the hoop king takes on his sporting peers at their own game.

Shaq will swim against Michael Phelps, the Olympic champion, fight the former world boxing champion Oscar De La Hoya and challenge Serena Williams to a set of tennis in the Disney series.

But will the England star play ball? Negotiations are under way through the traditional medium of Twitter.

"Dear david beckham," tweets Shaq. "I kno u heard about my *Shaq Vs* show, anyway u will never score a goal on me, I challenge you lil man."

With no reply forthcoming, O'Neal upped the ante. "David beckham I kno u hear me, dnt be scared, dnt make me call u out, u will never score a goal on me." And finally: "Dnt make me tweet to 2 million people that yur scared of shaq, u betta respnd, if u scared get a dog."

With Shaq on his back, as well as the Galaxy boo boys, perhaps Becks should invest in a rottweiler.

The Times 29 July 2009

— issues challenges to other
famous sporting figures

— some he will
compete against

— using Internet to
generate interest

— challenging David
Beckham

This is how two students responded to the question.

Grade D response

Shaq does a lot of things to attract viewers. He has challenged David Beckham to play him at soccer. He has challenged other sporting people as well for his Disney series. He is also insulting Beckham which might appeal to some people and make them interested in him.

Grade C response

Shaquille O'Neal wants to attract viewers to his television show so he has challenged a number of sporting figures, who are well-known. He will swim against Michael Phelps, box the ex-world champion Oscar De La Hoya and play tennis against Serena Williams. Finally, he generates interest by trying to get David Beckham on the programme and by pretending to threaten him on Twitter: 'if you scared, get a dog'.

ACTIVITY

Decide exactly why the second answer is better.
Think about:

- the precise details used
- the way the ideas are organised and put together
- how the Grade C response starts
- how the first sentence is explained
- how the student deals with the points related to David Beckham.

EXAM TASK

Re-read the report about Shaq and Becks.
How does Shaq try to persuade David Beckham to come on to his show?

Examiner's tip ★

Start with a general statement then put in as many details as you can to explain it.

Remember

- **Make sure you select evidence that is appropriate to the question or to the point you are making.**
- **Put material together with care, so that relevant points are linked together.**

Using quotations and examples effectively

Learning objective

- To learn how to use evidence to support the points you make.

⭐ **Examiner's tip**

Always use the Point, Evidence, Explanation technique (P.E.E.) in your answers. If you do, the marker knows where you got the idea from and that you can explain the effect of each detail in the text.

What are the essential features of evidence?

When you write about non-fiction texts in the exam, you will need to use evidence from the text to support your points.

What this **evidence** is depends on the question being asked but you are most likely to be using a direct quotation from the text or picking out details about the text's layout or presentational features.

Checklist for success

You need to

- remember that any analytical points you make require proof from the text
- select **brief** quotations – usually no longer than two lines
- refer to detail and make your examples precise, rather than offering generalised thoughts. For example, 'We know the rescue has been successful because the woman in the picture is smiling. This makes us think…'

ACTIVITY

Here are two examples of evidence. What does the second example include that the first one does not?

The family looks silly and happy.

The family looks silly because they are wearing cat costumes and we know they are happy because the parents are smiling and the boy is playing.

The second example is better, because of the evidence and explanation supporting the points being made.

Focus for development: Using evidence well

It's important to select the best quotations to be convincing in your exam answers.

Read this letter which was sent to a local newspaper, in which the writer makes a series of points about his disappointment when trying to find peace on a day of remembrance in his local churches.

NO PEACE TO BE FOUND IN THE HOUSE OF GOD

September 11th is a date we all know – the anniversary of the attack on the Twin Towers in New York. Over three hundred firefighters died that day – and as a firefighter myself, it is not a moment I will ever forget.

Each year, when not working, I try to find some peace to remember the fallen. I live in the country, so my local church is always open and I use that as my sanctuary.

However, this year, I was visiting your city and was saddened to find all the churches locked. I can understand why, with all the vandalism that takes place, but I was upset that there was apparently nowhere for me to go.

When I e-mailed the church nearest to my mother's house, I got a short, sharp reply saying that the church would not be open. The message was not even signed.

I drove around the district in the morning, but it was the same everywhere. Since all places of worship were closed, my wife and I headed for the Cathedral. We knew that would be open every day.

How foolish we were! The noise inside was unbelievable. We hoped for peace and meditation – what we got was chatter and laughter from those working inside and loud comments from other visitors who were viewing an exhibition inside. With the busy bustle from the shopping area, we might just as well have been in the city's market.

Sanctuary? No peace inside

We moved as far as we could from the disturbances and sat in the front pew, only to have a female cleric arrive with a visitor in a suit: they stood beside us and discussed the planned visit by the mayor the next day, where he should sit and what he needed to do. They had no manners and no respect for us or the building.

When we crossed to sit at the other side, a man came in and sat beside us and repacked his chocolate bars and crisps in his Morrison's bag. Unbelievable!

I know the church is trying to attract new worshippers by encouraging all kinds of people to enter, not just the old and committed. But I for one will never set foot in the Cathedral again.

Where there should have been peace, there was noise and disturbance. Heaven alone knows what the builders of such a beautiful shrine to the almighty would think, when worshippers are treated so badly.

ACTIVITY

Copy and complete this table, which focuses on what the man's feelings were and the evidence for this in the letter.

Point	Evidence	Explanation of effect
He struggled to find a peaceful place	•	•
Several unfortunate and noisy incidents upset him in the cathedral	• 'We hoped for ... what we got was chatter and laughter from those working inside' • •	• Contrast between first part and second part of sentence – what they wanted and what they got... • •
He is very unhappy about the changes to the Cathedral	•	•
He uses powerful language to emphasise his feelings	• •	• •
The ending sums up his emotions	•	•

A good answer will use this P.E.E. technique.
For example:

> He uses powerful language to emphasise his feelings:
> 'Heaven alone knows...' He sounds upset and we can
> imagine the emotion as he says those words.

However, if you can move beyond a relatively simple explanation (P.E.E.) into **analysis**, with extended thoughts about the evidence (P.E.**A.**), you will gain better marks. For example, by adding extra thoughts to the example above:

> ... we can imagine the emotion as he says those words.
> They are particularly appropriate with his call to 'heaven',
> for he is in a cathedral and it is to heaven that he is
> looking, for its peace. Whereas many people might say
> casually 'Heaven knows...', he is writing what he really
> means.

Notice how the student has explored the meaning of one word in detail.

Examiner's tip ★

*Looking closely at individual words can lead to higher marks. Where possible, try to think about a word's **connotations**. This means what it suggests or any associations it has. For example, the word 'red' literally means the colour red, but its connotations are passion, romance, anger or sometimes warning.*

EXAM TASK

Write a response to this question, trying to use the P.E.A. approach.

> **Why does the writer of 'No peace to be found in the house of God' feel so strongly about what happened that he had to write the letter?**

- Explain why the writer was in the Cathedral.
- Work through what happened and his feelings.
- Support each point you make with evidence – in most cases, a quotation – and explanation or analysis.

Remember

- **Find evidence for each point, then explain or analyse it.**
- **Good answers are usually sprinkled with short quotations.**

Drawing inferences

What does inference mean?

When you make an inference, you look beyond the obvious thing someone has said or written, and think about what they are suggesting. You read 'between the lines'.

So, if someone writes, 'her hairstyle is really quite interesting', you might wonder what 'interesting' really suggests and conclude that the writer was less than impressed.

ACTIVITY

What might be being suggested in each of these examples?
- 'Anyone who sees your paintings can tell that you try really hard.'
- 'Don't worry: every grey hair you grow makes me love you more.'
- 'No one will be losing their job today.'

ACTIVITY

What can you work out about this family, from the picture?
A few things are obvious, but you will need to **infer** others.

Focus for development:
How texts make suggestions

Sometimes, we gain an impression from a whole text; at other times, we respond to particular words or phrases.

On your own, read the newspaper report below. Then answer these questions, which focus on what the text suggests.

- Which words or phrases suggest the gardener's actions are not normal?
- Explain what each one makes the reader think.
- How does the picture add to this impression of the gardener?
- What is the attitude of the writer to what has happened? Is he amazed, shocked or amused, for example? Find evidence to support your view and comment on how the writer's viewpoint affects the reader.

Wednesday, November 25, 2009 **Sun** 35

MADNESS ON A RIDE-ON MOWER

Are you off yer hedge?

By RICHARD WHITE

A POTTY gardener trims his hedge — using a sit-on lawnmower and a CRANE.

Drivers screeched to a halt as they watched the grinning man slice through the foliage after getting a pal to hoist him skywards.

He spent 20 minutes balancing precariously on top of the 6½ft high bush in Cambridge, New Zealand.

One passer-by said: "His wife was horrified, he's lucky he wasn't killed."

Sun gardener Peter Seabrook said: "This certainly isn't a method I'd recommend. Apart from the obvious danger, he probably didn't get the even cut he wanted." r.white@the-sun.co.uk

Here are two students' responses and the marker's comments on how they wrote.

> *The writer is amused because at the end he says 'he didn't get the even cut he wanted'. At the start, he calls him 'potty' too...*

This is from a **Grade D** response – it has well-chosen support and shows understanding, though the quotation is not explained. The student understands the writer is amused but fails to add detail and clarify the point.

> *The writer is telling us the story with tongue-in-cheek because he quotes a gardening expert at the end 'he didn't get the even cut he wanted'. He is making a joke of the fact that after all the gardener's efforts, he did not make a success of trimming the hedge.*

This is from a **Grade C** response. The point is proven and explained. The student also makes an inference about the writer's attitude which is explained appropriately.

As we read **biography** and **autobiography**, we enjoy finding out about a particular person and the events in their life, but we also make inferences about them and their character. We interpret them through the words the writer chooses.

This is an **autobiographical** extract, in which the writer meets a bookseller in Afghanistan.

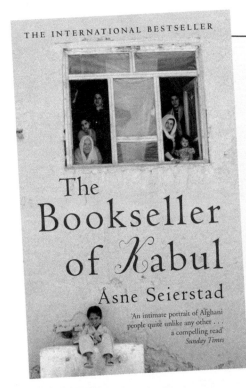

THE INTERNATIONAL BESTSELLER

The
Bookseller
of *Kabul*
Åsne Seierstad

'An intimate portrait of Afghani
people quite unlike any other . . .
a compelling read'
Sunday Times

One day he invited me home for an evening meal. His family – one of his wives, his sons, sisters, brother, mother, a few cousins – was seated on the floor round a sumptuous feast.

Sultan recounted stories, the sons laughed and joked. The atmosphere was unrestrained. [...] But I soon noticed that the women said little. Sultan's beautiful teenage wife sat quietly by the door with the baby in her arms. His first wife was not present that evening. The other women answered questions put to them, accepted praise about the meal, but never initiated any conversation [...]

On a foggy day in February I moved in with the family. [...] I was given a mattress on the floor next to Leila, Sultan's youngest sister, who had been assigned the task of looking after my well-being.

'You are my little baby,' the nineteen-year-old said the first evening. 'I will look after you,' she assured me and jumped to her feet every time I got up.

Sultan had ordered the family to supply me with whatever I wanted. I was later told that whoever did not comply with this demand would be punished.

The Bookseller of Kabul, Asne Seierstad

ACTIVITY

Produce two lists of points in answer to these questions, with quotations to prove them.

- What do we know about life in Sultan's home?
- What is the writer's view of it all? (For example, what might she be thinking when she writes, 'The other women ... never started any conversation'?)

A student writes...

It always seems easiest to just copy out sections of the text when answering ...

Answer...

Always keep quotations brief: a couple of lines at most. Only include the parts of the text which are relevant to your answer.

EXAM TASK

Turn your lists of points about the extract into a full answer to this question:

> *What sort of life does the writer find in Sultan's home and what does she seem to think about it?*

Make sure you identify details in the text and comment on

- the effect they have on the reader
- the writer's view (make inferences about what she is suggesting).

Remember

- **Focus on events but also make inferences and comment on what is being suggested.**
- **Look for what you can say about people's attitudes or views.**

Writing about presentational features and language

What does writing about presentational features and language involve?

Presentational features are usually the first things we notice in a text – the pictures, headings and text boxes. They are there to create an effect: to make the reader react or think in a certain way.

You will need to answer a question about these features in the exam and show you understand how they **link to the purpose** of the text.

There will also be a question in the exam on exploring the writer's **choice of language** and the effects this creates.

Checklist for success

- You need to decide how the presentational features are used and explain **how** the language affects the reader.

When writing about the presentational features of a text, you might find it useful to follow these three steps:

- Decide on the purpose and audience.
- Identify the writer's point of view.
- Work though the features, commenting on how each one is intended to affect the audience – what it makes them think or feel – and linking them to the text's purpose.

ACTIVITY

Read this section from a longer text.

Working in a group, discuss these questions:

- What is the purpose and audience of the text? How do you know?
- Which presentational features would you comment on?
- What would you say about how each one is used?
- How do the features link to the language used in the text?

HAVE YOU GOT money flu?

Here's how to fight off the spending bug

Whether it's keeping up with the constant string of parties or your inability to resist the 'bargain' sales, affluenza (living beyond your means) is highly contagious at this time of year. Luckily for you, after a quick consultation with our experts, you can boost your immunity *and* your bank balance.

SYMPTOM YOU CAN'T SEPARATE 'WANT' FROM 'NEED'

OK, it's winter and of course a nice wool coat is essential, but do you *really* need a brand new one? We're all guilty of spending on the non-essentials, but if you regularly put off paying the gas bill because you've convinced yourself you 'need' something else, it's a problem.
CURE: "Work out how much cash you have left *after* paying off your bills," says Katie Edwards, from debt experts Ladies In The Red (www.ladiesinthered.com). "If all you have left is money on your credit card, that's *not* spare cash. Prevent irrational spending by locking your credit card in a box, hiding it and giving the key to a trusted friend. Then sew some new buttons on your old coat."

Woman cannot live on shoes alone

SYMPTOM YOU CAN'T RESIST TREATING YOURSELF

SYMPTOM YOU STRUGGLE TO KEEP UP WITH YOUR FRIENDS

SYMPTOM YOU CAN'T RESIST THE SALES

When asked how presentational features were used in this text, two students responded like this:

Grade D response

> We know that the woman is obsessed with her shoes because she is staring at one of them and there are other shoes all around her. Her fridge is full of shoes but she cannot eat them because women cannot live on shoes alone. We can see that there must be something wrong with her and so it links with the headline – 'Have you got money flu?' We know she must have a kind of illness, especially because 'money flu' is in red and stands out ...

Examiner's comment: Understanding is shown throughout, and the beginnings of explanation ('because she is staring' and 'we can see that there must be something wrong with her'). However, there is no clear sense of why the features are there or how they are being used – or of the purpose and audience for the text.

Grade C response

— identifies purpose and audience

> The writer wants to stop women spending money unnecessarily. The picture is of a typical young woman (with painted toenails and make-up) who is clearly unhappy, and gazing at a golden shoe, like Cinderella. She will not go to the ball, because she has got 'flu'. The word is highlighted in red, like her T-shirt and nail varnish, and like the subheadings. This links to the idea of being 'in the red' or in debt, as in the name of the expert's website 'www.ladiesinthered.com'.

provides evidence

links red features in text and picture

— offers extended explanation

Examiner's comment: This is a Grade C response. The purpose and audience are set out in the first sentence and, rather than being written about individually, the effects of the presentational features are linked as the notes above show.

Read through the examiner comments on the Grade C answer, then complete your own response

- using ideas from your group discussion and evidence from the text
- linking presentational features to purpose and audience.

Focus for development: Language features

Language features will be present in any text analysis. The important thing is not to try and write about them all. Instead, focus on the ones that are most relevant to the question. To write about the language, you might follow these three steps:

- Identify what the text is saying and the writer's viewpoint.
- Decide on the writer's attitude – whether he/she is amused, excited, being coldly analytical or whatever.
- Find at least four words, phrases or sentences that are typical of the text and which you could analyse: for example
  - a simile
  - a metaphor
  - a short sentence
  - a gripping opening.

⭐ **Examiner's tip**

Focus on trying to find language which is 'typical' of the text. It is then easier to say why it has been used – it will be appropriate for the writer's purpose and will fit with his point of view.

ACTIVITY

Re-read the 'Money flu' text on page 37 again and make notes on the first two steps above.

Then copy and complete this grid, adding any extra language features you wish to comment on.

Language feature	Link to purpose	How it is used
Women cannot live on shoes alone	Text is saying some women waste too much money on non-essentials	<ul><li>Variation of 'cannot live on bread alone'</li><li>Paying the bills is more important than shoes</li><li>To amuse</li><li>Link to picture – shoes like food</li><li>'alone': she looks alone!</li></ul>
how to fight off the spending bug		
affluenza		

On your own, read the text below carefully.
Then write your response to these questions.

- How are the presentational features used in this article?
- How has the writer used language to interest the reader?

SHOPTALK

HIGH STREET BUYER'S GUIDE ruki.sayid@mirror.co.uk

Glamazon? I think not

THE huge warehouse could be just another faceless building nestling in the shadow of a motorway.

Yet this grotty location off the M1 in Bedfordshire is a real life Santa's Grotto.

The warehouse, which is the size of eight football pitches, is run by one of Britain's busiest online stores – amazon.co.uk.

Tens of thousands of boxes are piled high, while row upon row of metal shelves house countless racks of books, CDs, DVDs, video games and toys.

The interior not only looks like the world's biggest library, it has the same air of silent toil.

At times the only sound is the stamp of the machine that scans parcels and puts on an address label.

This was a rare glimpse behind the scenes at Amazon which expects to process at least a million orders a day at Christmas.

Allan Lyall, the firm's vice-president of European operations, says: "We are on to an order within four hours of a customer placing it online. At their click of a mouse, we swing into action as the product is picked from the shelf, packed, scanned, labelled and out."

There are 1,000 staff at the Marston Gate warehouse near Milton Keynes – and Amazon has 3,000 more in four other areas

With Brits expected to spend £7billion on Christmas and almost nine out of 10 adults buying online, the company has to be slick. Which is why I was told off for moving an item several feet from its original location.

It's a rigid system with no room for frivolity.

The pickers methodically go about their business, electric scanners in hand, piling goodies into boxes.

The boxes are then transported on conveyor belts to the packers who encase them in cardboard, stick a barcode on and pop them on another moving belt to be machine weighed, addressed and stamped before being sorted into areas for next-day delivery.

The 24-hour business may not have the fairytale Disney feel of Santa's work-shop but for millions of armchair shoppers looking for a merry click-mas, Amazon does the job.

Allan says: "We can even take an order at 8.30am on Christmas Eve and guarantee same-day delivery in London and Birmingham."

Savvy online shoppers can cash in on the e-tailers' free delivery for orders that can wait three to five days. This will leave a little extra cash to spend on carrots for the reindeer.

BOOK BEHIND THE SCENES
Ruki in the massive warehouse

PICTURES: IAN VOGLER

WIN SUPERHERO BEN10'S JACKET

SUPERHERO Ben10 is starring in a new film which had its world premiere in London and airs on Cartoon Network on Saturday.

Ten fans who attended the screening of Ben10: Alien Swarm, won one of his trademark leather jackets. And we have the 11th to give away after being worn by Perri Kiely, pictured with Alesha Dixon, who performed at the bash with Diversity.

Send your entries to: Daily Mirror, Shoptalk, Ben 10 Jacket, PO Box 6867, London E14 5AN, to arrive by Friday, December 4. Include your name, address and daytime phone number.

The Editor's decision is final and usual Daily Mirror rules apply.

Who performed at the Ben10: Alien Swarm world premier?
A) Jedward.
B) Diversity.
C) JLS.

Comparing texts

Learning objective

■ To understand how language comparison questions work in the exam.

 Examiner's tip

It is vital to compare things that are actually comparable, for example how sentence length or particular words are used in the texts. 'Comparing' metaphors with alliteration, for example, is unlikely to earn the best marks.

Will there definitely be a comparison question in the exam?

You will always have to compare two texts. At Foundation tier, you will need to compare the **presentational features** of the texts. At Higher tier, you will need to compare the **language** in the texts.

Checklist for success

Here are two different ways of comparing for you to consider. You might

- make a general statement of comparison, then work though features, comparing them as you go:

    picture in Text 1 / picture in Text 2

    colour in Text 1 / colour in Text 2

- work through Text 1, writing about its features – for example, a simile, use of alliteration, pun – then work through the features of Text 2 in a similar way, but mentioning how these differ from Text 1.

Comparing presentational features

Here are two football products: a matchday programme and a sports magazine cover. Take a careful look at their presentational features.

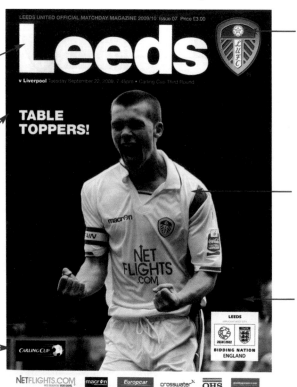

makes club and badge prominent

heading dominates programme – other necessary information very small above it

catchy subheading; stands out in white

player celebrating

shows crowd and referee, but not centre of attention

shows sponsor's logo clearly

puts title behind head – Michael Owen is more important than name of magazine

focuses on famous player to attract readers – looks like a man worthy of respect

makes people want to read lead article (can't read it elsewhere)

uses red as main colour for whole cover, matching the shirt colour

attracts readers with different sporting interests

quotation to grab attention

sense of fans watching but Owen is the focus

big names to attract football fans

shows variety of material on offer inside

October 2009
SKY SPOR
magazi

EXCLUSIVE LIVE SPORTS GUIDE
UEFA Champions League
Four Nations Rugby League
Heineken Cup
Coca-Cola Football League
ICC Champions Trophy
La Liga
Super League Grand Final
And full 31-day listings
for October

EXCLUSIVE
"He deserves more respect"
Jamie Carragher on Michael Owen and Liverpool v Manchester United

Rangers v Celtic
Why there's nothing like an Old Firm match

PLUS
Stuart Barnes on Brian O'Driscoll
Ronnie O'Sullivan answers your questions

ACTIVITY

Make lists of
- the presentational features that are similar
- what is different about the presentation of the two texts.

Examiner's tip

At home, practise comparing whenever you can, by reading
- *magazine covers – deciding why they are different*
- *adverts – looking at how they are designed*
- *newspaper reports and articles – comparing the language and pictures.*

Here is the opening of a **Grade C** response comparing the presentational features of both front covers:

> Because a programme is produced mainly for the home fans, buyers would know the player. By having the young player looking excited in the Leeds programme, it would attract the home fans. It helps if readers know a footballer on a magazine cover, so the picture of Michael Owen, who plays for England, must have been chosen to get football fans generally to buy the magazine.
>
> The texts obviously have things in common. In each case, the focus is on the player and the crowd is fuzzy in the background because they don't matter. The first thing you notice is the difference in attitude of the two players. Michael Owen looks cool and serious, as if we should have respect for him. The Leeds player looks younger and much more excited, as if he has just become a 'Table Topper.' He seems to be screaming, which shows his happiness. His white kit stands out against the darker background to make it seem bright and attractive. That headline says that Leeds are at the top of the league – in white again, to match with the kit – whereas the other cover has mostly red showing because that is the colour of Owen's shirt...

ACTIVITY

Work with a partner to analyse the **Grade C** response.
- At the start, locate the comparisons and the mention of purposes and audience.
- Find all the points of comparison.
- Find all the explanations of why things are there and how they are used.
- Identify any ideas that are developed beyond just a simple point.

On your own, complete the comparison of the two football texts.

Comparing language

This is the start of an article from a national newspaper:

> Let's think the unthinkable: is anything in life more boring than football?
> It seems more important than any other element of life in modern
> Britain, but in reality it is about as exciting as queuing at Sainsbury's. A
> typical afternoon? Ninety minutes of watching distant figures running
> around chasing a lump of leather; one goal – a scrambled effort as
> twenty-two athletes throw themselves into a heaving, muddy
> melee; thirty pounds paid and nothing to show for it but a
> soaking pair of trousers and a sore throat.
>
> Dull, dull, dull. Who cares about the FA Cup? Even the World
> Cup? The British are better at cycling and swimming – that's
> what we should be getting excited about, if anything, not the
> League Cup or the Egg Cup…

ACTIVITY

You are going to compare the language used in this newspaper article with the language used on the cover of *Sky Sports Magazine* (on page 41). Start by

- noting down some initial points of comparison
- listing four or five language features of each text to write about.

In this case, you are going to use this three-step structure to compare them:

- First, offer general comparative statements.
- Next, write in detail about the language on the magazine cover.
- Then, writing about the article's language, make any comparisons you can.

A student writes…

Do we have to make a comparison using four or five features? That sounds a lot.

Answer…

In any comparison, you will have to decide how many points you are able to make, and how many direct comparisons you can find.

EXAM TASK

Write your own comparison of the way language is used on the cover of *Sky Sports Magazine* and in the newspaper article.

Use the notes you made on the two texts and follow the three steps provided above.

Remember

- **Decide how you are going to organise your comparison.**
- **Link ideas clearly when comparing the texts.**
- **Do not just make general statements – make sure you explain or analyse details of the texts' features.**

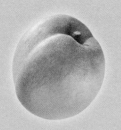

Nature perfected the fruit.

We perfected the pack.

SPC Nature's Finest fruit is picked when perfect and then packed in juice with no added colours or artificial flavours. Find it in the packaged fruit aisle.

Fuss free fruit.

www.surprisingfruityfacts.co.uk
'SPC Nature's Finest' is a Registered trademark of SPC Ardmona Operations Ltd.

Extended Exam Task

How does this advert attempt to tempt the reader?

Write about the

- purpose and likely audience
- colours and the two sections
- pictures
- main messages in the text
- language used.

Evaluation: what have you learned?

With a partner, use the grade checklist below to evaluate your work on the Extended Exam Task.

- I can write appropriately about purpose and audience, presentation, language and the writers' viewpoints.
- I can link what I say to the texts' purposes.
- I can support my ideas with relevant evidence from the texts.

- I can understand texts' purposes and audiences.
- I can write about presentation, language and viewpoints in texts.
- I can use some appropriate evidence for my ideas.

- I can comment on the purpose and audience, presentation and language of the text, using some evidence.

- I can comment on some things about the text that are relevant, mentioning purpose and audience, colours, pictures and the language.

You may need to go back and look at the relevant pages from this section again.

Exam Preparation
Unit 1A: Reading Non-fiction Texts

Introduction

In this section you will

- find out the exact facts about, and requirements of, Unit 1A, the Reading section of the exam
- read, analyse and respond to the sorts of texts you will face in the exam
- answer the sorts of questions you will face in the exam
- assess the quality of sample answers by different candidates
- evaluate and assess your answers and the progress you have made.

Why is exam preparation like this important?

- If you know exactly what you need to do, you will feel more confident when you sit the real exam.
- You need to be able to work under timed conditions: in the sample tasks you can learn what is required of you in an hour.
- Answering the questions yourself, then judging your answers against answers written by others will help you see what you need to do to improve your own work.

Key Information

Unit 1 is Understanding and Producing Non-Fiction Texts.

- It has an exam of **2 hours**, worth **80 marks.**
- It is worth **40%** of your overall English GCSE mark.
- Section A of the exam is on Reading.
- Section B of the exam is on Writing.

Section A Reading

- The reading part of the exam is **1 hour** long, and is worth **40 marks**.
- It is worth **20%** of your overall English mark.

The reading exam

You will have to read three non-fiction texts.

- The **Foundation Tier paper** will have **five** questions:
  - **Question 1:** finding relevant information in a text **(4 marks)**
  - **Question 2:** explaining what is suggested in a text **(4 marks)**
  - **Question 3:** explaining what is suggested in a text **(8 marks)**
  - **Question 4:** analysing how language is used in a text **(12 marks)**
  - **Question 5:** comparing how presentational features are used in two texts.

    (12 marks)

- The **Higher Tier paper** will have **four** questions:
  - **Question 1:** finding information in a text **(8 marks)**
  - **Question 2:** analysing the presentational features of a text **(8 marks)**
  - **Question 3:** explaining what is suggested in a text **(8 marks)**
  - **Question 4:** comparing the language used in two texts **(16 marks)**

The Assessment

The assessment objective for reading (AO3) states that you must be able to do the following:

- Read and understand texts, selecting material appropriate to purpose, collating from different sources and making comparisons and cross-references as appropriate.
- Develop and sustain interpretations of writers' ideas and perspectives.
- Explain and evaluate how writers use linguistic, grammatical, structural and presentational features to achieve effects and engage and influence the reader.

Targeting Grade C

Some of the key differences between a Grade D and a Grade C are as follows:

Grade D candidates	See examples on pages 52, 57 and 58
<ul><li>show some understanding of texts</li><li>use evidence to support what they say</li><li>are able to interpret the text</li><li>can compare texts and make connections between them.</li></ul>	**D**

Grade C candidates	See examples on pages 52, 53, 55, 56 and 58
<ul><li>show clearly that the texts are understood</li><li>use appropriate evidence to support their views</li><li>offer relevant interpretations of the texts</li><li>make clear connections and comparisons</li><li>leave the reader in no doubt that they know why and how particular features have been used.</li></ul>	**C**

Item 1

Marathon runner Ron Hill tells of when he was a boy and his dog fell though some frozen ice.

The dog that nearly drowned

I called and called and Bruce began to make his way back, but after a couple of feet the ice became too thick and Bruce couldn't make any further progress. He tried to climb on to the ice but his paws just kept slipping off. After three or four minutes his efforts began to get weaker and weaker and he began to whine. I just couldn't leave him like that, he was loved like one of the family. I'd got him in, so it was up to me to get him out again. I looked around; but there was no one about and I slipped off my clothes until I had on only a pair of swimming trunks, which I was going to wear under my shorts in the afternoon.

I kneeled on to the ice and began to crawl out towards the dog. As I edged closer I could feel the ice beginning to bend, so I stretched out flat trying to reach as far forward as I could for his paws. I slithered slowly out and was just reaching for his collar when the ice gave way and in I went. The shock was terrific! It took my breath away, and all I could gasp was, 'Aagh!' My first thought was of getting my legs caught in weeds or submerged branches, but then I had to think of getting out. I trod water and tried in vain to slide on to the ice myself. I couldn't do it. I tried to push Bruce on to the ice. Again, no success, so I began to smash the ice with my fists. It was slow progress as I was out of my depth and Bruce had his paws on my shoulders for support.

Eventually I reached the trunk of an overhanging willow tree and, with one hand grasping this, yanked Bruce by his collar on to solid ice, then pulled myself up on to the bank.

The Long Hard Road, Ron Hill

By James Parry

VENTURE out today on a wildlife ramble and you'd be lucky to see anything much bigger than a rabbit or squirrel. Perhaps a fox (although only if you live in a town). Yet moves are afoot to plot the return of bigger animals long-vanished from our landscape. Yes, we're talking wolf. Possibly lynx. Maybe even bears and bison. It's hard to imagine how this might work but the process of bringing back some of our lost wildlife has already begun.

Although Britain has a good record on wildlife conservation our countryside is a tame old affair. Our ancestors did a great job of cutting down British wildwood and hounding to extinction the animals that lived there.

The last native brown bears were probably wiped out during Roman times, although bears were imported regularly thereafter for the so-called sport of bear-baiting, a favourite entertainment of Queen Elizabeth I. Good Queen Bess was so keen on watching bears fights with dogs that her favourite nobles competed with each other to obtain as many bears as possible for when Her Majesty came to stay. Thankfully she wasn't as extreme as one European count who used to fire live bears out of cannons and then try to shoot the hapless beasts as they hurled through the air.

'Red Kites are busy scavenging road-kill off the M40'

Meanwhile in Britain there were hardly any big animals left to hunt. Once the larger carnivorous mammals and birds of prey had been exterminated attention turned to smaller fry such as wild cats, martens, polecats, hawks, falcons

WALK ON THE WILD SIDE

Daily Express Thursday October 1 2009

NICE TO SEE YOU: Beasts set to return to the UK include, clockwise from left, wolf, elk, lynx and white-tailed eagle

Britain is being 'rewilded' as large animals that once roamed our country are introduced again

and owls. […] Only with the advent of the First World War, when most young estate workers and keepers were sent off to the trenches, did the pressure let up and give surviving predators a chance to bounce back.

Some species haven't needed asking twice. Buzzards and marsh harriers are now more plentiful than for at least 150 years. Polecats are appearing in places where they have not been seen for decades. Red kites, given a helping hand with young birds imported from Sweden and Spain, are busy scavenging road-kill off the M40. […]

NOW the stakes are being upped. In May this year a group of wild beavers were reintroduced to Scotland to the Knapdale Forest in Argyll and immediately set about felling trees and building a dam. It was as if they'd never been away.

But even bolder plans are afoot elsewhere. Paul Lister, the owner of 23,000-acre Alladale Estate in Sutherland, has already released wild boar and elk on to his land and hopes to introduce wolves, lynx and brown bears over the next few years. […]

BUT wolves need space. With the population of Britain spiralling towards 70million it is difficult to see how they could ever "fit" in a densely-populated country like ours. Wolves can probably never really roam free here again. The most we can expect is a huge enclosure in which they live wild but in a controlled environment.

Is it worth the effort or should we just accept that the spirit of the wilderness has no place in Britain any more?

DESTRUCTION OF THE RAINFORESTS CAN BE FELT ALL OVER THE WORLD. HELP STOP IT.

The clearing and burning of rainforests is responsible for 17% of the world's CO_2 emissions and contributes directly to the melting of the polar ice-caps.

Tell the world to stop tropical deforestation by sending a Rainforest SOS.
Visit www.rainforestSOS.org or text SOS and your full name to 60777*

THE PRINCE'S RAINFORESTS PROJECT

RAINFOREST SOS

Targeting Grade C in the Foundation tier exam

Foundation tier questions

Answer these questions.

Read **Item 1,** 'The dog that nearly drowned' by Ron Hill.

1. What four things did Ron Hill do to try to rescue his dog?

1	
2	
3	
4	

4 marks

2. What do we learn about the sort of person Ron Hill was?

Find details from the text and say what they tell us about him.

4 marks

Now read **Item 2,** 'Walk on the wild side'.

3. To what extent does the writer feel that wildlife has a place in modern Britain?

Answer in two sections, beginning:

- 'The writer suggests that wildlife has a place in modern Britain by saying…'
- 'The writer is less positive about the place of wildlife in modern Britain when he says …'

8 marks

4. How does the writer use language to make the article informative and interesting for the reader?

Answer in two sections:

- Language to make it informative.
- Language to make it interesting.

12 marks

Now look again at **Item 2,** 'Walk on the wild side' and look at **Item 3,** 'Destruction of the rainforests can be felt all over the world'.

5. Compare the ways in which these items have been presented in an effective and attractive way.

Compare them using these headings:

- pictures and colours
- headings, subheadings and captions.

12 marks

Total: 40 marks

Targeting Grade C in the Higher tier exam

Higher tier questions

Answer these questions. (Refer back to the three texts on pages 47–49.)

Read **Item 2,** 'Walk on the wild side'.

1. What do we learn about the way wildlife has been treated in Britain? **8 marks**

Now read **Item 3,** 'Destruction of the rainforests can be felt all over the world'.

2. How have presentational features been used to make the text effective? **8 marks**

Now read **Item 1,** 'The dog that nearly drowned'.

3. What do we learn about the relationship between Ron Hill and his dog? **8 marks**

Now you need to refer to **Item 1,** 'The dog that nearly drowned', and to **either Item 2 or Item 3.** You are going to compare two texts, one of which you have chosen.

4. Compare the ways in which language is used in the two texts. Give some examples and explain what the effects are. **16 marks**

Total: 40 marks

Exploring Sample Responses Foundation tier

Targeting Grade C in the Foundation tier exam

1. *What four things did Ron Hill do to try to rescue his dog?*

Example 1

1	He took off his clothes and went on to the ice because he felt it was his fault and there was no other choice if the dog was to be saved.
2	He crawled across the ice to try to be as safe as possible until it broke under him.
3	He smashed the ice with his fists because there was no other way of getting to the side.
4	He allowed the dog to rest its paws on his shoulders because it was worn out from trying to escape.

Examiner feedback

The candidate selects four sensible and separate things, all of which are relevant. He also includes detail with his choices – for example, giving two very accurate reasons for his first choice. He resists the temptation to simply copy out sections of the text.   **Suggested Grade: C**

2. *What do we learn about the sort of person Ron Hill was?*
   Find details from the text and say what they tell us about him.

Example 2

> Ron Hill loves his dog. He says, 'he was loved like one of the family'. He felt he was responsible for the dog being in the water, so he has to try to get him out. He took off his clothes.
>
> He is brave because he goes out on to the ice to help his pet. We know he can swim but also he is tough because he smashed the ice with his fists. He even manages to get the dog out at the end and also to get out himself so he must have been quite fit but he must have been very cold and obviously wet.

Examiner feedback

This response has some valid points (we know he loved his dog and the point is supported; he is brave because he risks the ice; he must have been fit because he got both of them out) but other points tell us nothing about him ('He took off his clothes'). We get some retelling of the story rather than appropriate selection of detail with comment.   **Suggested Grade: D**

Read the following responses to Questions 3 and 4 and judge how well you have done against the quality of these answers, bearing in mind the Examiner feedback.

3. To what extent does the writer feel that wildlife has a place in modern Britain?

   Answer in two sections, beginning:

- *'The writer suggests that wildlife has a place in modern Britain by saying...'*
- *'The writer is less positive about the place of wildlife in modern Britain when he says...'*

Example 3

focuses on the positive →

offers effective detail

gives opposite viewpoint

provides detail in support

The writer suggests that wildlife has a place in modern Britain by saying that 'the country is being 'rewilded' as large animals that once roamed our country are introduced again'. This is presented as a fact.

In the article, he mentions lynx, bears and maybe bisons could be brought here. He tells us that buzzards and marsh harriers are more common than before, and there are polecats and red kites. In Scotland, there are now beavers and might soon even be wolves. All these things suggest there is a place for wildlife in Britain.

The writer is less positive about the place of wildlife in modern Britain when he says at the end that there will be no room for wildlife because of all the people. Not only that, he has already told us that the British are horrible to animals, like using bear baiting and hunting and shooting birds and animals like wild cats. Anyway, he does not think that wolves will ever be able to roam free.

← gives a quotation for support

← sums up and relates back to start

← ends strongly

Examiner feedback

This answer deals with both sides of the argument and offers supporting detail for what is said, which is well selected. There is insight into the writer's ideas, which are clearly understood. This also moves way beyond copying from the text, organising the material and summing up the writer's viewpoint with phrases such as 'there will be no room for wildlife because of all the people' and 'All these things suggest...'

Suggested grade: C

4. How does the writer use language to make the article informative and interesting for the reader?

Answer in two sections:

- *Language to make it informative*
- *Language to make it interesting.*

Example 4

<u>Language to make it informative</u>

Ron Hill uses lots of facts to make it clear what is happening, like 'the ice became too thick'. There is also repetition to make it all come to life: 'weaker and weaker'. We also know he loved his dog because he uses a simile: 'like one of the family'. He uses short sentences sometimes and that shows exactly what was happening and how he was feeling: 'I couldn't do it'. He also uses some good verbs which tell us things, like 'yanked' which was when he pulled the dog suddenly out of the water.

<u>Language to make it interesting</u>

Some of the language makes it quite interesting. It starts with 'I called and called' which is repeated like he was repeating himself when he called. And later, he shouts 'Aagh' and we know he is in trouble. He sounds a bit like a snake too when it says 'I slithered slowly out' and then the ice breaks and he says 'The shock was terrific!' which doesn't mean it was good – it means he was really upset. That is why it ends with an exclamation mark.

Examiner feedback

This answer responds to both headings, offering relevant details on which to comment, but often falls short of real clarity in what is said. For example, 'yanked' and 'Aagh' are mentioned, but not the effect they have on the reader. When we read 'There is repetition to make it all come to life', we think that is a comment that could easily apply to any language, in any text. The mention of sounding like a snake is better, though the alliteration and the effect of the 's's is not really dealt with. The fact that the student knows about the effect of the exclamation mark deserves credit.

Suggested grade: D

ACTIVITY

Read the following response to Question 5 and judge how well you have done against the quality of this answer, bearing in mind the Examiner feedback.

5. Compare the ways in which Items 2 and 3 have been presented in an interesting and attractive way.

Compare them using these headings:

- *pictures and colours*
- *headings, subheadings and captions.*

Example 5

opens with comparison

<u>Pictures and colours</u>

'Walk on the wild side' has animals, and the one that stands out is the snarling wolf. On the other hand, 'Destruction of the rainforests' is very peaceful, and the polar bear and frog seem happy together, to show the world could be happier.

Although the 'Walk' pictures are in black and white, they show the sort of animals being talked about in the article. The elk and lynx look beautiful, and the wolf and eagle fit well with the heading. The teeth of the wolf look wild. There is also a map, perhaps showing where the wild animals can be found in Britain.

'Destruction of the rainforests' is different. It's about global warming and it makes it look as if nature is getting together to say 'please stop', because you would not expect a frog and bear to be together. The blue sea behind them looks dirty, which fits with destruction, and the 'Help stop it', help address and number are in green at the bottom, because this is about try to be greener to save the planet. SOS is the warning in red.

It attracts you, but in a different way to 'Walk on the wild side'.

<u>Headings, subheadings and captions</u>

'Walk on the wild side' has alliteration in the title, to make the idea of a wild walk stand out. The pull-quotes are to attract the reader to certain ideas, and the best one is 'Red kites are scavenging road kill off the M40', which makes it seem like the wild life is dangerous. The caption under the picture says what is coming back, but also makes a joke ('Nice to see you') because they may not be very nice.

'Destruction of the Rainforests' is more serious. 'Help stop it' is short and seems to be shouting at us. The detail about the rainforests at the top is in small font, because they think we will read it after the big heading. At the bottom it is again telling us what to do, and the white writing on the black makes it serious. 'Rainforest SOS' is really noticeable and looks like an emergency is happening. It is not like 'Walk on the wild side' because it is softer and sadder but also demanding things.

Annotations (left margin):
- explains why features are used
- gives reason for colour choice
- appropriate vocabulary
- highlights the effect
- explained

Annotations (right margin):
- gives some interpretation of features
- more explanation needed
- partly explains pull-quote
- carries on comparison
- ends with sensitive comparison

Examiner feedback

This is a good answer which covers everything that has been asked, gives some clear and quite sensitive comparisons between the texts and backs up everything it says with detail. The black and white terror of 'Walk on the wild side' is set against the much more dreadful situation that is arising through global warming. We feel the candidate knows what the texts are about and ties the impressions created back to the texts' main messages.

Suggested grade: C

Exploring Sample Responses
Higher tier

1. What do we learn about the way wildlife has been treated in Britain?
Example 1

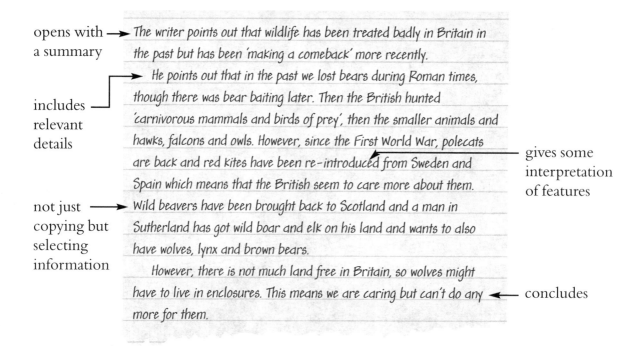

opens with a summary → *The writer points out that wildlife has been treated badly in Britain in the past but has been 'making a comeback' more recently.*

includes relevant details → *He points out that in the past we lost bears during Roman times, though there was bear baiting later. Then the British hunted 'carnivorous mammals and birds of prey', then the smaller animals and hawks, falcons and owls. However, since the First World War, polecats are back and red kites have been re-introduced from Sweden and Spain which means that the British seem to care more about them.* ← gives some interpretation of features

not just copying but selecting information → *Wild beavers have been brought back to Scotland and a man in Sutherland has got wild boar and elk on his land and wants to also have wolves, lynx and brown bears.*

However, there is not much land free in Britain, so wolves might have to live in enclosures. This means we are caring but can't do any more for them. ← concludes

Examiner feedback

This response has most of the important details, and they are used to make clear points. There is an appropriate first statement, setting out the basic situations, then and now, and then the response includes information about what was lost and what has been re-introduced. Crucially, the candidate selects what is relevant and the facts are blended with an overview – for example, in the last two sentences.

Suggested grade: C

2. *How have presentational features been used to make the text effective?*
Example 2

The text shows a polar bear and a frog together, with the frog on the bear's back, so this attracts the reader and makes us think they are together. Actually, the advertisement is trying to get people to help stop rainforest deforestation so it wants us to think about these animals and all the others like them. It has blue at the back, which makes it a bit summery. The title is in white but then 'Help stop it' is in green, because this is about green things. There is green writing at the bottom as well, to remind us of the message at the top and 'SOS' is in red because it also attracts our attention and it is as if the letters are burning.

Examiner feedback

This response identifies many relevant features and says things about them (such as 'it makes us think they are together') but it does not ever make clear comments about their effects. For example, it would have been helpful to say **why** the writer wants us to see the bear and the frog together (perhaps the reader sees different elements of nature sticking together as man destroys the planet). Similarly, towards at the end it shows understanding when pointing out that the letters 'SOS' appear to be on fire, but it would have been useful to say **why** the writer wanted to give that impression; and what is the advantage in creating a depressing impression overall. A better response would have said **how** these things affect the reader and what they make us think – linking all this to the purpose of the advertisement.

Suggested grade: D

ACTIVITY

Produce a better response by examining each of the presentational features and saying how it is intended to affect the reader.

Write about
- how the features help support the text's purpose
- each feature in turn, including mention of the picture, the colours, the headings, information in the text boxes and the overall layout.

ACTIVITY

Read the following responses to Questions 3 and 4 and judge how well you have done against the quality of the answers, bearing in mind the Examiner feedback.

3. What do we learn about the relationship between Ron Hill and his dog?
Example 3

begins with a summary that will be developed →

adds to our understanding of why the writer responded as he did

Ron Hill loved his dog, saying it was 'like one of the family'. This is why he could not leave the dog to drown, even if it meant getting into the water himself. He also feels responsible because he says he was the one who caused the dog to be in the water in the first place.

makes point, supports and explains →

We know how fond he must be. When he has taken off almost all his clothes in the freezing conditions, he risks a real disaster by keeping going even though the ice was 'beginning to bend'. When he actually falls in himself though, he does not just get out. First he still has to rescue his dog. He pushes him and even lets Bruce have his paws on his shoulders, which must have made it very tricky to break the ice with his fists.

retains focus on question

ends with conclusive idea →

It is also significant that he gets Bruce out first, then follows himself. This proves that they were very close.

clear points throughout

Examiner feedback

This is a very thorough answer which makes clear points about the relationship and backs up what is being said with quotation or detail from the text. Everything is relevant and each detail is presented in a logical order. Even in the final sentence, the response focuses back on the question. There is never the sense that the story is just being re-told.

Suggested grade: C

4. Compare the ways in which language is used in the two texts. Give some examples and explain what the effects are.
Example 4

Ron Hill uses repetition in his story, like 'I called and called' and 'weaker and weaker', which lets us know exactly what was happening. He also uses a simile to describe his dog ('like one of the family'), so Bruce was like a brother to him. He uses alliteration to describe what it was like on the ice: 'I slithered slowly out'. This makes it sound slippy. He also uses some exclamation marks so we know what a shock he had ('Aagh!'). There are a lot of short sentences, such as 'I couldn't do it' and this makes it more descriptive of what was happening. The last sentence though is quite long and that is as he escapes. He uses a verb – 'yanked' – to show how he pulled Bruce out.

The language in 'Walk on the wild side' is not telling a story, it is talking about animals and how they have disappeared. Unlike Ron Hill, it uses some old-fashioned words like 'Venture' and talks about 'Good Queen Bess'. It can be like someone is talking to us because some of the sentences aren't proper sentences, like 'Possibly lynx'. This is chatty, and it isn't like Ron Hill either. He also mentions 'hapless beasts' and calls the smaller animals 'smaller fry'. There are lots more difficult words, such as 'carnivorous' and 'predators' so you would have to be quite bright to read this. It is not as much fun as the Ron Hill text.

Examiner feedback

This response is sensibly organised so that it makes points about the first text and then makes comparisons as it moves through the second text. Some points are almost clear ('This makes it sound slippy') but the comments always fall just short of real relevance (for example, **how** the alliteration gives the sense of slippiness). The response compares the style, noting how the second text has chatty features and also compares the kind of vocabulary used. However, while the student shows some understanding, there is always more to say and they do not provide real insight into how the language affects the reader.

Suggested grade: D

If you only do five things…

1 Try to read at least one non-fiction text each day, always deciding on its purpose and audience.
2 Work out what the writer wants us to think and spot the techniques the writer uses to convince us.
3 Focus on how the writer uses presentational features and explain the effect of these in detail.
4 Select elements of the language you could comment on, such as alliteration or similes.
5 Make comparisons between non-fiction texts, for example comparing how they use pictures and colour. Structure your ideas so that they link and develop.

What's it all about?

Writing non-fiction texts means you have a chance to write a fantastic variety of texts, many of which will be very useful for life after school. What's more, a good letter, exciting news article or a snappy web text can be just as creative as a story or a poem.

How will I be assessed?

You will get **20% of your English marks** for your ability to write non-fiction texts. You will have to complete **two** written tasks in an exam lasting **one hour**. You will be marked on your writing of **two responses** – one **short**, one **long** – to two set tasks.

What is being tested?

You are being examined on your ability to

- write for specific audiences and purposes
- communicate clearly, effectively and imaginatively
- organise information in a structured way using a range of paragraphs
- use a variety of sentence structures and styles
- use a range of linguistic features for impact and effect
- write with accuracy in punctuation, spelling and grammar.

Purposeful Writing

Introduction

This section of Chapter 2 will help you to

- understand what a question in the written paper is asking you
- understand the meaning of the words, 'purpose, audience, and form'
- come up with good ideas and plan your writing.

Why is planning for purpose important?

- You need to **understand what you have to do** and, once you have done that, to **focus on how you get there**.
- The **plan** helps you stay focused and stick to what you want to write.

A **Grade E** candidate will

- plan with some idea of purpose in mind
- include several points and ideas, but possibly leave out several others
- not include all the correct layout or structure (such as the correct way to close a letter).

E

A **Grade D** candidate will

- plan with the purpose in mind, but without always thinking about the audience or form
- use paragraphs but not link them well, so the structure is not really clear
- include some, but not all, of the relevant features for the chosen form of writing.

D

A **Grade C** candidate will

- plan so that the organisation of his/her writing is effective, for example using clear paragraphing to sequence ideas
- use appropriate features and language to interest the reader.

C

Prior learning

Before you begin this unit, think about:

- what you already know about **purpose**, **audience** and **form**

- previous occasions when you have had to **come up with ideas** for a written task

- how well you structure your written work

- how easy it is to read your handwriting.

Could you jot down what you understand by these terms?

What did you do?
What techniques did you use?

Can others follow your ideas easily?
Why? Why not?

Understanding task, purpose, audience and form

What do these terms mean?

The **purpose** is the **reason for writing** or the **job** it has to do: for example, to persuade or to explain.
The **audience** means the reader or readers, the person or people you are writing **for**.
The **form** is the type or **genre** of writing: letter, article, report.

Checklist for success

- You need to correctly identify the purpose, audience and form in the writing task when you read your examination paper.
- You need to think about all three things when you write your plan.
- You need to make sure your piece of writing is in the right form, does the right job and is suitable for the named audience.

ACTIVITY

Here is a sample task. Look at what the purpose, audience and form are.

Sample title: Write a letter to the manager of your local football club persuading him or her to come to your school to give a talk on leadership.

Form (the type of text) = *letter*   **Audience** (the reader) = the *football club manager*   **Purpose** = to *persuade him* or *her* to come to your school to give a talk on leadership

In pairs, note down the **purpose**, **audience** and **form** in the following three tasks.

1 Write a leaflet for householders explaining some of the different ways in which people can save energy in their homes.
2 Write an article for a website called 'Great days out', informing families of your favourite place to visit.
3 Write a letter to your local supermarket manager advising him or her about how the shop could be made more appealing to teenagers.

Focus for development: Matching your writing style to your audience

When you have identified the purpose, audience and form, you need to choose the right style for the task.

Try to picture the audience in your mind's eye. Imagine how you might speak to that person and this will help you to decide how formal or informal your writing should be.

ACTIVITY

Exploring the terms formal and informal

You have been sent the two invitations below. Discuss with a partner:

- At which party would you dress formally? What does formal mean?
- At which party would you dress informally? What does informal mean?

Year 11 Prom *At The Palace Hotel* *Saturday 6th June* *Dinner and Disco* *Evening Dress*	*Hiya Guys! I'm having a barbeque* *to celebrate the end of exams (hooray!)* *Thursday 4th June* *My back garden – 6ish* *Love Keisha xx*

Now think about writing. What are the features of our language 'wardrobe'? Gather ideas in a grid like the one below.

Features of formal writing	Features of informal writing
Using standard English *Being polite*	*Using more chatty phrases*

EXAM TASK

Look again at the sample task on the previous page.

Write the first three or four sentences of your response. You could begin

Dear Sir, *We are writing in the hope that you may be able to find some time in your busy schedule to visit our school.*

Make sure

- you don't use slang or chatty language
- your grammar and spelling are correct
- you write in complete sentences.

Glossary
Standard English: the form of English that is generally thought to be grammatically correct and appropriate for polite, formal or professional situations.

Examiner's tip ★

Remember the standard way of beginning and ending formal letters.
Dear Sir/Madam   ends... Yours faithfully
Dear Mr/Mrs   ends... Yours sincerely.

Remember

- **Identifying the purpose, audience and form in the task will help you write in the correct style.**

Planning an answer

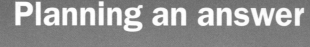

What does it mean to plan an answer?

When you plan an answer you are thinking ahead. You note down what you are going to do in a series of easy-to-follow steps.

Checklist for success

- To write a successful plan, you need to
  - answer the **main purpose** of the task
  - cover the **main points** you want to make.
- It is recommended that you spend **five minutes** planning each answer in the exam, then 20 minutes writing the short answer and 30 minutes the longer one. First, though, you need to come up with some **ideas**.

 Examiner's tip

You don't have to use a spider diagram. Try a list, a flowchart, or whatever works for you. The main thing is to get ideas down on paper!

ACTIVITY

Generating ideas

The task is:

form   audience   purpose

Write a **letter to** your **headteacher advising** him or her about **whether it would be a good idea to make the school day** longer by an hour and a half.

A student has started **generating ideas** using a spider diagram. With a partner, see if you can add any other ideas of your own.

letter of advice – longer school day, good or bad?

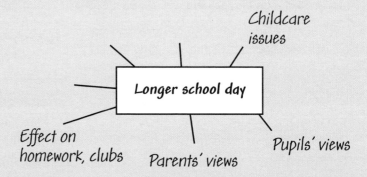

Focus for development: What makes a good plan

Read this plan based on the spider diagram.

Look at the plan with a friend and discuss the following.

- Would you be able to write an answer based on this plan?
- Is there anything else you could add which would help?
- Could it have been organised in a different way? For example, could the 'bad points' come first?

Plan
1. Formal start – Dear Headteacher, Thank you for asking me to advise ...
2. Good points: – less childcare for parents   – homework done in school, so gets it out of way
3. Bad points: – some pupils don't like school, so may be problems   – buses, train times?
4. End/conclusion: Overall, a good idea if parents are kept informed

Now look at this task.

First, take two minutes to generate ideas, using a spider diagram.

> A website called 'Classic Films' has asked users to review their favourite film, saying why they like it so much. Write about your film.

Now write a plan for six paragraphs. Take no more than four minutes. The first two have been done for you.

Spider diagram:
- My favourite film
  - Name of film
  - Basic story

1.	Introducing my film – what it's called
2.	Basic story ...
3.	(your ideas/notes)
4.	(your ideas/notes)
5.	(your ideas/notes)
6.	End/conclusion

Examiner's tip ★

As you plan, it's a good idea to jot down some good words or phrases you could use, for example, 'thrill-a-minute film', 'completely hilarious'. Jot them down beside your plan.

Remember

- **A good plan will help you write a clear and relevant response.**
- **Your plan will keep you calm and focused as you write your answer.**

Structuring your text

Learning objective

- To understand how different structures can produce different effects.

What does structure mean?

The **structure** of the text is the way it is **organised**: how it begins, develops and ends.

Checklist for success

To have a successful structure, you need to

- put your content in a suitable **order** (deciding whether to put your main point right at the start, for example)
- **organise** content effectively (deciding whether to group certain ideas together, or keep them separate, for example)
- make sure the structure **fits the form**.

ACTIVITY

Read this email sent to an employer to ask if they have any job vacancies. The student has forgotten that ideas need to be clear and meet the needs of the reader. His ideas are in completely the wrong order.

- Can you move the sentences around so that the ideas are in a more logical order? What should come first, for example?
- Then, rewrite or change any parts that don't work any more.

To: Brown Buildings Ltd

From: D Samuels

I've got 7 GCSEs (5 with grade Cs) and I have worked in a café for six months. So, if you have any vacancies can you let me know. Oh, by the way, I go to Peters Street High School. Plus, I'm 16. I work really hard too and I'm reliable.

I'm writing because I saw your advert in the paper.

Yours

D Samuels

Focus for development: Finding a logical order

Read this response to the task on page 64 about lengthening the school day. If it were longer, it would be a Grade D response.

> Dear Mr Robson
>
> We should make the school day longer. It's a great idea, and I thoroughly recommend that you go ahead with the change. Yes, there are some negatives, but they are not many.
>
> The good points are that kids get to do their homework, that parents don't have to pick them up til later and this frees them up to do shopping or stay at work. A bad point, though, is that kids will probably get bored at school if they stay too long and they'll miss buses and trains.
>
> More good points could be that kids will spend more time with their friends and this will help friendships.
>
> I hope this helps you make a decision.
>
> Yours sincerely,
>
> David

Talk about these questions with a partner.

- What is the structure here?
- Where does David's 'decision' (what he thinks) come?
- Where does David talk about the good points and where about the bad points?

As this is a formal letter, it needs
- a polite opening
- clear paragraphs in which the ideas are separated out
- connectives to help link, explain or develop ideas, such as 'so', 'therefore', 'In addition' etc.
- a conclusion in the right place – after the different sides of the issue have been put across.

Improve the letter by reorganising the paragraphs and following the plan on page 65.

Give each paragraph a key point and make sure the tone is formal enough.

Develop your ideas fully. For instance, could you offer a solution to how the 'bad points' could be overcome?

A student writes…

What is wrong with giving the conclusion first?

Answer…

It can be done, but if you choose to start by saying what your opinion is, then you will need to do it far more politely than David did. Beginning like this may put off the reader.

Write your own email to an employer, introducing yourself, explaining what you have to offer and asking about job vacancies.

Decide what kind of job you are applying for.

Make sure your tone is suitably formal.

Remember

- Put your ideas in a logical order.
- Make sure the structure suits the purpose and form of the task.

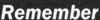

Grade Booster

Extended Exam Task

Now generate ideas, write a plan and decide on a structure/sequence for this question:

> *Write an article to go on the school website in which you persuade your year group to volunteer to work for local charities.*

Remember to follow this process:

Generate ideas → Plan → Decide on structure

Then, if you feel ready, write the opening two paragraphs of your article.

Evaluation – What have you learned?

With a partner, use the grade checklist below to evaluate your work on the Extended Exam Task.

C
- I can write detailed plans with a view to interesting the reader.
- I can organise my writing clearly and choose generally appropriate language, linked to the purpose and form.

D
- I can write plans but they are not always as detailed as they might be.
- I can understand the task, purpose, audience and form and generally produce writing which is relevant in response.

E
- I can write a basic plan which attempts to be relevant to the task, purpose, audience and form.
- I can begin to write in an appropriate style.

F
- I can identify some ideas to write about.
- I can show that I am aware of the task set.

You may need to go back and look at the relevant pages from this section again.

Communicating Clearly, Effectively and Imaginatively

Introduction

This section of Chapter 2 will help you to

- communicate clearly
- select vocabulary for its effect on the reader
- use a variety of sentences accurately
- structure and organise paragraphs
- use a range of accurate punctuation
- begin to engage the reader.

Why is communicating clearly and accurately important?

- Your ideas may be wonderful, but you need to make sure what you have in your head is clear to the reader.
- You also need to make the reader interested in what you have to say.

A Grade E candidate will

- attempt a range of sentences and use some accurate punctuation
- use fairly simple vocabulary, with some attempt made at choosing words for effect
- use some paragraphs but without much sense of overall structure.

E

A Grade D candidate will

- attempt a range of sentences, though not always chosen for their effect on the reader
- use mostly accurate basic punctuation
- select a wider vocabulary, but not always appropriately
- use paragraphs but not always link them effectively.

D

A Grade C candidate will

- use a wider range of sentences, thinking about their effect on the reader
- use a generally accurate range of punctuation and a varied and sometimes imaginative vocabulary
- use clear, logical and linked paragraphs to structure his/her writing
- produce writing that interests the reader.

C

Prior learning

Before you begin this unit:

- Make a quick list of any ideas you have about how and when to use paragraphs.
- Note down the different sorts of punctuation marks you can use in writing (for example, full-stops, capital letters and commas) and, if you can, say when and why you use them.
- Look over your past work and pick out any particular difficulties you had with paragraphing or punctuation.

Structuring paragraphs

What does structuring paragraphs mean?

Paragraphs are generally made up of **several sentences**. Deciding how you start your paragraph and what you include in it affects the meaning.

Checklist for success

- You need to use a **topic sentence** to state the main point or idea of your paragraph.
- You need to make sure the sentences in the paragraph are **linked by connectives** where appropriate.

Glossary

Connectives are words or phrases used to link ideas. There are several different types:

To show time or sequence: 'firstly', 'later', 'finally'.

For contrast: 'however', 'on the other hand'.

To show logical order: 'as a result', 'consequently'.

For developing ideas: 'moreover', 'in addition'.

ACTIVITY

This paragraph comes from a task in which the student was asked to advise a younger pupil how to cope with everyday life in school.

Topic sentence introduces first point of advice in response

Second sentence clearly linked to the first by use of the pronoun 'it' (the bell)

> My first piece of advice would be to make sure you arrive well before the bell goes. When it does, there will be a stampede of students into the front hall. As a result, any small Year 7 who is hanging around by the office will be crushed!

Third sentence is linked to the others by a connective and develops the point.

Now write a second paragraph about doing Games or PE. Advice could be about PE kit, getting changed – whatever.

- Start your second paragraph with a **topic sentence** that makes it clear what your next bit of advice is about in this paragraph. You should refer to Games or PE directly.
- Use at least two further sentences which provide **more detail, or explain the first**.
- If you need to, use **connectives** such as 'because' or 'however'.

Focus for development: Your first paragraph

Although topic sentences are excellent for introducing the main idea in a paragraph, you might like to start your very first paragraph in a more exciting way. Here is the opening paragraph to the advice text for Year 7s.

> 'Can you help me please? I've lost my bag, my best friend and my form room!' These were my first words to a teacher on my first day at secondary school. They sum up everything that can go wrong for a new pupil, and for that reason I am going to give you the benefit of five years' experience in big school. Most importantly, I am going to give you advice on surviving that first day.

Discuss these questions with a partner.

- What technique has the writer used to **grab the reader's attention?**
- How does it make the text **more interesting?**
- At what point do you find out the **main subject** of the text?

There are other ways you can write your first paragraph. For example, you could use a vivid description, an anecdote, a conversation, or even a question.

EXAM TASK

Write the first two paragraphs in response to the following task.

> Your Headteacher has asked for suggestions for someone you know to visit the school and talk to your year group. Write a letter to him or her suggesting someone and persuading the Head why this person would be suitable.

- Make sure the first paragraph grabs the reader's attention.
- The second paragraph should deal with the first main point you want to make.

Remember

- Opening paragraphs should grab the reader's attention.
- Paragraphs usually have a topic sentence that introduces the main idea.

Varying paragraphs

Learning objective

- To understand how to vary your paragraphs for effect.

What does varying paragraphs mean?

Paragraphs are usually made up of several sentences. If your paragraphs are all the same length they may not be as interesting to read.

The order of paragraphs in a text affects how the reader follows your point of view.

Checklist for success

- You need to make sure the order of your paragraphs is **logical** and **clear** and that the paragraphs are **linked**.
- Generally, you need to introduce the subject in your first paragraph and sum up in your final one.
- You need to use a variety of paragraphs, some longer and some shorter. Don't just deal with topics in a mechanical and dull way.

★ Examiner's tip

It's important to start a new paragraph when you begin to write about a new point. The change of paragraph shows your reader you have something new to say.

ACTIVITY

Read these paragraphs from a Grade D review of a school production.

> This is a review of the school's production of West Side Story. It was really great. It had everything you could wish for. It had good acting and great dancing. It was definitely worth coming to see. Tickets sold out in minutes and we were quite lucky to get in.
>
> Amy Fisher did really well as Maria. She sang beautifully and acted well too. David Wellings in the part of Tony also made an impact. His acting was excellent and we all cried our eyes out when he was killed.
>
> The production design was very effective. The design really reminded me of the streets of New York. The art department did a great job. Miss Harris even got a special bunch of flowers at the end.

Discuss with a partner how the paragraphs could be improved.

Think about

- the opening paragraph's impact
- the content of each paragraph (vocabulary and sentences)
- the length and variety of the paragraphs.

Here is the ending from a higher grade response.

> *The production design was very effective. The art department had created a look that made you feel you were actually walking the streets of New York, and the lighting was moody and romantic. For a moment, you were taken out of the school and over the Atlantic. It was simply wonderful – like a dream.*
>
> *Then the play ended and the house lights came on. We cheered and cheered but reality had returned. We were in the school hall and it was a rainy Friday night. So much for romance!*

What is effective about the second paragraph?

EXAM TASK

You have been asked to write a review of any event at school – sporting, theatrical, musical, or a competition.

Write a plan of five paragraphs in response.

Paragraph 1: say what I'm reviewing and when it happened (grab the attention!)

Paragraph 2: first main point or area discussed

Paragraph 3: next point/development

Paragraph 4: final point/development

Paragraph 5: conclusion.

Remember

- Begin impressively.
- Make each paragraph create an impact through a range of sentences and good vocabulary.
- Use a variety of paragraph lengths for effect.

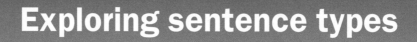

Exploring sentence types

Learning objective

- To learn how to use sentences accurately and effectively.

What are sentence types?

The way your sentences are constructed can affect your meaning.

Checklist for success

- You need to know that sentences should usually contain at least one main **verb** and a **subject**, and should make complete sense.
- You need to use a variety of sentences (**simple**, **compound** and **complex**) and to use punctuation and capital letters correctly.

ACTIVITY

Read these two extracts written by students to persuade readers that their favourite beach is the best.

This is a **Grade D response**.

> Combe Warren is always sunny. There are sunbeds and there are cafes everywhere and they have hot showers nearby. There are quad bikes to hire. You can see lots of private boats, plus there are also private flats you can hire.

This is a **Grade C response**.

> Combe Warren is always sunny, with sunbeds available whenever you want them. Hot showers are nearby, and there are quad-bikes for hire for those who have the energy. If you have the money, there are private boats for rent, with on-board satellite televisions, mini-bars and, most important of all, luxury ensuite bedrooms. There are also exclusive private flats alongside the beach.

Discuss the two responses with a partner. Try to be precise about why the Grade C response is better.

- What do you notice about the length of sentences in each response?
- What do you notice about the way sentences begin in each response?
- Which response provides more interesting details?
- What do you notice about the punctuation in each response?

Glossary
Verb: a 'doing' or 'being' word
I **am**
She **went**

Focus for development: Three types of sentence

Using a variety of sentences and punctuating them to make the meaning clear is essential for a Grade C and higher. The three main sentence types are: **simple, compound** and **complex**.

A **simple sentence** has a **subject** and **verb**. It must 'make sense' on its own:

subject   verb

Combe Warren is always sunny.

A **compound sentence** links two simple sentences (or clauses) together with 'and', 'or' or 'but':

*Combe Warren is always sunny **and** it has sunbeds and cafés.*

*Combe Warren is popular with holidaymakers **but** it is not as popular as Portland Bay.*

A **complex sentence** adds extra detail to a simple sentence (the main clause):

extra detail   main clause

*When it rains, **you can shelter in the cafés**.*

The **main clause** will make sense on its own but the extra detail (or **subordinate clause**), 'When it rains', does not.

If all your sentences were the same length they would be dull and repetitive, especially if they all began in the same way:

***There are** luxurious sunbeds. **There are** lively bars along the beach.*

It would be better to combine the sentences, adding extra detail:

***All along the beach**, there are lively bars and luxurious sunbeds, which I love.*

Placing the phrase 'All along the beach' at the start, emphasises the beach.

EXAM TASK

Write the opening two paragraphs of a response to this task.

Think about the worst trip, journey or holiday you have ever had.

Write an article for a new website, 'Nightmare Holidays', explaining what went wrong on your trip and why you would not recommend it.

Make sure your sentences start in lots of different ways.

ACTIVITY

Write down two more ways this last sentence could be written by changing the order of the three parts. In each case, what is being emphasised?

Remember

- **Use more than just simple sentences or sentences joined with 'and'.**

Varying sentence length for effect

Learning objective

- *To understand how your choice of sentence can have an effect on the reader.*

What does varying sentence length for effect mean?

Different lengths of sentence can produce different effects.

A **simple** sentence can express an idea simply or clearly, while a series of short simple sentences can create a sense of excitement and pace.

Longer, **complex sentences** can be used to explain or develop ideas, adding extra detail for the reader to think about.

Questions or **command** sentences allow you to address your audience directly.

Sometimes writers use **minor sentences** for impact and emphasis. These are sentences without a verb (*Christmas Day. A time of happiness.*). They force us to read slowly and pay attention to what they say.

Checklist for success

- You need to select the right form and length of sentence.
- Read your writing out loud to hear how your sentences sound.

ACTIVITY

Look at the different sentences used in these charity leaflets.

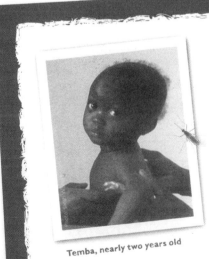

Temba, nearly two years old

EVERY MORNING CHILDREN LIKE TEMBA WAKE UP WITH MALARIA.
MANY OF THEM WILL DIE.

A goodnight kiss. A hug. Then, as they sleep, you hope that tonight your child won't be bitten by the mosquito that will take their life.

Temba was bitten by a mosquito carrying malaria, a disease which is the main killer of children under 5 in Africa.

Copy and complete the table below.

Discuss with a partner the effect of each sentence, thinking about the message and purpose of the leaflet.

ARE YOU ALONE?

DRAW THE CURTAINS.

SIT IN A COLD ROOM.

SPEAK TO NO ONE.

That's Christmas for 1 million older people in the UK.

[...] With your help we can change all this. Even a small donation could transform Christmas for lonely older people, enabling us to provide them with Christmas Lunch at a community centre, bringing them warmth, entertainment, and much-needed relief from their loneliness.

Sentence	What type of sentence is it (simple, complex, question, command, minor)?	Possible effect on the reader
Many of them will die.		
Temba was bitten by a mosquito carrying malaria, a disease which is the main killer of children under 5 in Africa.		
A goodnight kiss.		
Are you alone?		
Speak to no one.		
Even a small donation could transform Christmas for lonely older people…		

EXAM TASK

Work in teams to write the text for a leaflet for a charity of your choice.

- write a dramatic simple sentence for the slogan
- provide information using a range of simple, compound and complex sentences
- use rhetorical questions, or questions and answers, and command sentences to engage the reader.

Remember

- **Vary sentence length to create effects.**
- **Use questions and commands to involve your audience.**

Using punctuation accurately

What does accurate punctuation mean?

It means you are using the main punctuation marks correctly and in the right contexts, so that your writing is clear and effective.

Checklist for success

For a Grade C you should
- use punctuation marks accurately
- try to use as full a range as possible (see pages 80 to 81).

ACTIVITY

Read this student's response to a task about raising the school leaving age to 19. What has he done well? What needs to improve?

> It is clearly crazy to raise the school leaving age to 19. Everyone needs a break from education its a fact that many children would like to leave school when theyre 9 let alone 19. As my friend Jake puts it, more school. No way.

Focus for development: Basic sentence punctuation

Full stops and capital letters

Full stops exist to mark the end of a unit of sense.

Capital letters indicate the start of a new unit. They are also used to highlight names of people and places, days, months and titles.

> Schooldays are the best days of your life.
> I'm not sure I agree with that statement and my friend Jake doesn't either.
> Now it's nearly June, the pressure is on at Bilton High School, where they expect good results.

Commas

You use **commas** to

- separate items in a list (except the final two items which are joined by 'and' or 'or'):

  School has many facilities such as **a cosy canteen, great playing fields, brilliant IT facilities and a theatre space**.

- separate extra detail (subordinate phrases and clauses) from the main part of the sentence:

  Despite my best efforts, the team were absolutely useless, **so we were thrashed 10-0!**

  Lucy, **a really true friend***, lent me the money.*

- separate connectives that begin a sentence:

  Finally, *we were ready to go.*

  A day later*, the painting was finished.*

Apostrophes

Apostrophes put in the wrong place – or left out altogether – can lose you valuable marks. Remember, they are used to

- show **possession**. If the owner is **singular** (just one), it goes before the 's':

  Bilton High's Principal; my friend's schoolbag

  If the owner is **plural (more than one)**, it goes after the 's':

  pupils' coats; students' coursework

- show **omission** (when a letter or letters have been removed). The new word that is created is called a contraction and sounds more informal.

  you have not – you haven't

  you are winning – you're winning

EXAM TASK

Now write at least two paragraphs in which you argue for the school leaving age to be raised to 19. Begin with a topic sentence and then add further sentences.

Make sure you focus on the accurate use of commas and apostrophes.

ACTIVITY

Decide where commas should be added to make these sentences clearer.

> It's true that school has lots of qualities such as seeing friends teaching you new stuff and preparing you for life. However there's a limit to what school can do. Although school's brilliant it is only one part of your life, despite what teachers say. Life for all its faults is the best education.

ACTIVITY

Here are the final sentences from the same student. Rewrite them, adding or removing apostrophes to make it correct.

> Its clear to me that youll get the best quality of life if you leave at 16 or 18. Pupil's lives will be better if school ends sooner rather than later.

Examiner's Tip ★

Watch out for its/it's and your/you're.
it's = shortening of it is or it has
its = belonging to it
you're = shortening of you are
your = belonging to you

Remember

- **Check your sentences carefully for accurate punctuation.**

Using a range of punctuation

Learning objective

- To use the full range of punctuation, as appropriate, in your writing.

What does the full range of punctuation mean?

There are many punctuation marks that can help your writing other than full stops, commas and apostrophes. To target Grade C, try using exclamation marks, question marks, speech marks, brackets, dashes and colons.

Checklist for success

- You need to use a range of punctuation.
- You need to make sure it is accurate and appropriate.
- If you can, try to use it for effect.

ACTIVITY

Exclamation marks add impact and are used to show humour or emotion such as anger or surprise.

Shopping in the sales is possibly the worst experience I have had in a long time!

When the doors to the centre opened it was like someone had fired a starting pistol!

Add one exclamation mark and one set of brackets to make this text 'come alive'.

> I absolutely adore shopping in the sales. The sight of those red banners and half-price stickers is enough to drive me crazy. I empty my pocket-money tin which is usually full of 20 pence pieces, persuade my dad to advance me a fiver for washing the car and then head off to town.

Examiner's tip

Don't over-use exclamation marks or your text will seem to 'shout out' from the page. It is best not to use them in a formal text.

ACTIVITY

Discuss with a partner how this writer uses the following two types of punctuation.

Brackets

Having children is one of the most wonderful (and most expensive!) experiences of your life.

Dashes

Babies demand a lot of time, energy and love – not to mention sleep – but are well worth it.

Now try it yourself. Add brackets to this sentence to highlight a particular part of it.

Shopping in the sales is an expensive and physically dangerous experience.

Examiner's tip

Don't over-use adjectives! You'll make less of an impact on your reader if every noun has an adjective before it. Be selective to be successful.

EXAM TASK

Either: | *Write the first two paragraphs of your own response to the task on page 84.*

Or: | *Use the response below as a starting point and add two more paragraphs of your own in a similar style.*

The best beach you could possibly wish for is Rolliwell Bay. You couldn't find a more relaxing, more refreshing or more beautiful place. With fluffy sand, calm clear water, and exceptional views,...

Examiner's tip

Think how you could answer this task in an unusual way to engage the reader. Does your perfect beach have to be sunny and sandy? Perhaps you would prefer it with stormy waves and dangerous cliffs?

Remember

- Build ideas using vocabulary, choosing specific nouns and adding detail with adjectives.
- Try to keep your writing lively and interesting – come up with a variety of words and phrases.
- Engage your reader by painting a picture with your choice of words.
- Get the tone right (formal or informal) for your audience.

Grade Booster

Extended Exam Task

Now write at least three paragraphs in response to this task.

> *Is there an everyday activity which you hate doing?*
> *Write an article for a magazine explaining what it is*
> *and why you dislike it so much.*

Make sure your focus is on communicating two or three ideas clearly and imaginatively through

- varied sentences
- appropriate, well-chosen vocabulary
- accurate and effective punctuation
- clear and logical paragraphing.

Evaluation – What have you learned?

With a partner, use the grade checklist below to evaluate your work on the Extended Exam Task.

- I can use an increasing variety of sentence forms, accurately punctuated.
- I can use logical paragraphs and clearly present main ideas.
- I can communicate my viewpoint and support it with some good ideas.
- I can use well chosen, but not especially varied, vocabulary.

- I can use simple sentences, and occasionally complex ones.
- I can sometimes use more varied vocabulary, but it is still rather limited.
- I can use paragraphs but they lack thought and variety.
- I can create a point of view but it is not well developed.

- I can use simple sentences, and attempt longer ones but often with inaccurate punctuation.
- I can use paragraphs mostly correctly but with little or no sense of their effect.

- I can use simple sentences and vocabulary.
- I can use paragraphs sometimes but not always properly or set out as they should be.

You may need to go back and look at the relevant pages from this section again.

Writing to Engage the Reader

Introduction

This section of Chapter 2

- looks at how you can interest your readers in your work
- explores how you can adapt form and style to your readers' needs
- develops your use of some particular language features.

Why is it important to engage your reader's interest?

- No one wants to read a text that is dull or does not provide what the reader wants.
- You will be more persuasive, appear knowledgeable, and be better understood if your writing creates impact.
- The higher grades at GCSE are given when the writing is not just clear but also makes the reader really take notice.

A **Grade E** candidate will

- have a sense of purpose and audience
- communicate his or her main ideas reasonably clearly
- choose some appropriate features to meet the audience's needs
- attempt to sustain and/or develop ideas.

E

A **Grade D** candidate will

- have a sense of purpose and audience
- develop and communicate his or her main ideas
- use some appropriate, if limited, language techniques to meet the audience's needs but the tone and ideas will not always be sustained.

D

A **Grade C** candidate will

- have a very clear sense of purpose and audience
- communicate his or her ideas clearly and appropriately
- clearly attempt to engage the reader using particular language techniques for effect
- clearly attempt to sustain and develop ideas.

C

Prior learning

Before you begin this unit, think about

- any particularly impressive texts, or parts of texts (maybe an opening to a story, or an end to a report?) you have written when your writing has really 'shone' and made an impact your teacher
- what keeps **you** interested in texts or engaged in what the writer has to say
- what techniques or approaches you already know that help your writing create an impact on the reader, or sustain their attention.

Adapting texts to purpose

Learning objective

- To understand how different forms require different features and language.

What does adaapting texts to purpose mean?

Often, you need to change your approach according to the purpose of a text (for example, an absence note wouldn't work as a 100 page novel!).

Checklist for success

- Use the common features for a specific text: for example, a headline for a newspaper article.
- Change the language to fit the situation: use serious language for a serious issue.

ACTIVITY

Look at the following front page of a two–page leaflet.

> *Playing sport is great for your health. In my opinion you really should give it a go, 'cos it's great fun and you will feel the benefit to your body. I used to be really unfit and a bit lonely but doing sport has made me fit and now I also meet lots of people which is great. I don't feel out of breath and my body is kinda toned now, which is also great. So, play sport and feel great!*

It makes some good points:

- Sport can help you get fit.
- Your body can become more toned – and look good.
- It can help with general breathing.
- Sport is great fun – you meet people.

However, it could be improved.

Discuss with a partner what is *wrong* with it as a leaflet.

Think about

- what the purpose of a leaflet usually is
- the presentational features you would expect to see
- how the language might need to change
- what other features might be vital.

Note down:

- What might be the leaflet's purpose (or purposes)?
- How has the writer tried to engage the reader with his/her use of language?
- What point of view emerges?
- How does the sequence of the sentences lead the reader into the detailed discussion?

Focus for development:
Improving the layout

Here is the same leaflet, with some improvements.

THINK SPORT'S A WASTE OF TIME? THINK AGAIN!

Playing sport:

★ Enhances and maintains fitness
★ Allows for better respiration
★ Exercises the muscles you never use
★ Is fun, friendly and sociable.

For more info visit sport4health.com or talk to your local doctor about opportunities to get fit locally. More info overleaf.

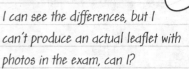

A student writes…

I can see the differences, but I can't produce an actual leaflet with photos in the exam, can I?

Answer…

No, but you can use appropriate language and layout features – for example, bullet points and headings – to make your text punchy and clear.

EXAM TASK

Draft a leaflet to warn people about the dangers of only eating 'fast-food' and 'takeaways'.

- Try to include a catchy heading – for example, notice how the sport leaflet repeats 'Think' and uses a question and command sentence to address the reader directly.
- Consider using bullet points and simple, clear and professional-sounding words and phrases.

Remember

- Make the language you choose fit the form.
- Consider basic features of layout.

Adapting language to purpose

Learning objective

- To understand how to write in different ways on the same subject.

What does adapting language to purpose mean?

In the exam, you will be told clearly what your purpose is: for example, whether to explain, argue or persuade. This will make a difference to how you write and what you say.

Checklist for success

- Choose your language carefully according to the task, purpose and audience.

ACTIVITY

Read these two articles on the same topic – CCTV surveillance.

EXAMPLE 1

> *I passionately believe that CCTV cameras are an invasion of our privacy. Nowadays they are on every street corner, in every shop and even in many schools. They are silent, secretive and scary. Do we really want every aspect of our lives watched? Certainly not!*

EXAMPLE 2

> *So what are CCTV cameras and why are there so many on our streets? The CCTV camera is a device, often owned by an organisation or business, which records on computer or tape the movements of people. The answer to why there are so many probably lies in rising levels of crime and the fact that some are concerned that there are not enough police on the beat. Others feel differently, saying that...*

Discuss with a partner:

- Which text is arguing a particular point of view?
- How do you know which text is arguing a point of view? (Think about the language and how it is written.)

Focus for development:
Writing to argue a personal point of view

Example 1 on page 90 uses some language features that are often used when you write to argue a personal viewpoint:

- the first person ('I')
- rhetorical questions ('Do we really want …?')
- emotive, powerful language ('passionately')
- lists, or repeated words ('every')
- patterns of three ('silent, secretive and scary').

ACTIVITY

Working on your own, complete the following paragraph arguing in favour of CCTV. Use at least two of the features listed above.

CCTV is needed in every city. Can we really allow …

Now compare your paragraph with a partner's. Identify the 'argue' features you used.

⭐ **Examiner's tip**

For questions like this, it is generally best to use quite a formal tone even if you think a chatty, conversational style might connect with some readers. Remember: you must sustain this tone throughout.

EXAM TASK

Write one or two more paragraphs of the text arguing in favour of CCTV. Try to use further features from the list.

Remember

- Subjects can be the same, but the way you approach them (to analyse, explain or argue for/against them) will affect the language you choose.

Using imagery for effect

What does using imagery for effect mean?

Imagery is the use of language techniques, such as similes and metaphors, to 'paint pictures' in the reader's mind.

Checklist for success

You need to make sure that when you are writing to describe something you create a clear picture for the reader in their mind's eye.

ACTIVITY

Here, Kathy Lette describes putting on fake tan in preparation for a holiday.

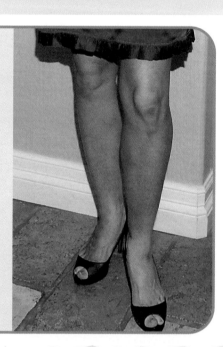

It said 'rich Mediterranean' on the bottle, but I was beginning to look more tandoori than tanning salon. My so-called 'tan' pulsated. It radiated. I looked as if I was wearing a tangerine wet suit, with darker elbow patches and kneepads. I was like a distress flare. People could employ me at the scene of a boating accident.

Good Housekeeping

Discuss with a partner two ways in which Kathy Lette has used imagery.

- Think about her use of **similes**.
- Think about her use of **powerful verbs** to describe how her tan looked and felt.

Glossary

Simile: a simile compares one thing to another thing using the words 'as' or 'like'.

Verb: a 'doing' or 'being' word.
I *was*
It *radiated*.

Kathy Lette used these techniques to make her writing come to life – and make us laugh. She has used description **related to the senses** to help us imagine how she felt.

Focus for development:
Describing the look and feel

ACTIVITY

Look at this task.

> *Describe the strangest outfit you ever had to wear and how it made you look and feel.*

Now create a simile that you could use in a response. You can develop one of the similes below or write one of your own. Try adding some extra adjectives to make it funny.

> *The huge, fluffy, white woolly coat my gran gave me made me look like ...*

> *The hat was grey, round and enormous; it looked like I was wearing a ...*

Now use **metaphors** to describe what it was like to wear the outfit. Try to include **powerful verbs**, too. For example:

> *The trousers strangled my legs they were so tight. My muscles throbbed and ached for a whole week.*

A student writes...

Similes are easy, but I don't get metaphors.

Answer...

Metaphors are when you compare one thing to another by saying it actually is something else, for example: 'In my pink, long, skin-tight trousers I was an overgrown flamingo'. It's a more powerful way of expressing an idea.

Examiner's tip ⭐

You need to judge when to use imagery. For example, in more logical texts, like explanations, imagery would not be so suitable.

EXAM TASK

Write an article advising students in Year 7 about what they should wear and bring to school.

Make the article lively – this is a 'survival guide' for your audience!

You could write about

uniform:
- how to wear the tie/uniform
- what your hair should look like

other matters:
- what sort of bag or pencil-case they should bring
- what coat to wear – or not!

Write at least two paragraphs, and use some amusing similes or metaphors to get your points across.

Remember

- Imagery can help readers to picture your ideas.
- Choose carefully when to use imagery; don't over-use similes.
- Powerful verbs can be as effective as long similes.

Sustaining your ideas and tone

Learning objective

- To keep to the ideas you decided on, building and developing them throughout.

What does sustaining your ideas mean?

It means keeping to the task, following what you set out to say, and using the right language from start to finish.

Checklist for success

- Be clear about your outcome – if you stated your aim at the beginning, have you kept to it at the end?
- Keep to the style you start with. For example, don't suddenly become informal (unless for deliberate effect) in a formal text.
- Try to engage and hold the reader's attention throughout.

⭐ **Examiner's tip**

For questions like this, it is generally best to use quite a formal tone even if you think a chatty, conversational style might connect with some readers. Remember: you must sustain this tone throughout.

ACTIVITY

Read the opening to the Grade C response to this task.

> It is often said that we are a nation of animal lovers. If that is true, why does the RSPCA report rising numbers of abandoned animals every year? Write an article in which you argue either for or against the idea that people should only be allowed a maximum of one pet at home.

> Do people really deserve to have pets? The RSPCA reports rising numbers of abandoned animals, and I would like to consider in this article whether one solution would be to simply limit how many pets a person can have. Perhaps there could even be a test to make sure people are fit to keep a pet in the first place. Animals are really important and I feel we should care for them properly.

Discuss with a partner:

- Has the student said what his intention is in writing the article?
- Is he actually answering the task?
- Does the style – so far – seem appropriate to the task?

Focus for development:
Planning to sustain your ideas

To be successful, you need to be writing in the same way at the end as you were are the start. Your ideas and tone need to be consistent.

ACTIVITY

Now read the final paragraph from the student's article about pet ownership.

> *I love animals and I think most people do. Pets become part of the family, and deserve to be cared for properly. Although some people want lots of pets, maybe it would be best if they just had one each and gave that animal all their love. If they deserve a pet, the pet deserves affection.*

With your partner, discuss these questions, finding evidence to back up your opinion.

- Does the ending sustain the ideas from the opening?
- Is the same style maintained? Is it still addressing the same audience?

EXAM TASK

Write your own article in response to the pet ownership task. Give yourself 35 minutes to plan and write it in – no more!

If you need a reminder of planning techniques, turn to page 64.

Remember

- **Your text must be consistent. Take a 'step back' to check your style, viewpoint and tone have been sustained throughout.**

Writing to persuade and advise

Learning objectives

- *To learn how to persuade and advise effectively.*

- *To be aware of techniques which can be used to persuade and advise.*

What is the difference between persuading and advising?

When you **persuade**, you try to make someone accept your point of view, or do what you want.

Advising is similar but the focus is usually on trying to help someone, which is not always the case when you are persuading (you may want someone to give *you* money, for example).

Checklist for success

- When writing to persuade, you need to ask yourself: will this convince the reader?
- For any piece of advice, you need to ask if it is detailed enough, so someone will accept your advice.

Focus for development: Convincing the reader

Persuading

You need to organise your ideas sensibly and use techniques to help persuade your reader that yours is the right point of view. You might

- simply focus on one viewpoint
- balance your view against the opposite point of view, as in an argument, but show that yours is better!
- use **emotive language** to convince the reader
- include examples and **anecdotes** to illustrate your ideas
- use rhetorical questions to hammer home what you say.

Notice how this **Grade C** response uses persuasive techniques.

> **Glossary**
> **emotive language** is language which touches the emotions: 'Tiny starving babies, crying out for food'
> **anecdote**: an extended example; a very short story

definite; allows no challenge →

list of three to impress →

extra ideas →

rhetorical question →

> *Stratford is a great place to live. It's got **the theatre, Shakespeare's birthplace and where he's buried**, but that's not why most people like living there. You don't have to worry about lots of heavy traffic (well, apart from the visitors going to see plays!) and you've got countryside all round, which can be fun, even if lots of people don't believe it. Most people would like to live with lovely clean air all around and being able to hear birds singing if they could, wouldn't they?*

← a touch of emotive language

Write the opening paragraph of an article to persuade the reader that a city of your choice is the most beautiful in the world. Use persuasive techniques.

Advising

Here are the main techniques you could use:

- setting out a problem, then giving a solution
- dealing with each part of the problem in turn
- using imperative verbs ('Remember', 'Do this')
- using a more sensitive approach ('Have you ever considered...?')
- using logic and evidence to support what you say.

ACTIVITY

Discuss with a partner how this Grade D advice might be improved by

- adding detail
- varying sentence length
- using a more sensitive approach.

You must find yourself a new boyfriend, and quickly. Things aren't going to improve. You need to tell him straight that it's all over. Don't be nice to him. He won't listen then. The important thing is to do it sooner rather than later.

EXAM TASK

Write a letter to a friend to advise them to work harder for their exams and to persuade them they will be glad later if they do.

Use effective persuasive and advice writing techniques.

Remember

- **People usually respond better if your advice and persuasion is sensitive rather than heavy-handed.**
- **Using suitable techniques will make your writing more convincing.**

Writing to inform and explain

What is the difference between informing and explaining?

The difference between these two types of text is important.

Information writing involves presenting facts and perhaps offering a personal interpretation of them.

Explanation writing involves going behind a set of facts and explaining why things have happened or how they can be improved. It means interpreting the information.

Checklist for success

- You can improve your writing to inform by adding facts and details. Think about how newspaper reports try to engage their readers.
- Writing to explain is best when it moves logically from information to explanation. For example, you might write:
  - what the situation is (information)
  - how it came about (information and explanation)
  - how we might resolve it (explanation).

EXAMPLE

This extract from a **Grade C** response **informs** about having to move home and **explains** the problems involved.

gives information about the change and begins to explain the problem

> I moved from my dad's house in Barnsley to live with my mum in Eastbourne and everything was different. Barnsley is where I had always lived and I knew what it was like. Eastbourne made me feel scared at first.
>
> My mum was renting this sort of apartment, in North Harbour. It was really posh. I had to get used to all sorts of new things. People spoke differently and couldn't understand me some of the time. Not only that, they made fun of me and that's really hard to get used to.

personal slant on the change

more details

introduces the main problem

develops explanation and shows feelings

Focus for development:
Clarity and effectiveness

Informing

Writing to inform usually contains facts and sometimes interprets them too. Research the facts when you can but be ready to invent them in an exam.

Explaining

When you give reasons for some facts, you might be explaining
- why something happened and the effect it had
- how someone feels about something.

ACTIVITY

Write a paragraph to inform your reader about what life is like where you live.

Include facts or statistics and interpret them (for example, 'So, we must do more to help the pensioners…')

ACTIVITY

Complete a table like this about where you live.

Problem with area	Explanation: how it came about	Explanation: how it could be solved
Vandalism	Not enough to do	More youth centres/evening activities

ACTIVITY

Read this Grade C piece by a student explaining what his area is like.

With a partner, identify the **information** and then the **explanations**.

My town is not the sort of place anyone would choose to live. There is nothing for young people to do because the council is not prepared to spend any money on what we need. At the same time, older people have to sit indoors and just watch television because since the college closed there aren't even night classes for them to go to …

EXAM TASK

Write a letter to a shop to
- inform them about the present you bought from them
- explain what went wrong with it.

Remember
- Use detail whenever you can to make your ideas more believable.
- When you are explaining, give reasons.

Writing to review

Learning objective

- *To learn how to write an effective review.*

What does reviewing mean?

A review looks back at something and examines it critically. It offers opinions. Good reviews look beyond the obvious and pick out different parts for comment.

Checklist for success

Learn from reviews in newspapers and magazines. See how they review television programmes, films, plays and music.

Reviews

Look at this **Grade C** review. It looks back on an event and criticises, with detail not just comment.

overview of event → *Everyone had been looking forward to our big day. We all thought we would raise hundreds of pounds for Macmillan nurses, but it went pear-shaped and everyone was really disappointed.*

details of what happened and begins to comment → *It started well enough, and even though the mayor did the opening, she wasn't as boring as we expected. Everyone rushed off to the stalls and started hooking ducks and things, but then the rain came down and we weren't prepared for it...*

ACTIVITY

Think about the last TV drama you watched. What would you say about it if you were asked to review it? Think about its strengths and weaknesses.

Strengths/weaknesses	Comments to make

Focus for development:
Sustaining an approach

This means

- structuring your ideas into an effective order
- using the same style throughout
- linking your opening and ending, so that you return to the ideas you began with.

Examiner's tip ⭐

Practise writing openings and endings, as they are so important. Set your own titles and just write those parts. The more you try it, the easier it becomes.

ACTIVITY

Read the start of this Grade E review.

> I went round to my mate Alfie's last week. We were going to the park but in the end we stayed in. The TV programme we watched instead was rubbish. I've seen better things on kids' programmes. It was all aliens and strange things and some man who pretended to be Scottish. What's that all about? It just wasn't real. Nobody would have believed it. The special effects were awful. I hated the music. The best thing was the coke and pizza we rang up for afterwards.

With a partner, discuss what needs to be improved.

- Break down the ideas, so that each one could form a paragraph. Add anything extra that is needed, including opinions. For example:
  1. When/where saw the programme: name of TV drama, who was in it, etc.
  2. Main character: Scottish. Not convincing. Clearly using a false accent.
- Use the student's thoughts about the film to decide what sort of ending the review might have. Write the ending, making up the details you need.

EXAM TASK

Write the review of your chosen TV drama, making sure you

- use an effective opening and ending
- analyse what happened
- include relevant detail
- give your opinions.

Remember

- **For reviews, you need to include details to support your opinions.**
- **Readers will be more interested if you include detail.**
- **Sustain your style and link your opening and ending.**

Grade Booster

Extended Exam Task

Draw on what you have learned about engaging the reader's interest to respond to this task.

> *Write an article for a cycle magazine offering advice to cyclists on how to deal with aggressive car and van drivers.*

Think about how you can

- create an impact with some powerful language and examples
- use a personal style which fits the text (an article for a magazine)
- make sure you develop your points.

Evaluation – What have you learned?

With a partner, use the grade checklist below to evaluate your work on the Extended Exam Task.

- I can offer a clear response to the purpose and audience and write with some success so that the audience is interested.
- I can use language for effect and can sustain an appropriate tone.
- I can develop my ideas and structure my writing effectively.

- I can write suitably for the purpose and audience.
- I can begin to develop ideas.
- I can sometimes use interesting language but occasionally my tone is not sustained.
- I can organise my writing but don't always link ideas well.

- I can communicate with some success and attempt to write a convincing response.
- I can use some features that are appropriate, so that at some points it reads like a suitable article.
- I can attempt to develop my ideas.

- I can write about the subject and offer a few relevant ideas, though the style is not convincing.

You may need to go back and look at the relevant pages from this section again.

Exam Preparation

Introduction

In this section you will

- find out the exact facts about, and requirements of, the written element of Unit 1B of the exam
- read, analyse and respond to two sample answers by different candidates
- plan and write your own answer to a sample question
- evaluate and assess your answer and the progress you have made.

Why is exam preparation like this important?

- If you know exactly what you need to do, you will feel more confident when you sit the real exam.
- Looking at sample answers by other students will help you see what you need to do to improve your own work.
- Planning and writing a full sample response after you have completed the chapter will give you a clear sense of what you have learned so far.

Key Information

Unit 1 is Understanding and Producing Non-Fiction Texts.

- It has an exam of **2 hours**, worth **80 marks**.
- It is worth **40%** of your overall English GCSE mark.
- Section A of the exam is on Reading.
- Section B of the exam is on Writing.

Section B Writing

- The writing part of the exam is **1 hour** long, and is worth **40 marks**.
- It is worth **20%** of your overall English mark.
- You will be asked to write **two pieces** of writing.
- One of the writing tasks is a **shorter task,** worth **16 marks**. You should spend about **25 minutes** on this task, including reading and planning time.
- One of the writing tasks is **slightly longer**, worth **24 marks**. You should spend about **35 minutes** on this task, including reading and planning time.

The Assessment

The Assessment Objective for Writing (AO3) states that you must:

- Write to communicate clearly, effectively and imaginatively, using and adapting forms and selecting vocabulary appropriate to task and purpose in ways that engage the reader.
- Organise information and ideas into structured and sequenced sentences, paragraphs and whole texts, using a variety of linguistic and structural features to support cohesion and overall coherence.
- Use a range of sentence structures for clarity, purpose and effect, with accurate punctuation and spelling.

Targeting Grade C

Some of the key differences between a Grade D and a Grade C are as follows:

Grade D candidates	See example on page 106 and 110
<ul><li>develop some points, attempting to match their style to the audience, but not always successfully</li><li>use paragraphs which are correct but not always well structured</li><li>begin to use a range of sentences, but do not always think about their effect on the reader</li><li>mostly use basic punctuation accurately</li><li>begin to use a wider vocabulary, but not always appropriately</li><li>spell simple words correctly and most attempts at more complex words will be recognisable if sometimes wrong.</li></ul>	D

Grade C candidates	See example on page 107 and 111–2
<ul><li>develop subject matter in more detail than those writing at the lower grades, showing a clearer understanding of form and genre</li><li>paragraph effectively to give structure to their responses and make their meaning clear</li><li>use a variety of sentence forms (short and long) for deliberate effect, although sometimes the effect is not always thought through</li><li>use generally accurate punctuation</li><li>occasionally make original choices of sentence type or vocabulary</li><li>spell more complex words with increasing accuracy.</li></ul>	C

Targeting C in the Foundation Tier Exam

The Two Writing Tasks

- You will have to respond to two writing tasks in your Foundation Tier exam.
- The most obvious difference between the two tasks will be in how much you might write in response. The first, shorter task is likely to be more straightforward, perhaps a letter to a friend, or something in which the format is short and more easily controlled. Whatever you do, don't spend more time on this than the longer second task.
- The second, longer task in the Foundation Tier exam may ask you to consider different viewpoints or develop your ideas a little more.
- The tasks will change every year, but you have been working on some typical questions in this section so far. Here are two more examples.

Short question [16 marks] 25 minutes	*Your local council has asked for suggestions for a new leisure facility for teenagers in your area. Write a letter suggesting an idea and why you think it would be good.*
Longer question [24 marks] 35 minutes	*Explain why you would or would not like your local town to be a car-free zone. Think about:* • *The advantages of getting rid of cars* • *The disadvantages of getting rid of cars* • *How you feel about cars in your local town* • *The overall effect of the change on your lifestyle*

Exploring Sample Responses

ACTIVITY

Read the extract on the following page from a student's response to the longer question above.
As you read it, decide how good it is.

Here are the key questions an examiner would look to answer:
- How clearly and effectively has the writer communicated his/her ideas?
- How well organised are the ideas and information ?
- How accurate are the sentences, spelling and punctuation?

Example 1

We should get rid of cars. I know we all think we need them but they are a pain too.

Our local town is just completely clogged up with traffic mainly at school times and Saturdays when people go shopping. You can hardly cross the road at school times. Still kids have to get to school and there aren't enough buses and some live a long way away. It means using a car most of the time.

On the other hand there are some buses and we could use them. Kids could get these buses and they could lay on extra ones. If it took cars off the road that would be good. Another thing is pollution. Basically cars give out lots of gases and pollute the atmospheare and if you live by the side of the main road it's really unhealthy. Having more buses might save the world.

Having said that if we tried to get rid of cars all together, that would cause problems for people who live outside the town. Like old people who can't walk to the bus-stop which is miles away. They might need the car. We have to think of them too.

Perhaps electric cars might be one solution. They are cars, yes, but they are very different. They are healthier for a start. It means people could get around without polluting, but they also go more slowly so there wouldn't be as many deaths on the roads. And pedestrains wouldn't be choking on fumes.

Getting rid of cars would not have a big effect on my lifestyle now because I can't drive. But my mum and dad do have to take me by car to lots of football games so it would effect them and me. If we couldn't take the car through town I might cycle more. Or I would walk to the bus-stop. The effect would be good on my fitness because I would walk or cycle more and I quite like being fit so overall it would be a good thing.

You know, I think we should do it. We should get rid of cars in the town.

Examiner feedback

The candidate has answered the task set and has given his/her opinion. However, the paragraphs do not build logically into a convincing argument: the response flits from idea to idea. Simple spellings are correct but there are some errors in more complex words ('completly', 'pedestrains'). Sentences are mostly accurate if a little dull and often short. In terms of style, the answer is reasonably formal but sometimes chatty ('kids', 'they are a pain'), and feels at times as if the writer might be talking to a friend rather than writing an exam response ('You know').

Suggested grade: D

Based on the examiner's comments, how would you improve the article to Grade C standard? Discuss these questions with a partner:

- How could the opening paragraph be improved?
- Can you find some sentences that might be joined together to make more complex sentences?
- Can you find all the spelling errors?
- Where could you introduce a rhetorical question or a quotation to interest the reader?
- How could the final paragraph be improved?

Now read this response to the same question by a different candidate.

Example 2

Introduces subject → The idea of getting rid of cars from our local town is an interesting one and there are advantages and disadvantages.

On the one hand it would be great to get rid of cars. For a start it would ← First paragraph deals with pollution
mean air pollution is not so bad. Also there would be less noise because if you live by the side of a main road it is horrible hearing cars racing by.

Good link to last paragraph → Another advantage would be to fitness. If we had to walk more or cycle more then it will improve health. This would mean the health service and hospitals would save money. We would need cycle lanes and more walking areas which would cost money but this would be worth it I think.

New paragraph to deal with disadvantages → On the other hand there are some disadvantages. For example what if you are a pensioner or disabled? You might need your car and not be able to get to a bus-stop. Of course there could be special cases for people like that.

Another point is shops and businesses. If you were a shopkeeper you might be well annoyed if people didn't come to the town anymore. They could go to
A bit informal → the enormous out-of-town supermarket which would mean driving even more! ← Use of exclamation mark to emphasise point
Also your business might be based on cars – like delivery or taxis. What would you do? In fact, this is quite a problem.

Covers the last bullet point in the task → Finally there is the effect on my life. I know I can't drive yet but I want to learn. I don't want to rely on my mum and dad. They already get fed up taking me everywhere! Also we live miles from a bus-stop so I am not sure how practical it is. I could cycle I suppose but am I really going to do that when it's raining cats and dogs. I don't think so. Perhaps the solution is electric cars. ← Electric cars idea could go in separate paragraph
Then we wouldn't have to worry about making the town car-free. Electric cars are quiet and don't pollute.

Overall I think it would be a bad idea to get rid of cars altogether. Too ← Last paragraph sums up but new point at end seems strange
many people would suffer like old and disabled people and you can't have buses going everywhere. I think cars are here to stay and whether we like it or not people need them for work, taking kids to school, and just general laziness. Besides I want to drive and have my own car which would be really cool.

Examiner feedback

This is a well-organised and clear response to the task with (most of) the paragraphs dealing with separate points for both sides of the topic. The points are quite well developed. Towards the end, the response does not have such a logical progression, which means the conclusion is not as effective as it could be. However, the vocabulary and sentences are varied and there is some thoughtful use of punctuation for effect. The writing is mostly accurate.

Suggested grade: C

EXTENDED PRACTICE TASK

Write an article for the local paper persuading local businesses (shops, cafés, banks) to sponsor events at the school's next 'Comic Relief' charity day. You will need to write about:

- What the sponsorship is for
- What events the charity day will include
- What the school can offer businesses in return

If you only do five things…

1 Read the task carefully and plan your answer around the form, audience and purpose required. Use the conventions of the writing forms you know.
2 Grab your reader's attention with the first paragraph; end by linking back to the main point or points you have made. Develop your ideas: points you make will usually have other points within them that can be drawn out.
3 Use a clear, logical sequence of paragraphs, each covering a separate point. Vary your paragraph lengths, for example long followed by short, for effect on the reader.
4 Use a variety of sentences – both in terms of length (short and long) and in terms of type (simple, compound and complex). Whatever else you do, make sure all your writing is accurately punctuated, clear and logical and uses a range of sentences and paragraphs.
5 Make your vocabulary specific rather than general, and avoid repeating words or phrases when there are better alternatives available. Use powerful imagery – especially similes and metaphors – to make your writing come alive. Try to use a range of other language techniques, for example rhetorical questions and patterns of three, for effect on the reader.

TARGETING C IN THE HIGHER TIER EXAM

The Two Writing Tasks

- You will have to respond to two writing tasks in the Higher Tier exam.
- The most obvious difference between these two tasks will be in how much you might write in response. The first, shorter task is likely to be more straightforward, perhaps a letter to a friend, or something in which the format is short and more easily controlled. Whatever you do, don't spend more time on this than the longer second task.
- The second, longer task may ask you to consider different viewpoints or develop your ideas a little more.
- The tasks will change every year, but you have been working on some typical questions in this section so far. Here are two more examples.

Short question [16 marks] 25 minutes	*A family friend from abroad is coming to visit your home town or area. Write to them and describe what there is of interest to see and do.*
Longer question [24 marks] 35 minutes	*Some people think it is wrong that members of the public are allowed to be humiliated in talent shows by celebrity judges. Write an article for a magazine in which you argue for or against this idea.*

Exploring sample responses

ACTIVITY

Read the extract on the following page from a student's response to the longer question. As you read it, think about whether it is closer to a D or a C grade, and why.

Here are the key questions an exam marker would look to answer:
- How clearly and effectively has the writer conveyed his/her ideas?
- How appropriate and well-chosen is the vocabulary?
- Does the structure and organisation guide the reader fluently through the ideas?
- Does the range of sentences, choice of language features, etc. have a strong impact on the meaning?
- Overall, does this text engage and interest the reader throughout?

Example 1

Talent shows are excellent

Talent shows have been around for quite some time and people love them. They stay in on Saturday night to watch them. I stay in myself to watch them. Whether it's X Factor or Britains got talent or even Celebrity Come Dancing they are all good. Let's face it, it's good to see people making an idiot of themselves. And some of them are actually quality – look at Leona Lewis for a start.

Some people have been saying we shouldnt be laughing at people who arent very good, but singers like Susan Boyle are a bit specal and if we didn't have the programmes we wouldnt ever hear from them. That is why I think the programmes should be kept on TV so it gives a chance to everybody. Even I would like to go on if I got the chance.

It's not fair at all that others criticise the judges. What have they ever done wrong? They have to say what is best and what is not so good about the performers and nobody is forced to go on so they have to take what the judges say and it shouldnt upset them. In fact, Simon Cowell is about the most popular man on television (I think he is) so that must mean that veiwers like him. We don't want to stop him doing what he does best. It's great when he gives that little look and you know he is hating what he is watching.

If people dont like talent shows they dont have to watch and if people dont want to be shown up they dont have to go on them. it's as simple as that. No one is being forced to do anything so the do-gooders who want to get things banned should be banned themselves. Then the rest of us can get on with watching what we like and laughing if we want.

Examiner feedback

This piece responds to the title and is satisfactorily, if mechanically, paragraphed. There is a range of ideas and a rhetorical question is used to add interest. However, there are some technical errors (punctuation and spelling) and the sentences and vocabulary lack variety. The student could, perhaps, have checked the writing more carefully and could have improved it to interest the reader more.

Suggested grade: D

With a partner:

- Identify and correct all the spelling and punctuation errors.
- Choose one paragraph and re-write it, improving the vocabulary and sentences and developing the ideas, adding detail where appropriate.

Now read this response to the same question by a different candidate.

Example 2

Headline grabs attention → **Celebrity rudeness**

We all love talent shows such as 'X Factor' and 'Britain's Got Talent'. These shows show people making fools of themselves as well as showing off their talents, such as singing and dancing. 'Best thing on the box,' my dad says, but my view is that it has all gone a bit too far and OTT. It's fine to have some criticism if you need to improve and you are not singing as well as you could, but if you are a poor person with some trashy job with no real talent, it's not fair to make you feel like a dummy.

Expresses personal opinion

States one main line of argument

Use of quotation for effect

Gives reason why the show is, perhaps, not acceptable

Uses short sentence for effect →

Sometimes, what is even worse is that the person who is criticised doesn't even realise what is happening. **That is terrible.** It is like a private joke between the celebrities and the audience. I think it is like bullying in school behind someone's back when they don't notice. For example, calling children a horrible name but not to their face.

States opposite point of view

The thing is, the shows would not work unless they had people making fools of themselves. If it was just people with talent it would be boring, and I admit that I am watching when these programmes come on. So I am as bad as the programme makers I suppose.

Uses connective to give sense of progression →

But you can't really stop people wanting to take part and no one really knows until someone opens their mouth whether they are going to be an idiot or a genius. I suppose you could choose not to show the really stupid ones, but probably some of them don't mind. **Perhaps they would rather be on telly even if it's making themselves look stupid?**

Uses rhetorical question for effect →

ctd.

This leads me to my final point. You would need to be from a different planet not to know what goes on in these shows. Everyone knows what they are letting themselves in for – nobody is completely innocent are they? And perhaps they like being shouted at by Simon Cowell. In fact, it might be the highlight of their lives, which is pretty sad – but it's their choice. No one forced them to sing out of tune or dance clumsily!

So, as long as there are people willing to humiliate themselves, I guess it's OK. I will continue watching and maybe one day I will be the daft one on stage making a fool of myself! Simon Cowell beware!

Exclamation at end of paragraph makes point strongly

Shows range of vocabulary

Effective conclusion and memorable finishing sentence

ACTIVITY

Before you read the examiner feedback, note down any improvements you think the student could make to his/her response. In particular, identify where and how some imagery might be used and a greater range of sentence lengths and types.

Examiner feedback

This is generally a clear, well-argued article with accurate sentences and linked and organised paragraphs. There is a good beginning and ending, and the candidate uses some variety of sentences, sometimes to good effect. There is a sense of how the text might affect the reader and the article is slightly informal only occasionally. The language is generally clear and there is some variety to keep the reader interested - the ending is unexpected and leaves a smile on the face of the reader.

Suggested grade: C

EXTENDED PRACTICE TASK

You are helping to organise a charity day at school to raise money for a hostel for homeless youngsters. Write a letter which will be sent to all parents, persuading them to come along to the charity day. [24 marks]

If you only do five things…

1 Read the task carefully and plan your answer around the form, audience and purpose required. Use the conventions of the writing forms you know.

2 Grab your reader's attention with the first paragraph; end by linking back to the main point or points you have made. Develop your ideas: points you make will usually have other points within them that can be drawn out.

3 Use a clear, logical sequence of paragraphs, each covering a separate point. Vary your paragraph lengths, for example long followed by short, for effect on the reader.

4 Use a variety of sentences – both in terms of length (short and long) and in terms of type (simple, compound and complex). Whatever else you do, make sure all your writing is accurately punctuated, clear and logical and uses a range of sentences and paragraphs.

5 Make your vocabulary specific rather than general, and avoid repeating words or phrases when there are better alternatives available. Use powerful imagery – especially similes and metaphors – to make your writing come alive. Try to use a range of other language techniques, for example rhetorical questions and patterns of three, for effect on the reader.

What's it all about?

We can all speak and listen, but if we develop our skills, we can communicate much better throughout our lives. Speaking and listening involves many skills that can be used elsewhere in English work and offers an immensely enjoyable change from reading and writing.

How will I be assessed?

You will get **20% of your English marks** for your Speaking and Listening ability.

You will have to complete three Speaking and Listening controlled assessments.

You will be marked on your

- presenting
- discussing and listening
- role playing.

What is being tested?

Your teacher will be judging your ability to

- speak clearly and purposefully
- organise your talk and sustain your ideas
- speak appropriately in different situations
- use standard English and a variety of techniques when speaking
- listen and respond to what others say and how they say it
- interact with others, shaping meanings through suggestions, comments and questions and drawing ideas together
- create and sustain different roles.

Presentations

Introduction

This section of Chapter 3 shows you how to

- give a presentation to an audience
- select a topic and structure your talk
- consider what content you might include
- use a range of techniques to boost your performance.

Why is it important to develop good presentational skills?

- We can all talk about topics, but to get good grades you need to demonstrate a range of skills.
- You will be more successful if you plan and structure your presentation and make it as lively as you can.
- You will use similar skills in other parts of your English course, such as when you are required to write in the examination.
- You may well use these presentational skills throughout your working life.

A **Grade E** candidate will

- give straightforward accounts and begin to adapt their talk for different audiences
- generally use Standard English appropriately
- show some variety in vocabulary and language structures.

E

A **Grade D** candidate will

- use different strategies to engage the listener's interest, with an increasing variety of vocabulary, appropriate for the task
- understand the need for Standard English.

D

A **Grade C** candidate will

- adapt their talk to the situation, using Standard English confidently
- engage the listener through their use of language so that information, ideas and feelings are communicated clearly
- the presentation will have a clear structure and interest the reader.

C

Prior Learning

Before you begin this unit, think about

- times when you have heard someone talk in a formal situation
- which speakers have interested you most and why
- how you have been taught to structure your formal essays.

Which of their techniques might you be able to use?

When you watched someone on a news programme or in assembly, or had an outside speaker in school, how did the speaker try to hold your attention? How did they begin and end their talk?

Which of the techniques could you use when preparing and delivering a presentation?

Understanding your audience

Learning objective

- To consider what an audience expects and how to respond to its needs.

What does understanding your audience mean?

Thinking about your **audience** is vital when making a presentation. You might be talking to a class, an individual, a group of people outside school or an assembly.

You need to **understand** what type of presentation is required. Is it

- factual
- argumentative or persuasive (supporting a point of view)
- entertaining?

Checklist for success

- You need to be clear about who you will be talking to and what is expected of you.
- You need to make sure your language, content and style are right for your audience.

ACTIVITY

You are going to make a presentation on how your school's rules should be changed.

How would you vary your style and content for these audiences?

1 the headteacher
2 your classmates
3 a meeting of interested parents.

In each case, ask yourself

- What will they already know?
- What do I need to tell them?
- How can I convince them to share my views?

Focus for development: Choosing the right words and style

You will gain marks by using a wide **vocabulary**. However, it must be right for the people you are talking to.

ACTIVITY

This Grade C presentation uses words that are appropriate for the audience.

> We all know what's wrong with the school rules. It doesn't take a genius to see that things need to be changed. Take the shirt rule for a start... Who decided that we can't learn anything if our shirt is out? How stupid is that?

Discuss with a partner:

- Who do you think the speaker is talking to? Give reasons.
- Why is the style right for this audience?

ACTIVITY

Examiner's tip ★

Always vary your words. It will be much more interesting than using the same words again and again.

Improve this extract from a Grade E presentation. The student is struggling to find interesting vocabulary.

> I know lots of you don't like *Scrubs* but I do. I watch it with my mum and dad. My dad loves it. I love it too. We watch it on Sky. The programmes are crazy but they are good. That's why I laugh at them. It's about doctors and what they are thinking and amazing things happen all the time. Sometimes there are, like, amazing dream sequences and everything.

Rewrite the extract, trying to improve the

- **choice of words:** especially when they are repeated
- **sentences:** many are short
- **content:** is some of it unnecessary?
- **style:** can you make it sound more interesting?

ASSESSMENT FOCUS

Write a presentation explaining what is best about your school.

You are going to make the presentation to visitors at parents' evening. Make it appeal to this audience.

In your actual assessment you will not be allowed to read from notes!

Remember

- Use different styles and approaches for different audiences.
- Focus on your choice of content, style and vocabulary.

Choosing a topic

Learning objective

- *To understand why a sensible choice of topic increases your chance of success.*

⭐ **Examiner's tip**

Some speaking tasks are more difficult than others. For example, it is harder to persuade someone that your football team is the best than to describe what happened during a match. You gain more credit for tackling something harder.

Why is choice of topic important?

If the **topic** is something you feel comfortable with, because you know about it, your presentation will flow better and be more detailed.

Checklist for success

- You need to choose your topic and approach carefully, so it interests your audience, not just you.
- You need to know as much as possible about your topic.

ACTIVITY

If you were choosing a presentation, which of these topics could you talk about most successfully? Why?

1. Argue that knife crime is (or is not) a real threat for young people.
2. Advise the parents of primary school students to send their children to your school.
3. Explain why teenagers prefer technology to real life.

Focus for development: Successful topics

ACTIVITY

- If you were choosing your presentation topic, what would it be?
- How would you approach your topic? Would you be describing, persuading your audience or putting forward an argument, for example? Give reasons why.

Discuss with a partner and decide why this Grade C response is better than the Grade D.

Think about

- how the ideas are organised
- which says more interesting things.

Some ideas are given to start you off. The Examiner's tip on the right will help you too.

Grade D

> I like school trips! When we went to Alton Towers, it was great. We weren't home until after eight. <u>I went round with Chesney and Squilly and we didn't see a teacher once.</u> It was fantastic. <u>Some of the rides were awesome and we had burgers for lunch</u>. They cost a fortune though…

random ideas

ideas jumbled together

Grade C

logical order

> The trip was a huge success. <u>We met at 6.45, which was really early for most of us, then the bus arrived at about seven.</u> I rushed straight to the back, to sit with Jenny and Asma, and a whole gang of us were on the back seat. <u>Mind you, we didn't feel like singing that early in the morning.</u> <u>I swear Lucy was still chewing her breakfast when she got on…</u>

ideas extended

humour

ASSESSMENT FOCUS

You are making a presentation to your class about school trips.

Decide on

- the main points you will make
- details you could use to support your points.

You might want to

- describe what is good or bad about school trips
- compare them with school days
- persuade your audience they are fun and educational.

Remember

- **You must know about a topic to talk about it confidently.**
- **You will be rewarded for showing your knowledge.**

Researching and developing content

Learning objective

- *To understand the importance of selecting and using content wisely.*

Why is it important to think carefully about content?

Unless your presentation has interesting **content**, you will not appeal to your audience.

Listening is different from reading. Points must be clear and easy to understand. If the audience misses a point, they can't go back to hear it again.

If the audience loses track of what you are saying, you will lose their attention.

Checklist for success

- You need to have enough information about your topic so that you can stay focused on the subject.
- You need to have details and examples to support your main points.

ACTIVITY

This extract is from a Grade C presentation: Muhammad Ali – why he was 'The Greatest'. The student has researched the topic well so she is clearly comfortable with it:

> Muhammad Ali is considered by many to be the greatest boxer of all time. He was first called Cassius Clay and he won the gold medal at the Rome Olympics in 1960 with that name. He became world professional champion later. When he became a Muslim, he changed his name to Muhammad Ali and refused to fight in Vietnam, in the war. He had his title taken from him, but he came back, some years later and won the world crown on another two occasions.

Discuss with a partner:

- How many facts does she include?
- How well chosen are the facts to show that Ali was 'The Greatest'?

Focus for development:
Selecting effective content

Be careful about what you choose to say. Just because you find a detail interesting doesn't necessarily make it vital to your presentation.

For example, the talk on Muhammad Ali only includes relevant facts that

- give a clear picture of what he achieved
- indicate he was a great fighter.

It also stays focused on the man because it is a presentation about why he was called 'The Greatest' – so it doesn't talk about the rights and wrongs of boxing, for example.

ACTIVITY

You have been asked to review a film you have seen recently and present it to your class.

With a partner, decide which of the following points you would include, and why.

Character details	Your range of hobbies
When you saw it	Why you watched it
Your favourite forms of entertainment	Length
Storyline	Best/worst moments
Themes	The last production you saw before this one
Opinions of others about it	Alternative ways of spending your time
Comparison with other similar productions	

(Of course, in a review you don't only get marks for your main points, but also for how you comment on them.)

ACTIVITY

Compare these extracts from two student reviews. Discuss with a partner:

- What does each review tell us about the programme?
- Are all the details relevant to the topic?
- Why is the second review better?

Grade D

I like *Boys will be Boys* and, obviously, most of you like it too. It's on twice a week on Mondays and Wednesdays, but you know that. It has three main characters, who are Steve, Imran and Ben. I was watching it with Jenny last week on Wednesday and we couldn't stop laughing. Jenny even knocked over a glass of water and we just howled. Her mum wasn't pleased, though...

Grade C

I think *Boys will be Boys* is a programme that would appeal to anyone. I thought about my own brothers when I was watching it. I laugh at them, and I laughed at the boys on the screen. The show made fun of Steve, Imran and Ben, but I have to say the girls seemed ridiculous too: Maeve with her hair and Sammy with her turned-up nose. She tries to be *so* superior...

Effective research

Because you will prepare your presentations in advance, you can always do some **research**. As you read about the subject, you need to be selective, finding information which best suits your purpose.

ACTIVITY

If you were researching the talk about Muhammad Ali and how he became a hero, which of these websites do you think might be useful? Why? Discuss with a partner.

1 Biography Channel – Muhammad Ali
   http://www.thebiographychannel.co.uk/biography_home/741:0/Muhammed_Ali.htm
2 Muhammad Ali Trivia
   www.whosdatedwho.com/celebrity/ trivia/muhammad–ali.htm
3 Muhammad Ali Timeline
   http://www.infoplease.com/spot/malitimeline1.html

Having found relevant material, you need to decide how to put it across effectively to your audience. For example, you might use

- diagrams or pictures
- PowerPoint slides
- anecdotes.

Ending well

ACTIVITY

Organise these facts into a conclusion for a presentation which argues that Ali deserves to be known as 'The Greatest'.

Write a conclusion that

- summarises your argument
- only includes relevant details
- leaves the audience with a positive impression of Ali (and of you as a presenter!).

> Voted top sportsman of the 20th century.
>
> World champion at the age of 22 in 1964.
>
> In 1996 lit the flame at the Olympics in Atlanta.
>
> Three times world champion. Finally retired in 1981.
>
> Won 56 fights and lost 5.
>
> Said he could 'Float like a butterfly, sting like a bee'.
>
> Parkinson's Disease diagnosed in 1984.

ASSESSMENT FOCUS

You are preparing to talk to your class about your favourite hobby. Complete a table like the one below, which is about running.

Summarise

- the points you would select
- why you would choose them
- how would you develop them.

Point	Why	Development
Running is healthy	Health issues important at any age	How much weight I lost / How my life changed as I became healthier
15 million British people run	Pleasure / Competition / Feeling of well-being	Age no barrier: Constantina Dita became world marathon champion at 38; Buster Martin ran in the London marathon aged 101

Remember

- **Content needs to be appropriate for your purpose and audience.**
- **Research if necessary but be selective in what you use.**
- **Using content well is the key to success.**

Structuring your presentation

Learning objectives

- To understand the importance of organising your ideas for maximum effect.
- To learn about effective openings and endings.

What does structuring your presentation mean?

In a **well-structured** presentation, the speaker knows what they are going to say, and in what order. Planning a strong opening and a memorable ending is part of the structuring.

Checklist for success

- You need to prepare your presentation in detail.
- You need to consider the different ways you can begin, develop and end your presentation.

ACTIVITY

You have been asked to give a short presentation about your favourite subject at school.

- List the points you might make.
- Put them into a logical order.
- How would you begin your presentation?
- How might it end?

A student writes...

Surely planning a presentation is just like planning an essay.

Answer...

In many ways, they are alike. However, when you are talking, you can interact with your audience, develop ideas on the spot and use different tones of voice.

Focus for development: Planning, openings and endings

A bulleted plan can contain all the information you need – and you can use it as a prompt while speaking.

ACTIVITY

Complete a table like this, developing your ideas about your favourite subject.

Main idea	Points to be included
Teachers	Miss Spivey (obsessed with Crimean War) Mr Jenkin (anecdote about haunted mansion)
Lessons	Lots of videos Fun quizzes
Trips	Warwick Castle Tower of London Portsmouth

Openings

Your opening **sets the tone** for what follows. It is vital to attract your audience's attention from the start. Here are some opening ideas for a presentation about going to the dentist:

- **rhetorical questions**:'Have you ever had the wrong tooth extracted?'
- **relevant humour**:'Have you heard the one about the dentist, the missing tooth and the court action for damages?'
- **powerful facts**:'Last year in Britain, 57% of children under the age of 10 had at least one tooth extracted.'

ACTIVITY

Use these techniques to write three different opening sentences for your presentation about your favourite subject.

Endings

A memorable ending can leave a powerful impression upon your audience. You could try

- a summary of your argument
- one final, convincing point
- a joke.

Which of these you choose will depend on your topic, purpose and audience.

Examiner's tip ✶

Practise your delivery. Powerful words are wasted if they are not delivered well.
You can present to a friend, to a mirror, or you could record yourself then judge your own performance.

ACTIVITY

Look at this ending and decide with a partner

- what was the purpose of the talk
- how the speaker hoped to impress the audience at the end.

Decide how the ending could be improved.

Grade D

So there is much we can do to help the environment. It's easy to leave it to everyone else but that's not what we should be doing. If you join with us today, we can work together tomorrow. Come and help us. Thanks.

ASSESSMENT FOCUS

Go back to the plan for your presentation on your favourite subject and decide how much precise detail you need to add.
Make sure it will interest the audience throughout.

Remember

- A detailed plan is essential for success.
- Openings and endings are vital parts of any presentation.

Using standard English, imagery and repetition for effect

Learning objectives

- To understand the importance of standard English in presentations.
- To understand how imagery and repetition can add to the quality of performances.

Glossary

Standard English: the form of English which is grammatically correct – not the more casual, chatty form you might use with friends.

Imagery: the use of imaginative comparisons, such as similes and metaphors.

Similes: the use of words 'as' or 'like' to make the comparison: 'She was as brave as a lion.'

Metaphors: the direct comparison of one thing with another: 'Her hair was a flowing mane.'

What does using these techniques for effect mean?

Using **standard English** will add a more formal tone, which is expected as part of your assessment.

Including **imagery** and **repeating** words or phrases will help engage your listeners and stress your key points.

Checklist for success

- You need to understand the differences in grammar and vocabulary between talking informally to friends and speaking in more formal situations. Listen to news presenters on television, to remind you what standard English sounds like.
- You need to plan some imagery and repetition into your presentation to create more of an impact.

ACTIVITY

Look at this extract.

With a partner:

- Identify the similes and metaphors.
- Find an example of repetition. Does it make the extract more or less interesting?
- Re-write the piece more formally in standard English, as if it was spoken by a BBC presenter.

> See, it's clear, init? There's them that's got the cash, sitting on it like some big greedy thing, and them that 'asn't. You gotta find some guy with big wads – and I'm talking major league money now, and make 'im cough up his big wads. Then yer charity's got wads of stuff to work with…

Focus for development: Standard English

Presenting in standard English means using correct grammar and avoiding very informal language, or **slang**.

- Try to speak in full sentences.
- Use 'school' vocabulary rather than street language.

Imagery and repetition

Imagery will make your presentation more interesting, while repetition can be used to touch your audience's emotions or hammer home a point.

ACTIVITY

Look at this extract from a Grade C presentation.

> I met a refugee from a country in Africa where the people have no freedom. She was like a scared rabbit. There was no sign of hope in her eyes. I felt really sorry for her. I felt sorry for her people too. That's why I'm doing this talk today. We have to help people like Mende. Without our help they will have no future, no tomorrow at all...

Use a table like this to list the imagery and repetition in the extract. Explain the effect of each example.

Imagery and use of repetition	Effect (how audience is expected to react)

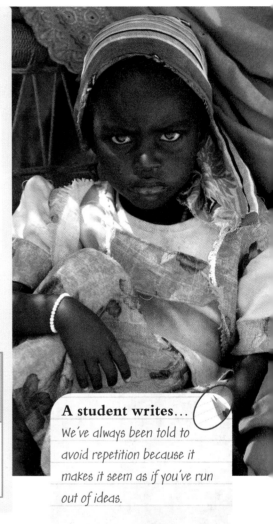

A student writes...

We've always been told to avoid repetition because it makes it seem as if you've run out of ideas.

Answer...

When you're using repetition for effect to hammer home a point, it will be seen as a strength, not a weakness.

ASSESSMENT FOCUS

Prepare the opening of a presentation about the job you would like to have when you are older.

Use standard English, some imagery and at least one example of repetition for effect.

Remember

- You will be expected to use standard English in most presentations.
- By including imagery and repetition for effect, you will make your presentation more impressive.

127

Using rhetorical questions, humour and exaggeration for effect

Learning objective

- To understand how rhetorical questions, humour and exaggeration can add interest.

Glossary

rhetorical question: a question asked to involve the audience, without expecting a reply – 'How could anyone ever think that?'

exaggeration: making things seem bigger to hammer home a point – 'I've told her a million times not to exaggerate.'

What does using these techniques for effect mean?

Using **rhetorical questions**, **humour** and **exaggeration** will help engage your listeners and bring variety to your presentation. You need to think about what each technique will make your audience feel or respond.

Checklist for success

- You need to use rhetorical questions, humour and exaggeration sparingly and only when suitable for your topic or audience.
- You need to plan in advance which of these techniques you will use.

ACTIVITY

Read this extract from a presentation to a group of headteachers.

With a partner, decide which questions, humour and exaggeration are inappropriate.

> So, how are you guys doing? I've got to say, you look pretty bored: I suppose you always do. Anyway, I've managed to cheer up thousands and thousands of conferences like this one, so it was worth your while turning up today. Actually, it's just as well you came today, because I don't suppose many of you will be around much longer. I bet your doctors are pretty busy, aren't they?

Focus for development:
Making presentations more interesting

Rhetorical questions

Rhetorical questions challenge the audience to think more actively about something. For example:

'Can this ever be acceptable?' – probable reaction: 'No!'

'Why, then have these changes been introduced?' – probable reaction: 'Tell me more.'

Add two rhetorical questions to this extract to add interest.

The royal family is something we should admire. They stand above politics and make us proud. Without them, the world would think less of Britain. Not only that, increasingly they seem so human: the two princes are just like ordinary young men you might meet anywhere.

Not everyone finds it easy to be funny. However, if you can add witty touches it often keeps the audience listening.

You could try using a funny **anecdote** (or short story) to support your point, for example: 'I caught measles on holiday. Well, actually, measles caught me. What happened was...'

ACTIVITY

With a partner, try to add a funny follow-on to these sentences.

- Anyone can dress well if they know where to shop.
- I try to help my cousin. Well...

Exaggeration

Don't over-use exaggeration, but it can have considerable impact. For example:

Crack SAS commandos couldn't track down and bring back my father when he's out for a night on the town.

ACTIVITY

Which of these exaggerations is more effective? Why?

- 'You'd have to go to the ends of the earth to find a better movie than this.'
- 'Literally millions of different kinds of bugs crawled out when we moved the stones to set up our tent.'

ASSESSMENT FOCUS

Write the opening of a speech about a person you admire – someone you know well, or someone famous.

- Explain why you admire them.
- Use rhetorical questions, humour and exaggeration.
- When you've finished, identify each feature by underlining it.

Remember

- Using rhetorical questions, humour and exaggeration can make your presentation more interesting.
- These features should only be used occasionally and if appropriate for your audience or topic.

Delivering your presentation

Learning objective

- To be best prepared to deliver a presentation.

Examiner's tip

Make sure any props that you pass round during your talk don't distract your audience.

Use PowerPoint to show your main points or to illustrate ideas, with photographs, diagrams or a short video. It will help guide you through your talk as well – but don't use it as a script. You get no marks for reading from the screen!

Examiner's tip

Making regular eye contact with your listeners shows confidence. A smile helps too.

How do you deliver a presentation well?

If you have **structured your ideas** and planned to use some **language techniques**, you should be ready to deliver your presentation with style. If you are not prepared, you could underperform.

Checklist for success

- You need to organise your presentation so that you know what to say in what order.
- You need to know how to handle your audience: this is crucial for your success.

Speakers deal with audiences in different ways: a stand-up comedian is likely to move around and joke with the audience, while a presenter at an awards ceremony will be more serious.

Focus for development: Establishing and maintaining a good impression

First impressions

First impressions count. If you seem calm and prepared, you will impress your audience. People notice body language: try not to look nervous.

ACTIVITY

In groups of four, improvise two scenes where a young person has a job interview at a supermarket.

- One interviewee knows about the job and is enthusiastic.
- The other knows nothing about the job and shows no interest.

Talk about the different impressions created.

Sustaining your role

Having created a good impression, you need to keep your confidence going throughout. Remember:

- Listeners can get bored quickly.
- A strong opening is wasted if it's followed by a muddle of points.
- Move through your planned material and head towards a clear ending.

Dealing with questions

You will probably have to answer questions from your audience at the end of your presentation. Try to think ahead to what they might be.

Good answers can often lift a Grade D presentation up to Grade C level.

ACTIVITY

Why is the Grade C answer to this question better?

> **Question:** What more *can* we do to help old people?

Notice that the Grade C answer has

- humour
- an extended idea (how to make them feel wanted)
- no irrelevant thoughts, such as 'sometimes I just give up'.

Grade D answer

We can do some things and try to help. Of course, they are usually grumpy so that's often it. I try sometimes, but sometimes I just give up. Whatever happens, we shouldn't though, because it's good to do their shopping and stuff like that...

Grade C answer

We can carry them across the road! No, seriously, we need to care more about them, take time to talk to them... All that stuff. They are happier if they feel wanted...

ASSESSMENT FOCUS

Create an impressive opening to the presentation:

My life out of school

Deliver the opening, then take questions. Ask for feedback on how you performed.

Examiner's tip ✭

If you anticipate some likely questions, you can have the information ready.

Remember

- **Prepare thoroughly.**
- **Impress your audience from the start.**
- **Sustain their interest to the end.**

Grade Booster

Extended Assessment Task

Produce a detailed plan for a presentation to your class, entitled:

> **What is the best sort of day out?**
> *Persuade your audience to accept your point of view.*

Or, you could choose one of these topics:

> - **Argue that there is no such thing as a good day out.**
> - **Argue that it would be better if people concentrated on making everyday life better rather than being obsessed with holidays.**
> - **Offer advice on how to enjoy your time on holiday and avoid problems.**

Make a note in your plan of the language techniques you will use at various stages, to interest your audience.

Pay particular attention to your opening, how you develop your ideas and your ending.

Deliver the presentation and ask for feedback.

Evaluation – What have you learned?

With a partner, use the grade checklist below to evaluate your work on the Extended Assessment Task.

- I can organise and deliver a structured presentation for a given audience.
- I can use presentational techniques and appropriate and effective language.
- I can hold the attention of my audience from start to finish.
- I can answer questions using some detail.

- I can plan and deliver a presentation to a given audience and use different techniques to interest them.
- I can begin and end relevantly and talk for an appropriate length of time.
- I can answer questions using some detail.

- I can express straightforward ideas.
- I can use some variety of vocabulary appropriately.
- I can begin to adapt talk for particular audiences.

- I can express ideas and use detail to add interest.
- I can use straightforward vocabulary and grammar and some standard English.

You may need to go back and look at the relevant pages from this section again.

Discussing and Listening

Introduction

This section of Chapter 3 shows you how to

- prepare for a discussion with one or more people
- speak and listen effectively in group situations
- improve your discussion skills.

Why is it important to spend time improving discussion and listening skills?

- Although we all talk and listen each day in many different situations, many people do not understand how to discuss topics effectively and skilfully.
- Discussion is not about simply making your point of view known; it is also about listening, responding and possibly changing previously held views.
- Persuading someone to agree with you is a skill that can be developed.
- Listening sensitively and accepting other people's views is a sign of maturity.

A **Grade E** candidate will

- make relevant contributions to discussions and respond positively to what others say
- follow discussions and ask straightforward questions.

E

A **Grade D** candidate will

- stay involved right through a discussion
- make effective contributions
- show they understand by responding appropriately to what is said.

D

A **Grade C** candidate will

- communicate clearly, using language that is appropriate to the situation
- listen carefully, developing their own and others' ideas and making significant contributions to discussions
- they are likely to ask questions, stimulate the discussion and are able to summarise what is said
- they stay focused on the subject.

C

Prior learning

Before you begin this unit, think about

- discussions you have watched on television.
- discussions you have taken part in at school
- discussions with friends

Who has appeared to be in control? How do they direct the conversation? Which people seem left out, and why?

How successful have they been? Why have they sometimes ground to a halt or not produced a conclusion? What can go wrong?

Who do you most likc to talk with, and why? When do you find conversations with friends annoying?

Preparing for discussion

What is there to prepare?

The kind of preparation needed will depend on the topic. For example, if you are discussing teenage crime, you may gather facts, figures and opinions from the Internet. If you are asked how your local area could be improved, you would probably collect other people's ideas and opinions.

Checklist for success

- You need to know what you will be discussing and, if appropriate, what your role in the discussion will be.
- You need to prepare ideas and information and note them down.

ACTIVITY

What would you find out in advance, to help you in this discussion?

> *In a group of four or five, come to an agreement about the five greatest-ever recording artists.*

Focus for development: Roles and research

Some discussions just happen naturally in class; preparation can help with others.

Chairing the discussion

You might be asked to chair a discussion. As chair, you need to have questions ready to ask and information ready to keep the discussion going. You must also be prepared to adapt to what anyone else says.

ACTIVITY

You have been asked to chair a discussion about how £5 million should be spent to improve your school.

Draw up notes you might use. For example:
- How will you start? (You could offer a range of ideas to be discussed).
- Will each person speak in turn?
- Will there be summaries?
- How will you end (in general terms)?

Adopting a point of view

You may be asked to take a particular point of view. If so, you need to be clear about what this is and prepare how you are going to support that viewpoint.

ACTIVITY

Imagine you are to be involved in the discussion about spending the £5 million.

You are supporting the view that half the money should be spent on new sports facilities and half on new teachers. Prepare your notes.

> **A student writes…**
> We did the £5 million discussion.
> I found some facts, figures and quotes to use and it was the first time I've performed like a 'star' in English.

ASSESSMENT FOCUS

Your teacher has warned you that you will be involved in a group discussion about whether there is still time to save the world from global warming.

You can choose whether to agree or disagree.

Make notes that

- support your opinion
- are in a logical order
- include some relevant facts, opinions and examples.

> **Remember**
>
> - **Prepare for discussions as much as you can, so you have more to say.**
> - **Never read from scripted notes.**
> - **Adapt your notes as the discussion develops.**

Developing strategies for confident talk

Learning objective

- To understand how to be, and appear, more confident in discussions.

How can anyone become more confident?

Confidence is important in all speaking and listening activities, including group discussions. If you are well-prepared (see page 134–5) you will show confidence in the way you speak.

Checklist for success

- You need to be prepared to offer views, listen carefully and ask questions.
- You need to work with people you feel comfortable with wherever possible.

Focus for development:
Improving your confidence

Speaking with confidence does not just mean speaking clearly. You also need to sound as if you **believe** in what you are saying.

Some hesitation is natural, because we think as we speak, but hesitating all the time would be a problem in an assessment.

ACTIVITY

Look at this short extract from a discussion.

The students are analysing advertisements they have just been given.

Who is more confident, Abi or Jenny? Why?

Abi:	So, does this advertisement work or not?
Jenny:	Well… there's the picture…
Abi:	Yes. *(Raises her eyebrows to Jenny)*
Jenny:	And the colours are good. I like them… Some of them…
Abi:	Do they have any effect though? Do they make us think?
Jenny:	Yes. No… Some… I don't know really…

Asking questions

Asking **appropriate questions** – which link with what someone has just said – can make you seem more in control and shows you are listening.

For example, you might

- ask for extra information: 'So, if maths is so wonderful, can you tell me why we need to learn about equations?'
- encourage reluctant speakers to join in: 'James – can you add to that point?'
- challenge people: 'You honestly believe that Spiderman exists?'

ACTIVITY

What questions might you ask in each of these cases?

Steph:	I've read some Shakespeare and the stories are utterly unbelievable.

(Ask for extra information.)

Anna:	I think she's right. Probably.

(Ask a question to encourage Anna to say more.)

Steph:	We shouldn't have to read Shakespeare; it's just a waste of our time.

(Ask a question to challenge what Steph has said.)

A student writes…

I never feel I'm saying enough in discussions. Other people say a lot more than me. But I think what I'm saying is important.

Answer…

Confidence is not just about talking at length. Careful listening, followed by a sensible comment or a good question, can show your confidence just as well.

ASSESSMENT FOCUS

To improve your confidence, discuss this topic in groups of three.

> *Should we should bring back hanging?*

- One of you should be the chair and introduce the discussion confidently.
- The others should take opposing viewpoints.
- The chair will use questions at different stages to help the discusssion.
- The chair will sum things up clearly.

Remember

- **Show confidence in a discussion and you will gain more marks.**
- **Be well-prepared and you should be at ease in the discussion.**
- **Know when to speak and when to listen.**

Developing and supporting ideas

What does supporting and developing an idea mean?

In conversation people often state an idea simply but fail to support what they say.

Being able to extend ideas or offer alternatives to ideas put forward by others moves the discussion on and gains you credit.

Checklist for success

- You need to know what you are talking about and to extend ideas in a discussion if you are going to be convincing.
- You need to listen carefully so that you can challenge or support what others say successfully.

ACTIVITY

If the points below were made in a discussion, how would you develop them (add information) and argue against them?

Copy out and complete the table.

Statement	Development	Opposite argument
'Football is a total waste of time.'		
'Nothing in life is more important than love.'		

Focus for development:
Extending and opposing ideas

Extending ideas

Discussions are usually better if you can make your ideas more detailed and encourage others to make their ideas clearer.

To improve your own points, add some supporting comments. For example:

- evidence (facts, statistics, details)
- anecdotes – short stories or examples to illustrate an idea
- others' opinions.

What evidence could you use to develop this point? Jot down some ideas.

> *Everyone should take more care to avoid sunburn.*

Add some **facts** and an **anecdote**. You can invent what you need.

To extend the ideas of others, you can use phrases like

- 'True! What else..?'
- 'And can you take that idea one stage further?'

To develop one of your own ideas, you can use phrases like

- 'Yes. And that reminds me of when…'
- 'Yes, I agree. Not only that, but…'

Opposing ideas

Discussions involving opposing views should not become disagreements. To argue your point in a controlled way, you can

- support a viewpoint
- try to change other speakers' minds sensitively.

Discuss with a partner:

Why is Mandy more successful in this argument that Dave?

Dave:	I think the advertisement is good.
Mandy:	Really? Why? Have you seen that picture?
Dave:	'Course I have. That's why I like it.
Mandy:	Typical. There's a pretty girl in it so you think it's good. I mean, yes, she's pretty but does the picture go with the product?
Dave:	Who cares?
Mandy:	Lots of us do, actually. Look at what it's saying…

ASSESSMENT FOCUS

Write down what you would say in response to these statements. Use the techniques you have learnt to develop ideas and challenge other views with tact.

> *There is only one good place to live: Australia. Australia has everything anyone could ever want. Only a fool would choose to live anywhere else.*

Remember

- **Extend and develop your ideas to make them more convincing.**
- **If you challenge other people's ideas tactfully and in detail, it is more likely to make them change their mind.**

Responding to talk

What does responding to talk mean?

You are assessed on your ability to **talk** *and* **listen**. Your physical reactions will suggest how well you are listening, and what you say will show how well you have understood the discussion.

Checklist for success

- You need to remember that both speaking and listening skills are vital in any discussion.
- You need to focus on listening carefully because what you hear affects how well you respond.

ACTIVITY

Think back to the last assembly you attended. Discuss with a partner:

- What were people in the audience doing which showed they were not listening? Think about students and staff.
- What was said in the assembly? What can you remember?
- How well did you and others **listen** on that occasion?

Focus for development: How you respond

Physical reactions

It is easy to identify who is not listening carefully, because of the way they behave. Try to avoid

- gazing out of the window
- muttering to someone else
- doodling.

Faces can be revealing too. Someone who is listening might

- raise eyebrows
- open or narrow their eyes slightly
- smile
- bite a lip.

What you say

What you say reveals how well you are listening because you respond appropriately. Poor listeners are easily spotted.

Examiner's tip

Don't force a reaction! If you are listening carefully your face will show it naturally.

Read this extract from a group discussion about who we should respect.

Shabnam:	OK. So we're going to put these people into order of importance. Lucy, can you start?
Lucy:	Princess Diana.
Steve:	I think she was over-rated. No one talks about her now. When did she die…?
Lucy:	There's Martin Luther King too. He was good.
Steve:	They all were, weren't they?
Shabnam:	My dad never liked Margaret Thatcher. What was she like?
Steve:	First woman Prime Minister…
Lucy:	President Kennedy… I don't know anything about him…

Discuss with a partner:

- How are Lucy's listening skills limiting this discussion?
- Why are the others better?

If you **listen effectively**, you can take in others' ideas and develop new ones.
Andi is a Grade C student. How do her listening skills show here?

Melody:	Let's face it, fashion isn't *that* important.
Andi:	Because? (*She looks quizzical and opens a palm, asking for clarification.*)
Melody:	There are lots more serious issues to think about.
Andi:	(*Andi shakes her head, smiling.*) But fashion brings people pleasure, doesn't it?
Melody:	Not much…

ASSESSMENT FOCUS

Discuss this in a group. Record the discussion, then play it back.

Is fashion really important?

How often did you

- 'disappear' from the discussion? (Were you still listening?)
- argue effectively?
- develop an idea?

Remember

- In discussions, listening is as important as speaking.
- Your listening ability will be clear in what you do and say.

Reacting to suggestions and summarising

Learning objectives

- To recognise what people are suggesting.
- To learn how to summarise.

What does reacting to suggestions and summarising mean?

Responding sensitively – not only to what people **say directly** but to what they **imply** – shows you are a good listener.

People often say things which **suggest** or imply something else: for example, 'I love your new dress. It's so… different.'

Summing up briefly what has been said in a discussion shows you have listened and understood well. It also helps to round off the discussion.

Checklist for success

- You need to listen carefully and show that you understand how to react to what is said.
- You need to be able to sum up what has been said.

Focus for development: Showing listening skills

Reacting to suggestions

Responding to what others are suggesting shows good listening skills – but your response must be appropriate.

> **ACTIVITY**
>
> In the discussion below, what is suggested by:
>
> Jenny at A   Daniel at B   Daniel at C?
>
> | | |
> |---|---|
> | **Daniel:** | Geography's like RE – a total waste of time. |
> | **Jenny:** | I agree. I've hated it since Year 7. I've had Mrs Bates every year and she's always had it in for me. (A) |
> | **Daniel:** | Too right. And I've had Mrs Cowen. How can she teach? She's too old to even know what's going on. (B) |
> | **Maisie:** | She said, 'An understanding of geography is vital if we are to understand the world around us.' You don't have to have a degree to know that's rubbish. |
> | **Daniel:** | She said, 'You've got to work hard to achieve anything.' That's like something my grandma would say. (C) |

Examiner's tip

Look out for what other speakers are suggesting, and challenge them if necessary.

142

Summarising

If you listen closely, you will be able to

- sum up what has been said in a discussion so far
- explain the main points of view at the end.

Making brief notes though the discussion will help, so nothing is missed. Notes are useful to

- group members, for weighing up different opinions
- the chair, for maintaining the balance between people with different views
- the summariser for commenting at the end.

ACTIVITY

Watch a current affairs programme in which there are guests representing opposing viewpoints.

- Note down the main points made.
- Summarise the viewpoints.

Examiner's tip ★

To summarise, use phrases like: 'On the one hand… whereas on the other hand…'. This shows you are balancing the views.

ASSESSMENT FOCUS

In a group, discuss this statement:

> **Out of school, most teenagers waste most of their time.**

- Whilst discussing, look out for suggestions and respond to them.
- Each member of the group can then summarise the discussion.

Remember

- **Good listeners will spot suggested ideas, and respond to them.**
- **If you can summarise accurately, you show you have been listening.**

Making significant contributions

What are significant contributions?

You are making a significant contribution if you

- support others in the group
- show understanding of others' ideas
- comment sensibly, helping to move discussions forward.

You need to be prepared to help direct discussions and sort out disagreements.

ACTIVITY

Working on your own, match these examples with the speaking and listening skills.

Examples	Skills
1 Right, to kick things off: why don't we like this story?	**A** Summarising
2 Are you sure, Satish? Let's just look at …	**B** Getting the discussion back on track
3 That's agreed, then. We think …	**C** Opening the discussion
4 Well, that's a totally different point. For now, can we get back to …?	**D** Challenging an opinion and focusing the discussion again

Focus for development:
Directing the discussion

A good performer will support others and, despite their own viewpoint, will ensure that all views are heard and all participants feel comfortable.

ACTIVITY

The extract on the next page shows the difference between two students working at Grade E, Cyndi and Jamie, and a Grade C student, Kylie.

Kylie:	So, is single-sex education a good thing or not? Jamie?
Jamie:	It's unnatural. We should all be together, right?
Kylie:	OK.
Cyndi:	Boys are a pain in school.
Jamie:	That's stupid. We're not any worse than the girls. They mess about with hair and stuff…
Kylie:	OK. So, you don't really agree. But wouldn't you both be happier if it was single sex? Jamie, if the girls are always messing about – you'd be away from them. Yes?
Jamie:	Not really. I like girls…
Cyndi:	I get sick of boys…
Kylie:	Could you both go to different schools then? A mixed one for Jamie, a girls' school for Cyndi?

Discuss with a partner:

- How does Kylie help the discussion? Look at each of her contributions.
- How might the others react to her suggestion at the end? Explain.

A student writes…

I like working in groups but I'm hopeless at leading the others. I always get swamped by their ideas.

Answer…

If you can't lead the whole discussion, try to guide the group through parts of it. Brief notes might help you stay in touch.

ASSESSMENT FOCUS

- In a group of three, have a discussion in which two take directly opposed viewpoints and the third guides the others to a friendly outcome. Choose from these topics:

  Football is more important than anything

  or

  … is the best band the world has ever known

- Then repeat with a different topic and different roles.

Remember

- **When guiding a group discussion, the priority is to try to avoid conflict and get agreement.**
- **Sensitive listening and the ability to encourage involvement and understanding make significant contributions to discussion.**

Grade Booster

Extended Assessment Task

Working as a group, prepare a discussion on the topic to the right. Then hold the discussion.

> *From the age of 14, young people should have much more freedom in every area of their lives.*

Each member of the group should

- decide on their initial viewpoint
- produce some bulleted notes and/or other materials for discussion
- come to the discussion with an otherwise open mind.

It is likely to help if

- one member chairs the discussion
- at least one person takes each side of the argument
- one member summarises the discussion for the rest of the class.

Evaluation – What have you learned?

With a partner, use the grade checklist below to evaluate your work on the Extended Assessment Task.

- I can listen closely and sympathetically.
- I can ask relevant questions and make significant contributions.
- I can also engage with others' ideas, recognising bias and using precise detail.
- I can stay focused throughout the discussion, offer detailed and relevant ideas and have the ability to summarise what has been said.

- I can sustain involvement and make effective contributions.
- I can show evidence of understanding and respond appropriately to what is said.
- I use some detail to clarify my ideas and listen throughout. Most contributons are relevant.

- I can respond positively to what is said.
- I can ask for clarification and make relevant contributions.
- I can also follow ideas and ask straightforward questions.

- I can make contributions and respond appropriately to the contributions of others.

You may need to go back and look at the relevant pages from this section again.

Adopting a Role

This section of Chapter 3 shows you how to
- approach the task when adopting a role
- develop a role successfully
- improve performances.

Why is it important to be able to adopt a role?

- It is one of the three tasks you must complete for the Speaking and Listening section of the exam.
- If you can adopt a role successfully, it shows understanding of the character you are portraying – and understanding others is a skill for life.

A **Grade E** candidate will
- show some understanding of aspects of characters and situations
- meet the basic requirements of different roles by using simple patterns of speech, gesture and movement.

E

A **Grade D** candidate will
- be able to prepare a performance and perform a role in a believable manner
- be able to interest the audience through intonation, movement and gesture.

D

A **Grade C** candidate will
- develop and sustain roles through appropriate language and effective gesture and movement
- engage watchers' interest by showing understanding of characters, ideas and situations
- give performances of appropriate length in which the character will be sustained throughout.

C

Prior learning

Before you begin this unit, think about
- soap operas and/or television series or films you watch

- how the characters were portrayed in any live theatre you have seen

- what the acting was like in any amateur drama you may have seen.

What is memorable about your favourite characters? How are facial expressions and gestures used? How are the most memorable lines delivered, and why?

How were they made convincing?

How might the characters have been made more realistic and interesting?

Getting into role

Learning objectives

- To learn how to explore a role and what is required when improvising it.

- To think about what can be done to improve performances and be more successful.

What does getting into role mean?

In your Speaking and Listening assessment, you will be asked to **improvise a role** using drama techniques. You might have to play a character from literature or someone from real life such as a doctor or cleaner, or you might have to represent a viewpoint in a discussion – supporting a new leisure complex, for example.

You need to prepare in advance to create and develop a **convincing character**.

Checklist for success

In order to portray a character convincingly, you need to explore

- their **history**: what has happened to them
- their **behaviour**: how they speak to others and act
- their **relationships**: with people around them
- their **motivations**: why they behave as they do.

ACTIVITY

Choose a character from a novel, play or poem you have studied.

- Make notes about this character for each of the areas listed above.
- In a group of three, imagine that your characters meet in heaven. Introduce yourselves, describing your life.

Focus for development: Planned improvisations

Look at the improvisation below, based on this situation:

A headteacher is meeting an angry parent whose child has been excluded for fighting.

What advice would you give these two **Grade D** performers, to improve their marks?

Think about what they say and their movements.

Paula:	(*sitting at her desk*) Hello, Mrs Garvey, please sit down.
Dawn:	Thanks. I wanted to see you. (*She sits down.*)
Paula:	What can I do for you?
Dawn:	I'm unhappy about Alice.
Paula:	I expected that. Could I get you a cup of tea?
Dawn:	No, thanks. I want to talk about Alice, she's very important to me.
Paula:	Fair enough. So, what can we do? (*She sips a cup of tea.*)
Dawn:	I thought you would know. I want our Alice back in school. She hasn't done anything wrong. (*thumping the desk*) You're the Head. Do something. You think she causes all the trouble. That's not true. You should look after her.
Paula:	Well, we'll see what we can do, Mrs Garvey…

ASSESSMENT FOCUS

With a partner, act out your own headteacher/parent interview.
Choose your own topic.

- First, make notes to help you play your role.
- Then decide together roughly how the conversation will start – develop – finish?

After performing, decide which were the most successful parts of your performance and why.

Improve any details and try again. Ask yourselves:

- Do we need to know more background about the characters or the situation?
- Could we change the mood to increase the interest for the audience?
  For example by building gradually to a big finish?

Remember

- Careful planning for your characterisation is essential.
- Try to make your character convincing.
- Preparing well with your group will help make your performance better.

Speaking in role

What does speaking in role mean?

Your performance will be more believable if you think carefully about a character's background.

However, to be really convincing you also need to pay attention to **how** your character speaks and **what** you say. Try to reveal what you **think and feel** through your words, not just say things which move the story along.

Checklist for success

Before you practise your performance, ask yourself:

- Have I prepared properly?
- Have I thought through what will happen and what I need to do at every stage?

After a practice run-through, ask yourself:

- Have I worked effectively as part of the group?
- What can I do to improve my performance?

Before the final performance, ask yourself:

- Do I know roughly what I will be saying at each stage?
- Am I secure in my character? Do I know how I will react?

A student writes…

How precise should we be about preparing our performance?

Answer…

You need to know enough before starting so that no one in the group will be surprised by events and everyone is aware of roughly what will be said. Beyond that, you improvise!

ACTIVITY

In these extracts a father, who is a single parent, is talking to his ex-wife …

Both students tell the audience similar information.

Discuss with a partner why the second one is better.

How does it

- express emotion?
- create a 'speaking voice' that sounds real?

Grade D answer

> I need some more money to help me feed the kids. Because you're their mum, it's reasonable that you should help to support them. They need shoes and new clothes. I can't do everything.

Grade C answer

> They're not just my kids. They're yours too. I need you to help support them because you know I simply don't have enough money. My wages can't stretch far enough and it's hard to even feed them properly, never mind buy new clothes…

Focus for development:
Speaking in character

Obviously you need to speak clearly, but you also need to speak in the way your character would. This means you won't always use Standard English.

ACTIVITY

Look at this **Grade C** improvisation in role as the Nurse in *Romeo and Juliet*. Discuss with a partner what features of her speech make it successful.

> Phew! I've had a hard day, I can tell you. I've been rushing around from morning 'til night. No rest! Not a chance. Everybody in this house wants something doing. And they ask muggins here to do it. Nobody cares about me. Couldn't give two hoots about old Nursie. None of 'em.

ASSESSMENT FOCUS

Work with a partner, each choosing two different characters from literature, the media or real life.

Demonstrating clearly how they speak, make a 30-second speech by each character.

Then your partner will criticise your performance, picking out

- what was convincing
- what was unconvincing, in terms of the character's personality and the words used.

Remember

- Focus clearly on **what** you say and **how** you say it throughout your improvisation.

151

Developing a role through expression and movement

Learning objective

- To understand how words can be supported by actions.

How can I develop a role through expression and movement?

As well as thinking carefully about the words your character would use (see page 150), you can develop a character by adding physical actions. This might be a limp, a mannerism such as furrowing your brows or showing anger with the jab of a finger.

However, to develop a role successfully though **gesture** and **movement**, you first need to understand the character's feelings.

Checklist for success

You need to observe people closely – their expressions, their movements and their peculiarities. Notice how they

- show feelings on their faces
- stand
- move
- show feelings in their mannerisms (for example, scratch their head, play with their fingers).

Focus for development:
Expression and movement

ACTIVITY

Choose someone both you and a friend should recognise from television. Make notes about them for each of the areas listed.

Then mime them doing something and ask your friend to recognise who they are.

ACTIVITY

Look at these **expressions**. Explain how you think each person is feeling.

Read these two statements:

- I'm happy here. There's nothing more I want from life than this.
- Things have got to change if we are going to get through this.

Create very different characters by speaking each of these statements as

- an old person
- a confident business person.

Concentrate on giving your characters physical characteristics, such as a bad leg or a habit of smoothing their hair. Make your facial expressions convincing.

Gestures and movements add to the feelings you want to show. For example:

- Hugging someone shows affection.
- Hands to the mouth could show shock.
- Arms wide apart could show welcome.
- A waved fist demonstrates anger (or triumph).
- Sitting down suddenly could register dismay.
- Walking away could show a struggle to accept what has been said.

ASSESSMENT FOCUS

With a friend, act out the extract below, using expression and movements.

- The first time, A is drunk and B is confused.
- The second time, A is frustrated and B is happy.

A: When the guy walks in…

B: Yeah… What?

A: Make sure it's safe…

B: It's safe?

A: Yes, safe.

B: Then what?

A: Get him.

B: Get him?

A: Yes. Are you stupid? Get him!

ACTIVITY

Imagine someone says each of these lines to you. Mime your reaction.

- We have no money left. We will have to move away, I'm afraid.
- She simply stepped into the road without looking. It wasn't the driver's fault. He couldn't stop.

What gestures and movements will you use?

Remember

- **Create an impression by how you react and move – but don't overdo it.**
- **Show your feelings even if you are not speaking.**
- **Support your words with expressions and movements.**

Maximising the impact

Learning objective

- *To learn how you can make the most of your role and gain good marks.*

What does maximising the impact mean?

To maximise the **impact** of your performance, show aspects of your character, sustain your role and finish strongly, leaving a clear impression of your character.

Checklist for success

- Plan exactly what you will do, what you will be talking about and how you will move and behave.
- Think seriously about how you will begin, maintain your role, and finish in a memorable way.

ACTIVITY

You are auditioning for a part in *Hollyoaks*. The part is a teenager who has just moved into the area and comes from a rich family but does not get on with their parents.

You have to walk into the café for the first time. How will you make an impact?

- What aspects of your character will you want to show?
- How will you behave towards the owner and other customers?

Focus for development: Making an impact

The opening

Performances can **start in different ways** but the opening is likely to establish your character.

ACTIVITY

You are 24 and have just arrived on holiday with a friend. You know no one else in the hotel. Your friend has gone out to look around and you go down to the pool.

In a small group, you are going to act out your first entrance. Imagine the people by the pool all go silent as you arrive. What will you do? What will be the first thing you say and to whom?

You might want to

- tell them about yourself
- tell them about your journey
- ask about the resort.

⭐ Examiner's tip

Talk to the people around you, but remember the audience too. Sometimes, actors on stage talk directly to the audience when they have something important to say.

The middle

Stay focused on your role:

- React in a convincing way, using speech, expression and movement.
- Keep focused and don't become distracted by the audience.
- Don't allow yourself to be excluded from the main action.

The ending

Your final appearance or your final speech will be your last chance to create an impact. It will help you if you can

- make a significant final contribution
- show you are the same person but, perhaps, also show how you have been affected by what has happened.

> **Glossary**
> **monologue:** an uninterrupted speech delivered by one person.

Interviews

Learning objective

- To understand how to act as an interviewer or interviewee.

When might I have to take part in an interview?

This might be in your **presentation** task – dealing with questions. Or it might be a **role** you are asked to adopt.

Checklist for success

You need to be successful as an interviewer and interviewee.

- A successful interviewer asks probing questions.
- An effective interviewee gives detailed answers.

ACTIVITY

Watch two different interviews on television, one involving a TV personality and one a politician.

Which interview is better and why?

What impression do we get of each interviewer and each interviewee from

- the language they use
- their facial expressions
- their body language?

Focus for development:
Good questions and good answers

Interviewing

ACTIVITY

In this extract, what does Sarah, the interviewer, do badly? Then what does she do well?

Sarah:	Tell us about your early life. ——— standard opening
Beata:	I was brought up in Warsaw, then we moved to England.
Sarah:	What did you first think of——— sudden switch university?
Beata:	I had a terrible time…
Sarah:	Yes. I think we all know that story. You have apologised, of course: but will the public ever forgive you for what happened…?

Answer…

It's fine to have a list of questions, but only as a guide. More importantly, you need to listen to the answers and respond to them by asking for more detail, commenting on what is said and changing your next question if necessary.

Being the interviewee

Prepare fully for the interview so that you know your subject well.
You need to be able to give detailed answers that will interest listeners.

ACTIVITY

What details and opinions does this **Grade C** student use to add interest to their answer?

Interviewee:
I had a great time as a kid. I was brought up in California. It was all sunshine and beaches. I loved it. When my parents said they were coming back to England, I was gutted. I didn't know anyone here and didn't know anything about the country either. I'd always been an American before.

— gives opinion in role

— good detail

ASSESSMENT FOCUS

Imagine you are a famous person of your choice.
Prepare to answer these questions in role.
Make up any necessary details.

- What are your earliest memories?
- Tell us about your time at school.
- How has fame affected your life?

Remember

- **You are assessed on your speaking and listening skills, so show both.**
- **Interviewers must be fully involved and interviewees must interest the audience.**

157

Grade Booster

Extended Assessment Task

In a group of three or four, plan an improvisation set in a workplace. A valuable item has gone missing and one person is accused.

Work though these stages:
- Plan what will happen.
- Divide the improvisation into scenes and decide what will happen in each one (or decide what will happen in one scene, if that is all there is).
- Make detailed notes on your character.
- Decide how you will play your role.
- Practise as a group.
- Discuss improvements.
- Have another run-through.
- Perform for the rest of the teaching group.

Take feedback on the performance, discuss it with your group, then improve your performance in the light of what you have learned.

Evaluation – What have you learned?

With a partner, use the grade checklist below to evaluate your work on the Extended Assessment Task.

- I can sustain and develop a role.
- I can use effective language, gestures and movement and show I understand how the character thinks and feels.
- I am convincing throughout and offer more than just simple characteristics.

- I can prepare a performance, perform in role and use appropriate language, gestures and movement.
- My role is believable and clearly different from the person I actually am.

- I can attempt to perform in role and can use simple patterns of speech, gesture and movement.

- I can create simple characters and react to situations in appropriate ways.

You may need to go back and look at the relevant pages from this section again.

Controlled Assessment Preparation
Speaking and Listening

Introduction

In this section you will

- consider examples from students' Speaking and Listening assessments
- look closely at how other students have responded to the tasks
- identify the strengths and weaknesses in their responses.

Why is preparation of this kind important?

- The example responses in this section allow you to take time to think about how well others speak and listen.
- It is important to learn from the examples of others.
- Taking the opportunity to consider and discuss how activities can be approached and how others have performed will help you to improve the quality of your own performances.

Key Information

Unit 2 is the Speaking and Listening assessment.

- It has three parts: **Presenting**, **Discussing and Listening**, and **Role Playing**.
- The three activities are worth **20% of your overall English GCSE mark**.

What will the assessments involve?

You will have to

- make an individual presentation
- discuss and listen as part of a group
- play a role.

You are likely to complete more than one assessment in each of the three areas, with your best mark in each case being used.

It is crucial that you avoid reading from notes in any of the activities. You are allowed to use notes if they are appropriate (for example, in the presentation), but you are expected to refer to them as you talk, not simply read them.

The Assessment

The assessment objective for Speaking and Listening (AO1) states that you must be able to do the following:

- Speak to communicate clearly and purposefully; structure and sustain talk, adapting it to different situations and audiences; use standard English and a variety of techniques as appropriate.
- Listen and respond to speakers' ideas and perspectives, and how they construct and express meanings.
- Interact with others, shaping meanings through suggestions, comments and questions and drawing ideas together.
- Create and sustain different roles.

Targeting Grade C

Some of the key features of Grade D and Grade C answers are as follows:

Grade D candidates	See example on page 161 and 163–4
<ul><li>interest the listener in different ways</li><li>use an increasing variety of appropriate vocabulary</li><li>understand the need for standard English</li><li>make effective contributions throughout discussions</li><li>respond appropriately to what is said</li><li>perform in role in a believable manner and interest the audience through intonation, movement and gesture.</li></ul>	**D**

Grade C candidates	See example on pages 162–3 and 165
<ul><li>adapt their talk to the situation</li><li>use Standard English confidently</li><li>interest the listener through their use of language</li><li>communicate clearly</li><li>listen carefully and develop their own and others' ideas</li><li>make significant contributions to discussions</li><li>develop and sustain roles through appropriate language and effective gesture and movement, and interest watchers by showing understanding of characters, ideas and situations.</li></ul>	**C**

Exploring Sample Responses

Individual presentation

This is an extract from a presentation about 'Why Work Experience is a good experience'.

Example 1

I had a great time on my work experience and I would recommend everyone to do it. I was working in a hospital in the kitchen and although I spent a lot of every day washing up, it was still fun. For a change, they let me clean the floors sometimes and although that sounds awful it could be great fun because I got the chance to use one of the scrubbing machines and they are really cool. You kind of lean to one side to make them go that way. The cleaners use them in school and they don't look like anything special but it can be a good laugh.

I also met some pretty good people and they helped me and showed me what to do. The other kitchen porter with me was called Raymond and he didn't have any teeth at all. He must have had pretty hard gums, because he seemed to eat most things. How can you get through life without teeth? There was also Annie who was about a million years old and she showed me how to rip the stem out of a lettuce and then turn it upside down and run water through it and all the leaves get cleaned at once. Pretty magic, that...

Examiner feedback

The response was delivered using only bulleted notes. It is focused on the title and suggests throughout that it was a good experience, though the examples given seem a little trivial – there might have been more important benefits to the student. There are some interesting touches about the people, though they are not developed as character studies. The opening and the language could have been improved.

Suggested grade: D

ACTIVITY

How might the response have been improved to Grade C level?
Think about
- how the opening could have been improved
- which vocabulary might have been made better
- what other kinds of details and ideas you might expect the speaker to include later
- how the speaker could really interest the listeners.

Now read this response to the same presentation title by a different candidate:

Example 2

rhetorical question → *Is work experience a good thing? I would say it is, and I have no doubts about that. I had a wonderful time working for Boots and I'd go back there every week if I could. They looked after me well: I had my supervisor, who told me what to do and kept checking that I was OK and knew what I was doing; and the other workers all treated me as if I was part of the team. I found out about what it is like to work in a big store and now know what it will be like when I leave school and enter the world of work.* ← situation established

why it was worthwhile

I want to start by talking about the interesting people you meet. You find out that adults can be fun to be with (and even that they can be childish at work when no one is around!) and going to work is great when you feel as if you have friends there. ← sense of order in the talk

an interesting aside

One of the girls – Annette – who worked on cosmetics was amazing. Looking at the layers of make-up she always wears, you would think that she was not real at all, but she had a fabulous sense of humour and made me laugh every day – much more than I ever do in school. One day an area manager was coming in, and you wouldn't believe what she did … ← individual as example

presents picture

complex sentence well controlled

start of anecdote

Examiner feedback

This begins well, giving some ideas about why the experience was positive, and then begins to work logically though them, starting with the people. Examples are used effectively. There is some variety of expression here (everything is not just 'good' or 'great') and the speaker gives a real sense of having enjoyed what happened – for example, the aside in brackets. At the end of the extract, she is moving on to deliver an anecdote. The style seems formal enough, sentences are varied and this is a good opening.

Suggested Grade: C

Discussing and Listening

This is an extract from a group discussion about transport and what could be done to improve it.

summarises Janey's opinion

Kane: So, you're saying we need more roads and it's as simple as that. Is it really just about building more roads and getting rid of more fields?

questions to get more information

Janey: Yeah… I think so… It would solve the problems… Simple.

Kane: But we have to think about the environment too.

a new angle

Janey: You're going to say we've all got to start riding bikes. Then we'll all get killed by the cars.

disagrees without offending Janey

Kane: Not if we're all on bikes. There won't be any cars, will there?

Janey: So how do we get to London? Grow wings?

Kane: No, grow more trains. Public transport's what we're supposed to be using, isn't it? Buses, trains, trams… that's the future.

touch of humour

Janey: I think that is just stupid.

helping Janey clarify

Kane: Why?

Janey: Because it is. I want to learn to drive and travel around and so does everyone else and I want to fly to holidays abroad. I don't see why I should miss out on everything.

own opinion challenges her

Kane: I think you'll have to. There's all this global warming stuff and transport's part of the problem. You know that. We have to change the ways we travel.

Janey: I hate all the grannies on the bus.

doesn't want to offend

Kane: Yeah. I know. Maybe we could have special buses for teenagers. You know, music on board and a disco upstairs and a make-up room for you.

lightens the conversation again

Janey: Hey…

Kane: OK. For you and your friends… with mascara on tap…
and lipstick racks on the walls…

Janey: Actually, that would be great!

Kane: And if it helped save the world, it would be worth every penny…

links back to what he feels is important

Examiner feedback

Janey is making useful contributions to the discussion and is following what is said. When she comments on us all riding bikes but getting killed by the cars, she is not perfectly logical. She develops a couple of points slightly and co-operates well with Kane.

Kane sustains the conversation and tries to impose some logic and development. He summarises and uses questioning effectively. His humour towards the end appeals to Janey, and he still manages to link it back to the main focus of the discussion.

Suggested grades: Janey D, Kane C

ACTIVITY

For each of these points made by Janey, decide how she could have developed them:

- We should solve the problem by building more roads.
- The idea of using public transport is stupid.
- Buses are full of old ladies.

How might she have countered these points made by Kane?

- There won't be any cars if we're riding bikes.
- Transport's part of the problem of global warming.

Adopting a role

Example 1

This student is speaking in role as Lennie, from *Of Mice and Men*.

(Sitting on a chair, facing the audience)

Me and George travel around together and we've been together for years. I used to live with my Aunt Clara but then me and George started travelling and we've been to lots of places. We were in Weed for a while and I made friends with a little girl there but then we had to leave and George made me hide in ditches and places and he said I'd done a bad thing but it's only 'cos I like to pet soft things. Sometimes I keep mice and then George makes me throw them away. He told Aunt Clara he'd look after me. When we got to the ranch, I made friends with Slim. He's a good guy. I don't like Curley though, but I like his wife 'cos she's purty. Candy had an old dog when we got there but that was shot. And we made friends with Crooks, but he lives in a room off the stable. He's on his own all the time, not like me and George.

JOHN STEINBECK'S CLASSIC NOVEL COMES TO THE SCREEN

Everyone has a dream, few dare to follow it..

Lenny did!

Of MICE AND MEN

Examiner feedback

The student has an understanding of Lennie's life and can talk as the character (in terms of the sort of details he might include, but also using 'purty'). Although some of the ideas are not well linked, that might be how someone who is not very clever might speak. However, it would have been better if the points were not quite so random and there was more development of ideas. There is no evidence here of Lennie using movement or gesture – he might have been better demonstrating his character by using more than just words to show what sort of person he is.

Suggested grade: D

In this second example, a student speaks as George, from *Of Mice and Men*.

Example 2

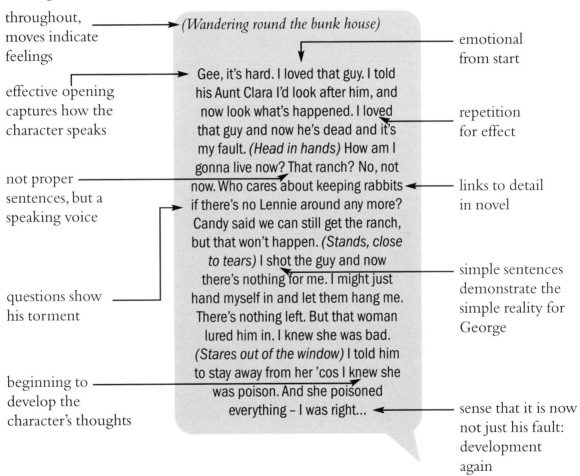

throughout, moves indicate feelings

effective opening captures how the character speaks

not proper sentences, but a speaking voice

questions show his torment

beginning to develop the character's thoughts

(Wandering round the bunk house)

Gee, it's hard. I loved that guy. I told his Aunt Clara I'd look after him, and now look what's happened. I loved that guy and now he's dead and it's my fault. *(Head in hands)* How am I gonna live now? That ranch? No, not now. Who cares about keeping rabbits if there's no Lennie around any more? Candy said we can still get the ranch, but that won't happen. *(Stands, close to tears)* I shot the guy and now there's nothing for me. I might just hand myself in and let them hang me. There's nothing left. But that woman lured him in. I knew she was bad. *(Stares out of the window)* I told him to stay away from her 'cos I knew she was poison. And she poisoned everything – I was right...

emotional from start

repetition for effect

links to detail in novel

simple sentences demonstrate the simple reality for George

sense that it is now not just his fault: development again

Examiner feedback

The student enters well into George's character – we get a clear impression of what the character is thinking through what he says and through his movements. We recognise his sorrow and possibly anger towards the end and the ideas seem to flow logically. The character is sustained and developed.

Suggested grade: C

Read through Example 1 on page 164 again, then act it out. There is no need to change the actual words. Just go through it putting in movement and gesture and notice how it is improved. If you can attempt an American accent, that would make it even better.

EXTENDED PRACTICE TASK

The local council has come up with an idea: there is to be a street festival in your area. Planning committees have been formed.

In a group of four, plan the grand procession. You need to have colourful floats which

- represent the community and the area
- will draw in people from outside the district.

You need entertainers who

- can move along with the procession
- offer a variety of skills and performances.

You will also have to consider, for security

- a police presence
- road closures.

Finally, you need to consider

- food and drink requirements for those taking part *and* those watching
- the route itself.

In your group, take on the roles of

- the chair who leads the discussion
- the festival organiser who also summarises the decisions at the end
- a local police officer
- a local business person.

Before you hold the discussion do some initial planning and make brief notes.

During the discussion, use the techniques and approaches you have learnt in this chapter.

If you only do five things...

1 When you are undertaking assessment tasks, avoid the temptation to use only simple words and short sentences – remember that you are rewarded for variety.

2 Attempt to speak appropriately in any given situation: formally, perhaps, for a presentation; speaking more 'normally', perhaps, if you are playing a character from a literary text.

3 If you are given the opportunity to plan, grasp it with both hands, because it will prove to be time well spent when you have to perform.

4 In discussions, pay attention to what others say: don't forget that listening is rewarded as well as talking. In role-play, try to really get into the character. Your performance will be more believable if you are thinking like the person and moving as they would move.

5 Take speaking and listening seriously. The 20% of marks awarded to it can be the difference between success and failure.

Unit 3A **Understanding Creative Texts** (Literary Reading)

What's it all about?

Reading a range of imaginative and creative texts enables you to explore some powerful ideas and ways of writing. This can be enjoyable, as well as feeding into your own writing and speaking work.

How will I be assessed?

You will get **20% of your English marks** for your ability to respond to a range of texts. You must study one or more Shakespeare plays, one or more texts from the English Literary Heritage and one text or a collection of texts from Exploring Cultures.

You will

- complete a Controlled Assessment task on **Characterisation and voice** or **Themes and ideas**, in which you cover one or more Shakespeare plays, poetry and one or more prose text (novel or short story) in **3 to 4 hours**

- write separately on the text from each of the three areas.

What is being tested?

You are being examined on your ability to

- read and understand texts, selecting material appropriately to support what you want to say
- develop and sustain interpretations of writers' ideas and perspectives
- explain and evaluate how writers use particular linguistic or grammatical effects (for example, imagery) to influence or engage the reader
- explain and evaluate how writers use structural or presentational features (such as rhyme patterns in poetry) to influence or engage the reader
- write about these effects and features in relation to 'characterisation and voice' and 'themes and ideas'.

Shakespeare: Characterisation and Themes

Introduction

This section of Chapter 4 shows you how to

- understand what a Controlled Assessment task on 'Characterisation and voice' and 'Themes and ideas' is about, in relation to *Romeo and Juliet*
- develop responses to tasks on these topics.

Why is it important to learn about characterisation and themes?

- They will be the focus of the responses you write.
- It is important to understand what they mean, how you can explore them, and how they relate to the Shakespeare play you are studying.

A **Grade D** candidate will

- show some understanding of the texts
- use appropriate quotations most of the time
- display some understanding of how the writer presents a character or theme, with some interpretation.

D

A **Grade C** candidate will

- show clear evidence that he or she understands the main ways in which a character or theme has been presented
- explain writers' presentation of character and theme clearly
- display understanding of various features of language and structure used by writers to create characters and explore themes
- support points with relevant and appropriate quotations.

C

Prior learning

Before you begin this unit, think about

- what you already know about analysing character and theme
- any recent text you have read in which a particular character made an impression on you, or in which a theme or idea really interested you.

> What do you understand these terms to mean?

> What do you remember about the character or theme? What kept you interested in him/her/it?

Introducing *Romeo and Juliet*

Why is it important to read Shakespeare?

Many of Shakespeare's stories and characters will already be familiar to you, even if you have not read or seen the plays. Words and phrases from his plays form part of our lives and everyday speech: for example, 'All the world's a stage'. But what was he really interested in writing about?

Here are two pupils discussing Shakespeare's play *Romeo and Juliet*.

Jude: Well, it's clear that the main character is Romeo. He's the one who chases Juliet. He does other things, too – he kills Tybalt, and then Paris.

Kaleem: No – Juliet's the centre of everything. She's the one Romeo falls for; she's the one who has to go against her parents.

Jude: Well, at least we agree on one thing. It's a play about hatred and family anger.

Kaleem: No, it's not! Without love there wouldn't *be* a play.

A student writes…

I get 'character' – that's about people and what they're like, right? But I don't get 'theme'.

Answer…

Don't worry, it's not clear cut as the two areas overlap. How people behave and speak can tell us what they're like (character) but it can also tell about an idea the writer is interested in (theme). For example, when Romeo climbs into his enemy's garden, he's brave (character) but it also reminds us this is a play about conflict (theme) because he could get killed.

ACTIVITY

With a partner, decide:

- Do the two students agree *who* the main character is? Why / Why not?
- Are they *just* talking about character (the people who do things in the play) or do they have anything else to say?

170

Focus for development: Predicting themes and character

The opening Prologue of *Romeo and Juliet* tells us a lot about the play to come. Read these notes a student has begun to make about character and theme.

'households' means 'families' so people mentioned straight away – that's character.

Like 'hatred' going back years. Is 'hate' a theme? What sort?

Don't get this – but sounds like this hate is making life dirty – almost sinful?

Two **households**, both alike in dignity,
In fair Verona, where we lay our scene,
From **ancient grudge** break to new mutiny,
Where civil blood makes civil hands **unclean**.
From forth the fatal loins of these two foes
A pair of star-cross'd lovers take their life;
Whose misadventur'd piteous overthrows
Doth with their death bury their parents' strife.
The fearful passage of their death-mark'd love,
And the continuance of their parents' rage,
Which, but their children's end, nought could remove,
Is now the two hours' traffic of our stage;
The which if you with patient ears attend,
What here shall miss, our toil shall strive to mend.

Glossary
civil: of the same town; belonging to fellow citizens (of Verona)
misadventured: ill fortuned
piteous overthrows: pitiful downfalls
strife: fighting
children's end: children's death
nought: nothing

ACTIVITY

Complete the notes above by answering these questions.

- Are any types of people mentioned (for example, parents)?
- Are there any references to words that could be themes (for example, 'hate')?
- Why do you think Shakespeare tells his audience so much about the story and ideas before the play begins?

ASSESSMENT FOCUS

Using your notes, write two short paragraphs explaining how the Prologue prepares the audience for some of the characters and themes to come.

- If you don't know the play, use the Prologue to predict what might happen.
- If you do know it, say how the Prologue looks ahead to what is to come.

Remember

- **Openings can you tell you a great deal about character and theme.**
- **Themes and characters are always linked.**

Writing about character: Romeo

Learning objectives

- To explain what you find out about Romeo clearly.
- To use a range of evidence to support your ideas.

What does writing about character mean?

Examiners will be looking for your ideas on *how* the character has been created (**characterisation**), with support from relevant evidence from the text. To simply comment on what the character is like is not enough.

You need to make deductions (like a detective) to find out about characterisation, using character pointers such as

- what the character **does**
- what the character **says**
- what other people **say about** the character
- how other people **behave towards** the character.

For example, here is the start of one student's investigation into Romeo – a list of some of the things he does in the play.

- Wanders around on his own dreaming about Rosaline
- Goes to the Capulet ball, disguised, and meets Juliet
- Secretly climbs into Juliet's garden and speaks to her
- Kills Tybalt after Mercutio is killed
- Secretly marries Juliet
- Goes to the tomb to meet Juliet; kills Paris after argument

ACTIVITY

Decide with a partner:

From the evidence in this list, what is Shakespeare trying to tell us about Romeo? Is he a

> brave romantic

> a typical teenager

> or an immature hothead?

Next, draw a line like the one below and put a mark where you think Romeo fits.

Brave romantic ←————————————→ **Immature hothead**

Focus for development: Selecting relevant evidence

In this extract a student has made a point and supported it with evidence.

> *It is clear that Romeo is just a typical teenager, probably only 14 or 15, falling in and out of love, because Shakespeare shows him moping around in Act 1 Scene 1, but then by the ball scene he has forgotten about Rosaline and fallen for Juliet.*

This is a good start as it

- makes the point (Romeo is a 'typical teenager')
- backs it up by explaining what Romeo does (mopes around).

Now it needs support from a suitable **quotation**. Here are two possibilities:

---

1 Romeo about Juliet

Did my heart love till now? forswear it, sight!
For I ne'er saw true beauty till this night.
(Act 1 Scene 5, lines 51–52)

---

2 Friar Lawrence to Romeo

Is Rosaline, whom thou didst love so dear,
So soon forsaken? young men's love, then, lies
Not truly in their hearts, but in their eyes.
(Act 2 Scene 3, lines 66–68)

Glossary
forsaken: pushed aside or forgotten

ACTIVITY

Discuss with a partner:
Which quotation best fits the idea that Romeo is a typical teenager falling in and out of love?

Examiner's tip ★

Evidence can be interpreted in different ways. For example, Romeo's 'moping around' in Act 1 Scene 1 could show that he isn't a typical teenager – after all, most teenagers in Verona are fighting in the street, not hiding away dreaming of a girl!

ASSESSMENT FOCUS

Now try to add part of your chosen quotation into the point made above. You could start like this:

> *It's clear Romeo is a typical teenager, falling in and out of love because the Friar thinks that ...*

Remember

- **Link your point of view to evidence from the play.**
- **Choose relevant quotations to support your points.**
- **Think about whether evidence can be interpreted in more than one way.**

173

Exploring character: Juliet

Learning objective

- To explore the differences between Romeo and Juliet as characters.

Checklist for success

Whatever your view of how a character is presented, you need to base your views on what *actually happens* in the text.

Here, a student has written about Juliet as a character. This view moves away from the idea that the story of Romeo and Juliet represents an ideal of romantic love.

> *Juliet is not a typical 'love-sick' sweet girl who just looks pretty – she's the one who takes action and shows real courage!*

There are some good points here, but

- the language is a little informal, for example 'love-sick'
- no real evidence is used to support the point that is being made.

ACTIVITY

Here are some notes made by the same student about some things Juliet does in the play.

- *Agrees to look at Paris to see if she likes him*
- *Falls for Romeo but doesn't realise he's a Montague (at first) and doesn't let it put her off*
- *Talks to Romeo in the garden and, despite hardly knowing him, suggests they marry*
- *Tells her parents she won't marry Paris, and is cruelly treated by her father*
- *Takes the sleeping potion, unsure whether it is deadly or not, and afraid of waking up in a tomb full of dead bodies.*

Which of these points could have supported the idea that she is brave and courageous?

★ Examiner's tip

Where possible, refer to Shakespeare and how he has presented characters and the techniques used. For example, 'Shakespeare conveys the idea that Juliet is an innocent, sweet girl through her desire to please her mother at the start of the play'.

ACTIVITY

A student has written the following paragraph to support the idea that Juliet is brave.

Grade D response

> Juliet seems brave when she considers whether to take the sleeping potion in Act 4 Scene 3. She thinks about waking up in the tomb too early.
> 'Shall I not then be stifled in the vault,
> To whose foul mouth no healthsome air breathes in'.

This response makes the point, adds evidence and a quotation, but does not

- embed the quotation fluently in the sentence
- refer to what Shakespeare does – with language in particular
- develop the point (about bravery).

Discuss with a partner how the Grade B response is an improvement.

Grade B response

> Shakespeare shows Juliet is a brave character when she considers whether to take the sleeping potion in Act 4 Scene 3. She has to face the possibility that she could be
> > stifled in the vault,
> > To whose foul mouth no
> > healthsome air breathes in.
> Shakespeare uses personification of the tomb to make it sound horrible, as if it is a monster with a mouth. However, although Juliet is very frightened, she still takes the potion.

ASSESSMENT FOCUS

Here is a further point with a supporting quotation.

Point	Evidence
Juliet is brave because she has to face her father's cruel words when she refuses to marry Paris (Act 3 Scene 5).	Capulet: 'And you be mine, I'll give you to my friend And you be not, hang, beg, starve, die in the streets!'

Now put these together to write a short paragraph which focuses on the language Shakespeare uses in this example to present Juliet.

Remember

- **Make your point and support it with relevant evidence.**
- **Embed the quotation where you can.**
- **Develop your point with further explanation or comment, especially about the language.**

Themes in *Romeo and Juliet*: fate and destiny

- *To consider key themes in the play and how to write about them.*

Why are writers' themes and ideas important?

Themes and ideas are what interest writers – and it is likely they will affect readers too. These themes emerge from the text as you read it (for example, the theme of 'growing up' in a poem about childhood).

Checklist for success

- You need to be able to trace the development of an idea or theme through a text.
- You need to explain your own viewpoint about the themes clearly and support what you say with relevant quotations and evidence.
- You need to interpret what the writer has to say about a theme or idea.

Here, a theatre director talks about his way of seeing the play.

> **Director**: For me, the play is about types of love, such as 'puppy love', family duty, love for your tribe or gang, and so on. This is why I used roses in my set design – they can be romantic, beautiful but also thorny and painful – and they wither and die too!

ACTIVITY

Discuss these questions with a partner or in a group.

- Do you agree with the director's view that the main theme of the play is different types of love? Base your answer on what you have read about the play so far.
- Or, do you think one of the themes below is more important?
  - Fate and destiny: the idea that you can't escape your future.
  - Conflict: the idea that the story couldn't happen without hate and conflict between families, between individuals and between old and young.

Focus for development: Language and themes or ideas

The idea of fate and destiny is strongly linked by Shakespeare in the language he uses to signs or omens that things will turn out badly.

Read these two quotations.

1 The Friar to Romeo, warning him about Juliet

> *These violent delights have violent ends,*
> *And in their triumph die; like fire and*
> * powder,*
> *Which, as they kiss, consume.*
> *(Act 2 Scene 6, lines 9–11)*

2 Juliet to Romeo, saying goodbye after their wedding

> *O God, I have an ill-divining soul!*
> *Methinks I see thee, now thou art below,*
> *As one dead in the bottom of a tomb;*
> *Either my eyesight fails or thou look'st pale.*
> *(Act 3 Scene 5, lines 53–56)*

Discuss these questions with a partner.

- How does Shakespeare hint at later events in the play in both these examples?
- What particular words or phrases does he use to suggest sad or violent outcomes?

Examiner's tip ★

Make sure you refer to the language Shakespeare uses, in this case powerful **imagery** linking events to ideas about fate. The **simile** of the gunpowder which is like passionate love is a good example because it links love to death and destruction.

ASSESSMENT FOCUS

Now, write a paragraph in which you deal with one or both of these quotations. You could begin…

> *Shakespeare draws the audience's attention to the theme of fate through his use of omens in the play, for example when the Friar/Juliet* [delete as appropriate] *….*

Remember

- **Plays (and novels) can be seen in different ways: some readers might focus on one theme or idea more than others but this doesn't mean the other views are 'wrong'.**
- **Themes can be detected in the language a writer uses.**

Themes in *Romeo and Juliet*: conflict

Learning objective

- To explore how different types of conflict develop in the play.

The Prologue to *Romeo and Juliet* mentions the 'ancient grudge' between the Montague and Capulet families. However, when you look more closely there are many different types of conflict in the play.

ACTIVITY

In groups, complete the spider-diagrams by answering the questions about the different types of conflict in *Romeo and Juliet*. Each one has been begun for you.

What caused it and how long has it gone on for? (Do we know?)

Which events in the play particularly show this conflict?

The Capulet and Montague grudge

Which characters are in conflict with which others?

Does the conflict between the families change between the start and end of the play?

Which parents and which children are in conflict during the play?

What events show this conflict taking place?

Parents and children

Why are these characters in conflict?

Other types of conflict

What about arguments between friends – Romeo and Mercutio?

Is there any 'self-conflict'? (When a character 'argues' with themselves over the right thing to do?)

Focus for development: Writing about conflict

The best way to write about your theme is to use clear stages.

> **Introduction to the theme:** Start with a paragraph that mentions all the forms of conflict in the play but without too much detail for now.

> **Development:**
>
> Decide on two or three points you want to make and write a paragraph on each. Link each paragraph to a separate scene or incident in the play. Include one example with some powerful language use.
>
> **Paragraph 1** **Point:** Shakespeare shows the Capulet and Montague grudge is very deep.
>
> **Evidence:** Capulet and Montague fight in the street despite their 'age' (Act 1 Scene 1).
>
> **Quotation:** Even the Prince can't stop them fighting and has to call them 'you beasts!' to get their attention.
>
> **Paragraph 2** **Point:** Shakespeare shows how conflict between young and old drives Juliet to do desperate things.
>
> **Evidence:** Juliet's father threatens her in a horrible way (Act 3 Scene 5).
>
> **Quotation:** Find your own…
>
> **Paragraph 3** **Point:** Shakespeare reminds us, even in the 'love' scenes, that conflict is never far away.
>
> **Evidence:** When Romeo speaks to Juliet on her balcony (Act 2 Scene 2).
>
> **Quotation:** Find examples of references to hate, death, dark/light.

> **Conclusion:** Use a summing up phrase, such as 'So, all in all we can see that…', to explain what you think Shakespeare wanted to say about hate and conflict in the play.

Examiner's tip

Start with a powerful quotation to gain the reader's attention, for example the Prince's words, 'All are punish'd' (Act 5 Scene 2).

Examiner's tip

*Look at how this **Grade C example** opens with a sentence that sets the background for the essay:*

> *It is clear that conflict is a really important theme to Shakespeare in the play. It can be seen in the hate between the families, the argument between Juliet and her parents, the personal grudges between Tybalt and…*

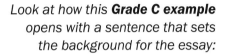

ASSESSMENT FOCUS

Look at the Development section of the plan and choose one of the suggested paragraphs (1, 2 or 3) to research and write.

When you have finished, compare your version with a partner's and assess whether you have included the point you wanted to make and a good explanation and evidence to support it.

Remember

- Use a clear, staged structure in your response.
- Make sure each paragraph comments on a different aspect of the theme.

Themes in *Romeo and Juliet*: love

Learning objective

- *To explore Shakespeare's presentation of different types of love in the play.*

A key theme is usually made up of different elements that contribute to the whole. For example, the elements listed in this student's plan make up the theme of love in *Romeo and Juliet*.

In developing a response on love, you would need to provide more detail on some of these types of love. For example…

Type of love	Example
Introduction: mention all types of love in play	Puppy love, duty, deep love, care, tribal love
Para 2: 'puppy/first love'	Romeo's love for Rosaline
Para 3: Dutiful 'love'	Paris for Juliet
Para 4: Deep love	Romeo and Juliet
Para 5: Caring love	Nurse for Juliet; Benvolio for Romeo? Friar for Romeo and Juliet
Para 6: Tribal love	Loyalty of Tybalt to Capulet family
Conclusion: sum up, focusing on one type as the most important	

Type of love	Example	When and where?	Quotation
Caring love	Friar for Romeo and Juliet	Friar thinks that marrying them will bring love and harmony to Verona (Act 2 Scene 3)	'For this alliance may so happy prove/To turn your households' rancour to pure love.'

Glossary
alliance: marriage, bringing people together

rancour: hate

ACTIVITY

Create a paragraph about 'caring love', using all the elements in the grid above.

A **Grade C** response would

- start by making a point about what Shakespeare wants to show about this idea
- give the example and support it with the quotation
- extend the point, referring to how this care compares with the Friar tending his plants carefully in Act 2 Scene 3 (for example).

Focus for development: The language of romantic love

There are some wonderful descriptions of love between Romeo and Juliet, but in your response the key is to explain them in relation to the development of the theme.

For example, you could comment on the way Shakespeare uses **imagery** related to light and dark to explore Romeo and Juliet's feelings for each other:

- When Romeo first sees Juliet he says:

> 'she hangs upon the cheek of night / As a rich jewel in an Ethiop's ear.' (Act 1 Scene 5, lines 44–45)

- In the same scene he also compares her to

> 'a snowy dove trooping with crows'

- Juliet, talking about spending the night with Romeo, says:

> 'thou wilt lie upon the wings of night / Whiter than new snow upon a raven's back.' (Act 3 Scene 2, lines 18–19)

- And when Romeo finds Juliet 'dead' in the dark tomb in, he says:

> 'her beauty makes / This vault a feasting presence full of light.' (Act 5 Scene 3, lines 85–86)

A student writes…

How do I go into detail about individual words and phrases?

Answer…

Look at the particular words Shakespeare chooses and other techniques he uses. For example, in 'a feasting presence full of light', 'feasting' conveys the richness of Juliet's presence and the alliteration of 'feasting' and 'full' adds to this richness and reflects the depth of Romeo's love.

ACTIVITY

There are many more images of light and dark in the play.

With a partner, look at the balcony scene (Act 2 Scene 2). Note down any examples of Juliet being compared to light/bright things.

ASSESSMENT FOCUS

Write a paragraph making a point about two of three of these examples, where Shakespeare presents the idea of love between Romeo and Juliet through images of light and dark. You could start in this way:

> Shakespeare uses the idea of light and dark to…

Remember

- **Themes often have many different parts and elements.**
- **Each of these elements is presented through events or through language that makes the reader think.**
- **Linking a broad theme to events or language choices is a key to better grades.**

181

Grade Booster

Extended Assessment Task

Write a response of around 600 words to this task.

> *Explore the way Romeo is presented as a central character in* **Romeo** and **Juliet.**

Write about

- how Romeo is presented through the things he says and does
- how he is presented through what others say about him and how they behave towards him
- what the language used by him and about him tells us.

For example, here is one student's plan.

Stage 1: Introduction (50–75 words) *Introduce subject in interesting way, e.g. quotation from Romeo? Or quotation about him? Will not reveal what I think at this moment, just explore different ways of seeing him.*	**Stage 3: 175–200 words (3 paragraphs)** **Paragraph 3:** *other elements of Romeo's behaviour and language: with Mercutio, Tybalt* **Paragraph 4:** *the final scene – Paris, death* **Paragraph 5:** *draw conclusions about his actions: fighting, exile, suicide.*
Stage 2: 150–175 words (2 paragraphs) **Paragraph 1:** *how Shakespeare presents Romeo at the start of the play* **Paragraph 2:** *how Shakespeare presents him in balcony scene. Draw conclusions about him as a lover and his relationship to Rosaline/Juliet.*	**Stage 4:** *Conclusion (50–75 words)* **Paragraph 6:** *sum up key points of Romeo's presentation and development.*

Evaluation – What have you learned?

With a partner, use the grade checklist below to evaluate your work on the Extended Assessment Task.

- I can show that I clearly understand and can explain the main ways in which writers present a character or theme.
- I can show how various features of language and structure work and can support my points with relevant and appropriate quotations.

- I can offer explanations that show some understanding of how the writer presents a character or theme.
- I can use relevant quotations to support points most of the time, and try to interpret what the writer has to say about character and theme.

- I can offer some explanations about what the writer has to say and show some awareness of the way a character or theme has been presented.
- I can use quotations to support points, but these are not always relevant.

You may need to go back and look at the relevant pages from this section again.

English Literary Heritage: Characterisation and Themes

Introduction

This section of Chapter 4 shows you how to

- understand what Controlled Assessment tasks on 'Characterisation and voice' and 'Theme and ideas' in relation to *A Christmas Carol* and a range of poems are about
- develop responses to tasks in these areas.

Why is learning about characterisation and themes important?

- You will only have to write on one of these two topics, but you need to be prepared for both because there are often links between them.
- It is important to understand what they mean, how you can explore them, and how they relate to the English Literary Heritage texts you are studying.

A **Grade D** candidate will

- show some understanding of the text
- use appropriate quotations most of the time
- display some understanding of how the writer presents a character or theme, with some interpretation.

D

A **Grade C** candidate will

- show clear evidence he or she understands the main ways in which a character or theme has been presented
- explain writers' presentation of character and theme clearly
- display understanding of various features of language and structure used by writers to create characters and explore themes
- support points with relevant and appropriate quotations.

C

Prior learning

Before you begin this unit, think about

- any 'typical' character types you remember from reading classic English stories and poems, for example the wicked stepmother or the poor innocent child.

How were the characters presented to make them memorable?

What were the key themes or ideas in these stories or poems?

Have you seen any modern film versions of stories which you would consider 'classic' texts from the literary heritage?

Writing about the writer's craft

Learning objective

- To learn and use a range of suitable technical terms and essay language when writing about texts.

Glossary
harlot: prostitute

blights: ruins

hearse: carriage which carries coffins

⭐ Examiner's tip

*Try to use and show you understand **technical terms** to do with poetry, such as 'verse', 'line' and 'symbol', when you are analysing a text. This will impress the examiner.*

Glossary
Symbol: when something represents or suggests another idea, such as poppies symbolising fallen soldiers in WW1.

Verse: a grouping of lines in a poem, often (but not always) rhymed.

Checklist for success

When you are writing about theme or characterisation:

- you need to use appropriate technical terms, for example 'chapter' when writing about novels, or 'verse' when referring to poetry
- you need to use words and phrases which explain what the writer is doing, for example 'the writer *suggests* that...'.

ACTIVITY

Read these last four lines from William Blake's poem, 'London'.

Then look at the extracts below from two students' responses to these lines.

> But most, thro' midnight streets I hear
> How the youthful Harlot's curse
> Blasts the new born Infant's tear,
> And blights with plagues the Marriage hearse.

Response 1

> The bit at the end of the poem has this idea which was really good that women pass on bad stuff to their kids.

Response 2

> The final verse conveys the idea that the mother is symbolic of how people pass on problems to their children and damage society in general.

The first student has done well to respond to these tricky lines, but the second student has written an even better response.

Discuss with a partner, where Response 2

- uses a **technical term** to do with poetry
- uses a **specific description** rather than just the word 'women'
- uses a word meaning 'represents' which describes the importance of the mother
- adds a **further explanation**.

Focus for development:
Commenting on writers' choices

Try making the ways you express ideas about the writer's work more varied. Here are some phrases you can use.

> **You could say:** *The writer...*
>
> *describes how... conveys the idea that...*
> *explains how/why/about... suggests that...*
> *comments on... reflects on... recalls how... tells the reader about... emphasises the idea that... questions how/whether/why...*

A student writes...

I can pick out what writers do, it's explaining it that's difficult.

Answer...

It will help if you get used to using a range of alternative words and phrases for 'says', such as 'conveys'.

ACTIVITY

Now read the first verse of the same poem 'London', by William Blake.

London
I wander thro' each charter'd street,
Near where the charter'd Thames does flow,
And mark in every face I meet,
Marks of weakness, marks of woe.

Discuss with a partner:

- Where does the poet 'wander' in London?

- What does he see in the faces of the people he meets?

Glossary
charter'd: here may mean 'controlled by powerful people' or 'mapped out' so there is no freedom about where to go
woe: pain and sadness

ASSESSMENT FOCUS

Complete this paragraph about the first verse, using at least one of the phrases from the box above.

In the _____ _____ of the poem, the writer _____ _____ he walks through London and notices _____ The effect of the repetition of _____ in the last two lines is _____

Remember

- **Use relevant technical terms to describe the poem and try to vary your essay language.**

- **Link each term to the effect it creates – don't just point them out.**

- **Use a range of words and phrases to explain how the writer presents his or her ideas.**

185

Exploring theme in English Literary Heritage poetry

Why is it important to explore themes?

Themes are the ideas or issues that seem to interest writers. For example, a Victorian author might focus on how new industry was affecting country people.

ACTIVITY

With a partner, read this poem by William Blake.

London

I wander thro' each charter'd street,
Near where the charter'd Thames does flow,
And mark in every face I meet
Marks of weakness, marks of woe.

In every cry of every Man,
In every Infant's cry of fear,
In every voice: in every ban,
The mind-forg'd manacles I hear.

How the Chimney-sweeper's cry
Every black'ning church appalls;
And the hapless Soldier's sigh
Runs in blood down Palace walls.

But most thro' midnight streets I hear
How the youthful Harlot's curse
Blasts the new born Infant's tear,
And blights with plagues the Marriage hearse.

ACTIVITY

William Blake is not interested in describing 'characters' as such. People *do* appear in the poem but they are types, not individuals, for example the Chimney sweep or the soldier.

Read the poem again together and make some notes about

- the 'subject' or theme of the poem. It is called 'London' – does that mean the poet is especially interested in the city? What is he concerned about?
- any particular words, phrases or lines that stand out. Are there any that are powerful or difficult to understand?

Here are three students discussing the poem's theme. Which view is closest to yours?

Ryan: Not any city – it's London, the capital. It's like he's having a go at the king 'cos he mentions the walls of the palace.

Joel: It's nothing to do with cities, it's people in general. He says they're weak and their minds have 'manacles' in them – that's chains isn't it? Like they're all sinners.

Jo: This is a poem about cities and how they ruin people. I mean you don't get 'harlots' in the countryside, do you?

A student writes…

All these ideas are great, but they're all different. They can't all be right can they?

Answer…

A good essay could well mention all these things, even if the theme was 'poverty in cities', or 'people's weaknesses'.

Focus for development: Researching William Blake

ACTIVITY

Read this background information about William Blake and what interested him.

William Blake (1757–1827)

English poet and artist, lived most of his life in London, and experienced turbulent riots against the government of the day. Whilst living for a short while in the Sussex countryside, he commented on the clarity and pureness compared with the 'vapours' of the city. From a very early age, perhaps as young as 4, Blake claimed to have seen visions, sometimes even seeing angels walking amongst ordinary people. 'London' comes from his most famous collection of poems, *Songs of Innocence and Experience*.

Find out more about William Blake using these websites:

http://www.william–blake.org/biography
www.bbc.co.uk/poetryseason/poets/william_blake

Find examples of Blake's illustrations – how would you describe them?

What did he witness in 1780 that might have influenced his work?

ASSESSMENT FOCUS

Now go back to the poem.

Write a paragraph explaining clearly what *you* think Blake is saying in his poem 'London'. Support your interpretation with two quotations from the poem.

Remember

- **Giving your own interpretation of the text can improve your grade, provided it is supported by quotation of evidence.**
- **Include information about the writer only when it is relevant to what you are saying about the text.**

Similar theme, different poem

Learning objective

- To respond to a similar theme dealt with by a different poet.

About 80 years after Blake wrote the poem 'London', Thomas Hardy wrote 'The Ruined Maid' a poem you will now look at. The key word to understand is 'ruined', which usually meant a woman whose reputation had been spoiled by sex outside marriage, maybe as the mistress of a rich man.

ACTIVITY

The poem imagines the first speaker meeting 'Melia in town, and noticing the change in her.

- First, read the poem to yourself.
- Then, to get an idea of the poem as a **dialogue,** read it aloud with a partner.
- Use different, distinct voices for each speaker if you wish. (You will need to decide if 'Melia's accent would change, or whether she is still a country girl at heart.)

The Ruined Maid

'O 'Melia, my dear, this does everything crown!
Who could have supposed I should meet you in Town?
And whence such fair garments, such prosperi-ty?'
'O didn't you know I'd been ruined?' said she.

– 'You left us in tatters, without shoes or socks,
Tired of digging potatoes, and spudding up docks;
And now you've gay bracelets and bright feathers three!' –
'Yes: that's how we dress when we're ruined,' said she.

– 'At home in the barton you said "thee" and "thou",
And "thik oon", and "theäs oon", and "t'other"; but now
Your talking quite fits 'ee for high compa-ny!' –
'Some polish is gained with one's ruin,' said she.

– 'Your hands were like paws then, your face blue and bleak
But now I'm bewitched by your delicate cheek,
And your little gloves fit as on any la-dy!' –
'We never do work when we're ruined,' said she.

– 'You used to call home-life a hag-ridden dream,
And you'd sigh, and you'd sock; but at present you seem
To know not of megrims or melancho-ly!' –
'True. One's pretty lively when ruined,' said she.

– 'I wish I had feathers, a fine sweeping gown,
And a delicate face, and could strut about Town!' –
'My dear – a raw country girl, such as you be,
Cannot quite expect that. You ain't ruined,' said she.

 Examiner's tip

The use of dialect words by a poet can sometimes present contrasts between particular places or characters.

Glossary

spudding up docks: digging up weeds

barton: barn or farmyard

megrims: headaches

ACTIVITY

Discuss the following with a partner.

- What **ideas** does Thomas Hardy seem to be interested in? Is he writing about city life like Blake on page 186, for example?
  - What contrasting characters does Hardy present to the reader?
  - How is this contrast shown? (How has 'Melia changed since she came to town, for example?)
  - What does Hardy appear to be saying about the effect of the town on 'Melia? What might be surprising about this?
- What sort of **tone** and **atmosphere** does the poet create? For example:
  - What is the effect of writing the poem in **rhyme** and with a **regular rhythm**? (Is it slow or does it bounce along?)
  - What is the effect of the repeated phrase or **refrain**, 'you ain't ruined / when one's ruined', at the end of each verse?

ASSESSMENT FOCUS

Return to the first question – whether Hardy is interested in city life. If so, does he approach it in the same way as Blake?

Write a paragraph dealing with this idea alone, but linking it to the **tone** and **structure** of the poem. Treat this like a final paragraph of your writing on this poem.

You could begin like this:

> Hardy conveys the idea that city or town life can...

Glossary

tone: the 'sound' or feeling of the poem, or of the voice of the poet (for example, jolly, calm, angry, superior).

structure: the organisation and order of the poem (How does it begin? Are there verses? Are any lines repeated? Do we hear more than one 'voice'?)

Remember

- **Link any comments on theme or ideas to the poet's choice of vocabulary or to the structure of the poem.**

Comparing theme in two different poems

Checklist for success

- You need to give equal weight to both poems in your response.
- You need to state clearly what the writer is saying in each.
- You need to analyse how he or she achieves this, focusing on similarities and differences as appropriate.

ACTIVITY

Read this task.

> ***How is the theme of ruin explored in any text(s) you have studied?***
> ***Write about the poems 'London' and 'The Ruined Maid', exploring how the writers use language and structure to explore how places affect people's lives.***

A student writes…

There's so much going on in the two poems, how can I fit everything I want to say into 500 words?

Answer…

If you get the 'story' of the poems out of the way in a couple of sentences, this will leave you plenty of time to explore the theme(s). For example, 'This is a poem about a girl who meets an old friend in town. She notices how well-dressed she is now and…'.

Use this plan to develop notes for your response.

Paragraph 1: Introduce the main comparisons between the poems

Paragraph 2: Introduce first poem, 'London' with a quick sentence explaining what it's about

Paragraphs 3-4: Analyse how Blake presents ideas on ruin through his choice of vocabulary and powerful images; the poem's 'voice'; the structure of verses and order of ideas; the overall tone and atmosphere

Paragraph 5: Sum up key idea in 'London'

Paragraph 6: Introduce second poem, 'The Ruined Maid' – quick sentence on what it's about

Paragraphs 7-8: Analyse similar features. Make any links or contrasts with 'London'

Paragraph 9: Sum up key ideas, commenting on a main similarity or difference in the poems

To this plan you need to add

- examples of the poet's language and structural choices
- your comments on the effect of each of these choices and how this effect is created.

Focus for development: Moving between poems

Although you will write about each poem in turn, it is useful, especially when writing about the second poem, to link back to the first if you can.

Here is an extract from a **Grade D** response.

> In 'The Ruined Maid' we don't find out anything about the poet, Thomas Hardy. In 'London' it is the poet who is speaking.

This draws out a good contrast but
- doesn't include relevant quotations
- doesn't analyse the effect of this.

Compare it with this extract from a **Grade C** response.

> Hardy doesn't refer to himself in 'The Ruined Maid', and the effect is that he is like a distant observer who has just recorded the conversation. On the other hand, Blake reveals that it is he who 'wanders' the streets of London and this creates a much more personal tone, as if he is telling the reader what to think about how the town ruins lives.

Be careful not to look for points of comparison that aren't there, however. For example, Blake talks about blood on palace walls but there is no obvious link to violent city life in 'The Ruined Maid'.

ASSESSMENT FOCUS

Work on your own version of the plan, adding examples from the text and comments you will make on their effect.

Then write a first draft of your comparison, based on the task opposite about the theme of ruin.

Remember

- **Refer to as many aspects of the poetry (vocabulary, structure, voice, imagery) as you can in your comparison.**
- **Include social and historical information, but only where they are relevant.**
- **Concentrate on what the writer has done to create effects and meanings.**

Characterisation and voice

Learning objective

- *To consider how writers present characters through description and speech.*

Why is it important to learn about characterisation?

Writers use many techniques to present characters, for example by providing descriptions of how they speak, dress, and move. They also show us how others respond or speak to them. (See page 172 for more on characterisation.)

Read this short extract from the well-known ghost story by Charles Dickens, *A Christmas Carol*.

Scrooge

Hard and sharp as flint, from which no steel had ever struck out generous fire; secret, and self-contained, and solitary as an oyster. The cold within him froze his old features, nipped his pointed nose, shrivelled his cheek, stiffened his gait; made his eyes red, his thin lips blue; and spoke out shrewdly in his grating voice. A frosty rime was on his head, and on his eyebrows, and his wiry chin.

ACTIVITY

With a partner, make brief notes on how Dickens brings Scrooge to life. Consider the effect of

- key adjectives, for example, 'secret' and 'frosty'
- similes (an image where Scrooge is compared to something else)
- different sentence lengths, for example the contrast between the lengthy first two sentences and the last sentence.

★ Examiner's tip

*If you were writing about how Dickens presents Scrooge in your assessment task, you would need to explain the **effect** of these techniques – how they show Scrooge as cold and hard-hearted.*

Focus for development: Characterisation through speech

How characters speak is also key in telling us what they are like, creating their voice and building up atmosphere in a story.

In this extract from 'The Monkey's Paw', a horror story by W.W. Jacobs, the mother is pleading with her husband to use a magical monkey's paw. She believes it can bring back their dead son.

ACTIVITY

Read the following extract, and look in particular at how the writer has used speech to convey character.

> Even his wife's face seemed changed as he entered the room. It was white and expectant, and to his fears seemed to have an unnatural look upon it. He was afraid of her.
>
> 'WISH!' she cried in a strong voice.
>
> 'It is foolish and wicked,' he faltered.
>
> 'WISH!' repeated his wife.
>
> He raised his hand. 'I wish my son alive again.'
>
> The talisman fell to the floor, and he regarded it fearfully. Then he sank trembling into a chair as the old woman, with burning eyes, walked to the window and raised the blind.

The writer tells us *how* the woman speaks in the first line: in the words 'cried' and 'strong voice'. Make a note of

- how the writer contrasts this with the way the husband speaks
- what other facts about how the woman looks and speaks convey the idea that she is very determined.

ASSESSMENT FOCUS

Write a paragraph in which you explain how writers use physical description and speech to present a character.

Use one example from *A Christmas Carol* extract and one from 'The Monkey's Paw'.

Remember

- **Character and relationships can be shown through detailed physical description, and through their speech.**
- **Look out for contrasts between characters.**

Establishing a character

Examiner's tip

*For a higher grade, focus closely on the language Dickens uses – what he tells us about Scrooge's **actions**, how he **looks** and how he **speaks** – and, how he is **contrasted** with other characters.*

What does establishing a character mean?

As we read *A Christmas Carol*, Dickens continues to build up or **establish** Scrooge's character as being cold and mean. He does this by contrasting him with other characters, by developing details of his character and by showing how he reacts to events.

ACTIVITY

- Look at the annotations one student has made to the extract below.

> Once upon a time – of all the good days in the year, on Christmas Eve – old Scrooge sat busy in his counting-house. It was cold, bleak, biting weather: foggy withal; and he could hear the people in the court outside go wheezing up and down, beating their hands upon their breasts, and stamping their feet upon the pavement stones to warm them. The city clocks had only just gone three, but it was quite dark already – it had not been light all day – and candles were flaring in the windows of the neighbouring offices, like ruddy smears upon the palpable brown air. The fog came pouring in at every chink and keyhole, and was so dense without, that although the court was of the narrowest, the houses opposite were mere phantoms. To see the dingy cloud come drooping down, obscuring everything, one might have thought that nature lived hard by, and was brewing on a large scale.
>
> The door of Scrooge's counting-house was open, that he might keep his eye upon his clerk, who in a dismal little cell beyond, a sort of tank, was copying letters. Scrooge had a very small fire, but the clerk's fire was so very much smaller that it looked like one coal. But he couldn't replenish it, for Scrooge kept the coal-box in his own room; and so surely as the clerk came in with the shovel, the master predicted that it would be necessary for them to part. Wherefore the clerk put on his white comforter, and tried to warm himself at the candle; in which effort, not being a man of a strong imagination, he failed.

Scrooge is counting his money – on Christmas Eve!

He is mistrustful

He is mean.

- Then jot down your own ideas about how Scrooge is presented as the extract continues. You can focus on the highlighted text if you wish.

'A merry Christmas, uncle! God save you!' cried a cheerful voice. It was the voice of Scrooge's nephew, who came upon him so quickly that this was the first intimation he had of his approach.

'Bah!' said Scrooge, 'Humbug!'

He had so heated himself with rapid walking in the fog and frost, this nephew of Scrooge's, that he was all in a glow; his face was ruddy and handsome; his eyes sparkled, and his breath smoked again.

'Christmas a humbug, uncle!' said Scrooge's nephew. 'You don't mean that, I am sure.'

'I do,' said Scrooge. 'Merry Christmas! What right have you to be merry? What reason have you to be merry? You're poor enough.'

'Come, then,' returned the nephew gaily. 'What right have you to be dismal? What reason have you to be morose? You're rich enough.'

Scrooge, having no better answer ready on the spur of the moment, said, 'Bah!' again; and followed it up with 'Humbug'.

'Don't be cross, uncle,' said the nephew.

'What else can I be,' returned the uncle, 'when I live in such a world of fools as this? Merry Christmas! Out upon Merry Christmas. What's Christmastime to you but a time for paying bills without money; a time for finding yourself a year older, but not an hour richer; a time for balancing your books, and having every item in 'em through a round dozen of months presented dead against you? If I could work my will,' said Scrooge indignantly, 'every idiot who goes about with "merry Christmas" on his lips should be boiled with his own pudding, and buried with a stake of holly through his heart. He should!'

ASSESSMENT FOCUS

Using your notes, write two paragraphs in which you say *how* Dickens establishes Scrooge's character in this extract.

- Try to refer to specific words, phrases and descriptions of Scrooge (for example, linked to his manner of speaking).
- You could also comment on anything that he does (for example, only allowing his clerk a small fire) and how he is different from Fred (his nephew).

Remember

- Consider the character's 'voice' as well as how they look and act.
- Support anything you say with well-chosen evidence.
- Comment on what the effect of any description is.

Character development: how Scrooge changes

Checklist for success

When writing about how a character develops throughout a text:

- you need to select two or three extracts which show how a character changes
- you need to provide relevant evidence from the text to support what you say.

ACTIVITY

Read the following fact file about Scrooge. Then discuss with a partner, what is the **main idea** Dickens wants to get across about Scrooge at the start of the story.

> ### Scrooge Fact File – the opening
>
> Scrooge is old, single, mean and hard-hearted.
>
> In the opening to A Christmas Carol we see him in his freezing office, his business partner having died many years before.
>
> He has a nephew, Fred, who kindly visits him each Christmas to wish him Merry Christmas, but is rejected.
>
> He has one employee, Bob Cratchit, whom he treats badly, gives a poor fire, and pays too little. Bob has a disabled son who may not survive.
>
> Scrooge has also refused to give any money to charity when visitors call at the office, saying that there is prison and the poor-house for those with no money, and that the population is too high anyway – a few deaths would help society!

ACTIVITY

Research what happened to people who couldn't pay their debts in Dickens's time?

Note down why was this particularly relevant to Dickens himself? Try going to **www.dickens-online.info/** to read his Biography.

Focus for development: a changed man

On Christmas Eve, Scrooge is visited by three spirits, including one called the Ghost of Christmas Present, who shows him around Fred's and Bob's houses so he can see what life is like beyond his own cold world.

In this extract, the spirit takes Scrooge to see Bob Cratchit's Christmas. Scrooge watches the poor family make the best of their dinner, and is interested in the unwell Tim.

> 'God bless us, every one!' said Tiny Tim, the last of all.
>
> He sat very close to his father's side, upon his little stool. Bob held his withered little hand to his, as if he loved the child, and wished to keep him by his side, and dreaded that he might be taken from him.
>
> 'Spirit,' said Scrooge, with an interest he had never felt before, 'tell me if Tiny Tim will live.'
>
> 'I see a vacant seat,' replied the Ghost, 'in the poor chimney corner, and a crutch without an owner, carefully preserved. If these shadows remain unaltered by the Future, the child will die.'
>
> 'No, no,' said Scrooge. 'Oh no, kind Spirit! say he will be spared.'
>
> 'If these shadows remain unaltered by the Future none other of my race,' returned the Ghost, 'will find him here. What then? If he be like to die, he had better do it, and decrease the surplus population.'
>
> Scrooge hung his head to hear his own words quoted by the Spirit, and was overcome with penitence and grief.

ACTIVITY

Note down which parts of the extract above you could use to show how Scrooge has changed from the story's opening.

ASSESSMENT FOCUS

Here is the beginning of a **Grade D** response.

> Scrooge is really mean in the first extract because he keeps the 'coal fire' to himself, but then in the later extract he is sad and depressed at what he sees.

A **Grade C** response will need to show us more closely how Dickens **presents** Scrooge.

- Use your notes to select (also from the extracts on pages 194–195) **particular descriptions** of what **Scrooge says and does**, and **how he is described.**
- Complete two paragraphs using these starting points:

  > In the first extract Dickens presents Scrooge as ... [add a quotation and your comment]

  > However, later when the spirit takes him to Bob's house, Dickens describes how Scrooge... [add a quotation and your comment]

  > The effect of these changes is to show that...

Remember

- **Show you understand a character's development by using direct evidence.**
- **Draw comparisons and contrasts between different sections of a story.**

Learning objectives

- *To select and fluently use the most relevant quotations.*
- *To plan a character response.*

Checklist for success

- You need to plan carefully to write a developed response on character in your Controlled Assessment.
- You need to include quotations to show how a particular effect is created.

ACTIVITY

With a partner, compare how these two students have written about Scrooge. Identify what is better about the second response.

Grade D response
When Scrooge realises it is not too late to change the future by being kind, he is delighted. *'I am as light as a feather! I am as happy as an angel, I am as merry as a schoolboy...'*

Grade C response
When Scrooge realises it is not too late to change the future, he says that he feels 'as light as a feather!', 'as happy as an angel' and 'as merry as a schoolboy'. Dickens's use of these similes suggests Scrooge has gone back to innocent childhood and, like an 'angel', can spread happiness. These positive descriptions contrast with the earlier unpleasant ones of him.

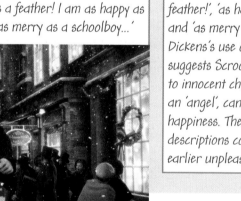

ACTIVITY

Here is an extract from the end of the story.

> Running to the window, he opened it and put out his head. No fog, no mist; clear, bright, jovial, stirring, cold; cold, piping for the blood to dance to; golden sunlight; heavenly sky; sweet fresh air; merry bells. Oh, glorious! Glorious!

Complete the following paragraph in which you comment on Dickens's characterisation of the 'new' Scrooge.

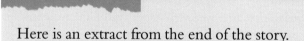

Dickens develops his characterisation of Scrooge through the way he _____ *The atmosphere created is one of* _____ *and* _____ *This changes the way we see Scrooge because* _____

Focus on

- the adjectives used, for example 'golden', to describe the setting
- Scrooge's behaviour (what he does).

Focus for development:
planning a character response

Here is a plan one student has written in response to a question about how Scrooge's character is presented and developed throughout the story.

Introduction: Sum up very briefly **the key facts** about the story and what happens to Scrooge by the end. (1 paragraph)

Development:

1. Write about the **opening chapter / Stave**, and how Scrooge is introduced. Comment on:
- his physical description (1 paragraph)
- how he behaves towards others. (1 paragraph)

2. Write about **Chapter / Stave 3**, when Scrooge visits Bob's house.
- Sum up what he sees and its effect on him; focus on the questions he asks and his regrets. (2 paragraphs)

3. Write about **Chapter / Stave 5**, when Scrooge awakes from his dream and realises he can still change the world. Comment on the contrast in his character, for example:
- his changed behaviour – how he moves and what he says. (1 paragraph)
- what he does – the actions he takes, like buying a goose for Bob. (1 paragraph)

Conclusion: End with a **general comment** summing up the way Scrooge has changed throughout the story, and perhaps choose an appropriate quotation to finish. (1 paragraph)

ASSESSMENT FOCUS

You have already made notes on several quotations that would fit this plan.
- Add them to the plan where you think they would be most appropriate.
- Read each of the key sections mentioned and add further examples from the story and quotations that you could use.

Remember

- **Plan your response about character.**
- **Refer to the first and last times the character appears.**
- **Build in further points about the character's development, and quotations.**
- **Analyse the language the writer uses, don't just add evidence.**

Grade Booster

Extended Assessment Task

Write a response of around 600 words to this task.

> *'How is the theme of change presented in any text(s) you have studied?'*

Make sure you

- consider how the idea or theme is presented at the start of the text (including subtle hints and suggestions)
- look at how the theme or idea is developed through characters or by significant events, moments or situations, and how it may have changed by the end
- explore how the theme is presented through use of language, setting, movement, key detail, imagery or structure.

Evaluation – What have you learned?

With a partner, use the grade checklist below to evaluate your work on the Extended Assessment Task.

- I can show that I clearly understand and can explain the main ways in which writers present a character or theme.
- I can show how various features of language and structure work and can support my points with relevant and appropriate quotations.

- I can offer explanations that show some understanding of how the writer presents a character or theme.
- I can use relevant quotations to support points most of the time, and try to interpret what the writer has to say about character and theme.

- I can offer some explanations about what the writer has to say and show some awareness of the way a character or theme has been presented.
- I can use quotations to support points, but these are not always relevant.

You may need to go back and look at the relevant pages from this section again.

Exploring Cultures: Characterisation and Themes

Introduction

This section of Chapter 4 shows you how to

- understand what is involved in a Controlled Assessment task on 'Characterisation and voice' and 'Theme and ideas' in relation to *Of Mice and Men* and a range of poems
- develop responses to tasks in these areas.

Why is learning about characterisation and themes important?

These two topics will be the focus of the responses you write.

It is important to understand what they mean, how you can explore them, and how they relate to the Exploring Cultures texts you are studying.

A **Grade C** candidate will

- show clear evidence that he or she understands the main ways in which a character or theme has been presented
- explain writers' presentation of character and theme clearly
- display understanding of various features of language and structure used by writers to create characters and explore themes
- support points with relevant and appropriate quotations.

C

A **Grade D** candidate will

- show some understanding of the texts
- use appropriate quotations most of the time
- display some understanding of how the writer presents a character or theme and offer some interpretation.

D

Prior learning

Before you begin this unit, think about

- any memorable stories set in different (non-UK) settings you have read
- whether there are particular themes or issues that arise in texts you have read set in, or written by people from, different cultures.

How important was the setting – and the effect it had on the characters – to the story?

Where writers 'belong' to two cultures, for example British and that of a country overseas, what ideas might they choose to write about?

Exploring characterisation in *Of Mice and Men*

Learning objective

- *To explore how an author presents a character through his or her actions.*

Checklist for success

You need to understand the different techniques a writer uses to present and develop a character in a text. These will relate to

- the writer's **physical description** of the character
- how characters **speak** and **what they say**
- what the character **does** – or **how they respond** to particular acts or events.

ACTIVITY

Characters' actions, however, always have a background to them. We are going to look at the presentation of character in the novel *Of Mice and Men* by John Steinbeck. Read these basic background notes started by a student.

> The novel is set in 1930s California during a time of job shortages and economic problems. Lennie and George are two homeless men moving from ranch to ranch looking for work. Lennie is rather backward and slow and George tries to keep him out of trouble. He often fails and feels both responsible for, and irritated by Lennie.

Discuss with a partner:

How might the social and historical background affect Lennie and George's relationship and the way they deal with others?

Think about

- the job shortages
- having to travel a long way to find work
- not having their own permanent home.

You can find out more about the Great Depression of the 1930s in the USA here:
www.bbc.co.uk/schools/ gcsebitesize/history/mwh/usa

How a character first appears is often vital to our understanding of them. This might be in what they do, or how they are described.

Here are some of the things we find out about Lennie in the first part of the novel.

Lennie – what he does

- (before the story begins) Lennie touches/grabs a girl's dress in the town of Weed, making her think she is going to be assaulted; this causes Lennie and George to leave town and hide from the townspeople.
- Lennie accidentally kills a mouse he has been stroking; then tries to keep it when George tells him to get rid of it.
- At the ranch, Lennie works hard to lift grain once they get their jobs.

ACTIVITY

The writer has chosen these events for a reason. Here are three possible explanations. With a partner, discuss which seems most likely:

A The writer wanted to show that Lennie is a hard worker and the earlier events had no real meaning.

B The writer wanted to show that although Lennie is strong, his clumsiness and strength, as well as his slow brain, can lead to real problems.

C The writer wanted to show that Lennie was cruel and strange.

Of course, looking at these opening events is not enough to judge Lennie. Characters often change and develop, or new things are revealed about them during the novel.

Examiner's tip

What a character does early in a story can provide clues to his or her later behaviour. For example, how is the incident with the pet mouse echoed later in the story?

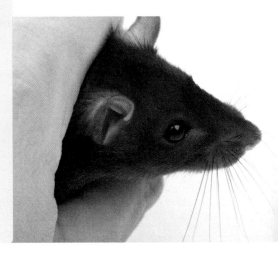

ASSESSMENT FOCUS

Write a paragraph in which you explain how the characters might be affected by the historical background, such as the job shortages and having to travel to find work. Use your discussion and research from page 202 to help you.

Remember

- **What we are told about the background of characters can reveal a lot.**
- **Writers often want to establish their main characters early on, through their actions.**

Analysing character

Learning objective

- To understand how writers use specific details such as movement and speech to convey character.

Why is it important to analyse character?

When you analyse character, you show that you are not just making basic or general comments, but are looking closely at individual words, sentences and structures to explain characterisation.

Read this extract from the first chapter of *Of Mice and Men*.

> His huge companion dropped his blankets and flung himself down and drank from the surface of the green pool; drank with long gulps, snorting into the water like a horse. The small man stepped nervously beside him.
>
> 'Lennie!' he said sharply. 'Lennie, for God's sake don't drink so much.' Lennie continued to snort into the pool. The small man leaned over and shook him by the shoulder. 'Lennie. You gonna be sick like you was last night.'
>
> Lennie dipped his whole head under, hat and all, and then he sat up on the bank and his hat dripped down on his blue coat and ran down his back. 'Tha's good,' he said. 'You drink some, George. You take a good big drink.' He smiled happily.
>
> George unslung his bindle and dropped it gently on the bank. 'I ain't sure it's good water,' he said. 'Looks kinda scummy.'
>
> Lennie dabbled his big paw in the water and wiggled his fingers so the water arose in little splashes; rings widened across the pool to the other side and came back again. Lennie watched them go. 'Look, George. Look what I done.'

ACTIVITY

Answer these questions briefly.

- What evidence is there in this extract to support the idea that George looks after Lennie?
- What adjectives would you use to describe Lennie, based on this extract? For example: serious, mad, angry, happy or wise?

Here is a response that doesn't show real analysis.

> *George watches over what Lennie does and warns him about the water, which he thinks is 'kinda scummy'.*

- It makes a point about George 'watching over' Lennie.
- It provides evidence with the reference to the water and it being 'scummy'.
- It doesn't analyse the language used.

Rewrite the paragraph adding a reference to at least one of the following and its effect:

- the adverbs used to describe how George speaks or acts ('sharply', 'nervously')
- the way George has to repeat Lennie's name.

Focus for development: Analysing literary devices

John Steinbeck cleverly uses a number of literary devices such as simile and metaphor to present a picture of Lennie.

ACTIVITY

Copy and complete this grid, deciding which image is a simile and which a metaphor, and then say what each one suggests about Lennie.

Quotation	Simile or metaphor	What it suggests about Lennie
'drank with long gulps, snorting into the water like a horse'		
'Lennie dabbled his big paw in the water'		

ACTIVITY

Of course, there is much more the extract tells us about Lennie.

- What evidence can you find that suggests Lennie is childlike?
- What evidence can you find that he wants to please George, but at the same time doesn't always listen to him?

A student writes…

I can pick out language features easily, like the way Lennie repeats simple words. Isn't that enough?

Answer…

Explaining the effect on the reader is the vital thing, for example: 'The repetition is childlike, showing Lennie's limited vocabulary.'

ASSESSMENT FOCUS

Using your understanding of Lennie so far, write a paragraph about how he is characterised by his actions, physical appearance and speech in the extract opposite.

Remember

- Writers use literary devices such as simile and metaphor to present characters.
- Focus on what these tell us, not just on spotting them.

Developing a response to character

Learning objectives

- To gather key evidence about Lennie which can be used in an extended task.

- To learn how to use that evidence in a response.

Why is it important to develop a deeper understanding of characterisation?

So far, you have looked at a small section from the start of the novel about Lennie. However, the task you are set is likely to ask you to focus on one scene and then provide further references to show your wider knowledge of the text.

It is therefore helpful to have a wider knowledge of Lennie's actions in the text.

Here is a summary of the main things Lennie does in the novel. It just needs finishing off.

Lennie's actions
• *Scares girl in Weed, forces George and him to hide and escape*
• *Accidentally kills mouse he finds*
• *Works hard on ranch*
• *Given puppy by Slim*
• *Crushes Curley's hand when attacked*
• *Accidentally kills puppy by 'petting' it too hard*
• *Talks with Curley's wife in barn and...*

You might want to write about any of these key moments, so having a bank of quotations describing Lennie from all of them will be useful.

- Some of these quotations will be **physical descriptions** provided by the writer:

> 'he walked heavily, dragging his feet a little, the way a bear drags his paws.'

Some of them will be **things the character says**:

> 'I done a real bad thing,' he said. 'I shouldn't of did that. George'll be mad.'

Some will be **descriptions or speech about the character by others**. This is George about Lennie:

> 'When I think of the swell time I could have without you, I go nuts. I never get any peace.'

- Choose one of the key moments from the list on page 206 and find one or two quotations that add to our understanding of Lennie.
- If possible, note down how that moment, and the quotation, link to what we know about Lennie from other key moments.

Focus for development: Using the evidence

Read this short extract by a student writing about Lennie.

Grade D response

> Lennie is very childlike. This can be seen when he is at the pool. It says:
> 'he smiled happily'
> This is when he had drunk the water.

This works quite well because it

- makes a point about Lennie's character (that he is childlike)
- supports it with a quotation
- gives a general explanation afterwards.

ACTIVITY

Now discuss with a partner how this response is better.

Grade C response

> Lennie is very childlike. This can be seen when they were at the pool at the beginning and he 'wiggled his fingers so the water arose in little splashes'. The verb 'wiggled' suggests he is just like a little boy getting pleasure from very simple things like making ripples. We see similar childish joy later when Lennie is given a puppy by Slim, for example.

ASSESSMENT FOCUS

Write two sentences in which you put together the following point and evidence.

Point: Lennie doesn't mean any harm.

Quotation: Slim says 'He ain't mean' (or choose your own quotation).

Explanation: Try to add to and develop the point. You could begin like this:

> Although Lennie does some terrible things, it is clear he...

Remember

- **Select the most relevant quotations.**
- **Build your quotations into your sentences, explaining your point of view.**
- **Develop or explain your point fully, if possible referring to the language used and its effect.**

Learning objective

- *To plan and draft an extended response.*

Planning an extended response

Checklist for success

- You need to make sure you explain your ideas clearly and logically in your extended response. This means having a clear focus for each part of your essay.

Here is a basic plan that a student has developed to a question about Lennie's character and the techniques used by the writer to present him.

Introduction: *Say something about who Lennie is, and what happens to him (but keep it very brief) and what this might mean.*

Development:

- *How Steinbeck describes his appearance, how he moves and speaks and what he does. Focus on imagery (simile and metaphor) and descriptive adjectives. (2 paragraphs)*
- *How Lennie's behaviour is presented + examples. (2 paragraphs)*
- *How other characters describe him and act towards him. Contrast with George? Focus on spoken language. (2 paragraphs)*

Conclusion: *Sum up how the writer presents Lennie and give an overall description.*

This doesn't include all the details, such as the quotations or events to refer to. These can be added as part of a more developed plan.

For example, here is a development of the section about Lennie's physical description.

- *Lennie looking and moving like an animal – Chapter I (paragraph 2)*
- *Lennie speaking in childlike way – end of Chapter I (about his dream) and talking to the dead puppy at the start of Chapter 5 (paragraphs 3 and 4)*
- *Lennie and the mouse*

ACTIVITY

Add more detail to the section about how other characters speak about Lennie and act towards him. Decide what you are going to say about others' attitudes to Lennie (for example, those of Curley, Slim and George) and where this evidence will come from.

208

Focus for development: Writing in clear paragraphs

Each paragraph in your essay needs to have a clear purpose. To do this, use a topic sentence to start the paragraph off. This sentence should make clear what your point or focus is.

For example, here is a paragraph from a similar essay about George.

Topic sentence introduces the main idea

Quotation/ evidence

Explanation/ follow-up

> *The writer presents George as someone who is alone and needs company.* When he meets Slim, *George tells him that he 'ain't got no people'.* This is one of the reasons *he travels with Lennie and looks after him.*

Write a paragraph in which you explain Lennie's childlike character.

- Start with a topic sentence: for example, *'Lennie's childlike character is developed when…'*
- Provide evidence/quotation.
- Explain the idea fully.

Linking paragraphs

If you are developing an idea about Lennie, make sure you use suitable **connectives** to link examples and evidence. For example, if you had already made a point about Lennie's childlike nature in one paragraph, you could say at the start of the next paragraph:

> **In addition**, we see Lennie's childlike character when …
>
> Lennie's childlike character is **also** shown when …

Examiner's tip ⭐

If you want to be really clever and vary your paragraphs you can begin one with a quotation, and then say what it shows. Make sure, though, that the paragraph flows logically from what you have written in the previous paragraph.

ASSESSMENT FOCUS

Now write a further paragraph from the essay, using one of the linking phrases above. If you want to make a different point, for example that Lennie's physical strength is **not** childlike, use a contrasting connective such as 'however' or 'on the other hand'.

Remember

- **Develop a basic plan for your response on characterisation.**
- **Flesh it out with more detail, for example which events, quotations to use.**
- **Consider how each paragraph will focus on a point from your plan.**

Writing your own response on characterisation

Learning objective

- To research and plan a response to a characterisation task on Of Mice and Men.

Checklist for success

Start by focusing on the task. Look at this example:

> *How does John Steinbeck present a key character in* **Of Mice and Men**? *Consider his use of structure and language devices.*

In this case, focusing on the task means looking closely at

- **one character** – so stick to the character you select

- **language devices** the writer uses, such as imagery (similes and metaphors), powerful descriptions, how characters speak or interact in dialogue, repetition, and the effects of these choices
- **structure** – the **order of events** or the **structure of a particular moment** in the story, for example how Lennie panics *then* breaks Curley's wife's neck in the barn.

Now read these summaries of what three characters from the novel do.

George	Curley's wife	Slim
• George first appears at pool with Lennie at start. • Speaks up for Lennie at the ranch. • Reveals to Slim about Lennie and what happened in Weed. • Talks to Candy about the dream farm and begins to believe his dream might come true. • Visits the brothel with the others. • Steals Carlson's gun after Curley's wife's death. • Shoots Lennie at the pool.	• Curley's wife appears in the bunk-house 'looking for Curley'. • Appears in Crooks' hut, when he is talking with Candy and Lennie, and threatens Crooks when they refuse to talk to her. • Talks in the barn to Lennie: tells him of her dream. • Lets him stroke her hair, panics and is killed by Lennie when she struggles.	• Slim is introduced at the time when Curley's wife comes into the bunk-house. • Gives Lennie one of his puppies. • Talks to George and gets him to reveal Lennie's past. • Allows Carlson to kill Candy's dog. • Comes up with plan to cover up Lennie having broken Curley's hand, to stop Lennie getting the sack. • Persuades George after the killing that catching Lennie won't do any good. • Comforts George after Lennie is shot.

ACTIVITY

- First, choose a **character** and a **key moment**, for example Slim and his first appearance.
- Make detailed notes on this key moment, including important quotations and their effect:
  - what happens in this moment, and where it fits in the book
  - how Slim is described
  - the way he speaks and moves; how others respond to him
  - what his actions tell us about him.
- Then, **plan your essay, following the format below.**

> **Paragraph 1**: Introduce the character quickly and efficiently. Refer to his role/job.

- Then, **allocate at least 3 paragraphs for the key moment** you will focus on. For example:

> **Paragraph 2**: Steinbeck's physical description of Slim which emphasises his 'majesty' and leadership qualities (how imagery is used, for example).

> **Paragraph 3**: How he is described as speaking and acting around the others.

> **Paragraph 4**: Any other important actions (for example he drowns the 'extra' pups).

- Then, **link what you find out to other times Slim appears**, and how he acts and is described.

> **Paragraph 5**: Mention two or three other moments when he appears and what he does.

> **Paragraph 6**: Explain whether his actions supports, or goes against, what Steinbeck tells us about him when we first met him.

> **Paragraph 7**: Conclude by summing up how Steinbeck characterises Slim across the novel as a whole, and what impression we are left with as readers.

Examiner's tip ⭐

When you are briefly summing up events to avoid a boring retelling of the story, try dropping in a short quotation, for example 'After the incident in Weed when George and Lennie had to "hide in an irrigation ditch all day…"'.

ASSESSMENT FOCUS

Now draft your essay.

Remember

- **Stick to your selected character.**
- **Focus on how the writer presents the character, especially the language devices used.**
- **Write logically and clearly.**

Themes in Exploring Cultures poetry

What are themes?

These are the particular interests of the writer that emerge as you read a text, for example the theme of 'growing up' in a poem about childhood, or 'conflict' in a play about family relationships.

Checklist for success

You need to

- follow the development of an idea or theme through a text
- use relevant quotation and evidence to support what you have to say
- show how language and structure are used to develop the theme or idea.

So, how could you identify a theme in poetry?

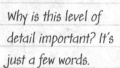

A student writes…

Why is this level of detail important? It's just a few words.

Answer…

Much of the enjoyment of reading poetry – rather like song lyrics – is all the connections the words and images create in your mind. Only by seeing all the possible meanings of a word can you understand its power – and words can also combine to create a powerful overall atmosphere or tone.

ACTIVITY

Take this line from a poem.

> *You scar me…*

Discuss with a partner the different ways that the word 'scar' can be used. Think about how it can be used literally (to mean a physical scar) and as a metaphor.

ACTIVITY

If you saw the line above in a poem about a relationship, what conclusions could you draw about the poet's feelings for the other person (who has scarred them)?

Write a sentence or two explaining your ideas, like this:

> *I think the poet has…*
> *I think the poet is talking about how…*

ACTIVITY

Many writers use strong similes or metaphors to convey their feelings about a relationship.

Discuss these three examples from poems with a partner.

For each one, decide whether explanation A or B is more relevant, or why both could be correct.

Lines from a poem	What it might say about my/our relationship
Shall I compare thee to a summer's day? Thou art more lovely and more temperate.	**A** I can't use typical comparisons to describe how beautiful you are because you are prettier than a summer's day. **B** You're not as nice as a summer's day so there's no point comparing you to one.
You were water to me deep and bold and fathoming	**A** You overwhelmed me with cruelty and I couldn't escape. **B** Like water, you gave me life, supported me, and you had a deep understanding of me.
My eyes looked out from you *My first god*	**A** You explained the world to me; you were the first person I admired. **B** You were the person I looked up to and who controlled my life, but now I have grown up other people have taken your place.

ASSESSMENT FOCUS

When writing about a theme, you need to interpret imagery like the examples above. That means to come up with your own explanation about what the images suggest or tell us.

Write a paragraph in which you compare or contrast **two** of these quotations and what you think the writer is suggesting about the people described. For example:

> *The writer of the first extract seems to suggest that the person he is describing is ...*
> *In the same way / However ...*

Remember

- **Focus in detail on individual lines and words in poetry.**
- **Consider all the possible meanings and effects of any images used.**

Exploring themes in 'Praise Song for my Mother'

Learning objective

- *To explore in detail how a poet uses language to convey ideas.*

Checklist for success

- When dealing with a poem for the first time, you need to read it, make notes and write down questions in order to get 'inside' it.

ACTIVITY

Song links to childhood?

Birth? Or washing, nourishing child?

what's 'mantling'?

- Read the poem by Grace Nichols to yourself and look at the annotations below that one student has begun.
- What impression of the poet's voice and reflections of her Guyanan childhood come through in the poem?

Praise <u>Song</u> for my Mother

You were
<u>water to me</u>
deep and bold and fathoming

You were
moon's eye to me
pull and grained and <u>mantling</u>

You were
sunrise to me
rise and warm and streaming

You were
the fishes red gill to me
the flame tree's spread to me
the crab's leg/the fried plantain smell
      replenishing replenishing

Go to your wide futures, you said
Grace Nichols

The theme of the poem

It's clear that the theme centres around the poet's relationship with her mother. But what makes it special and personal *to her?* You need to investigate more fully.

ACTIVITY

First, make your own notes and queries about the poem.

The language

- What words, phrases or lines stand out? Are any particularly powerful or striking? Why?
- What kinds of language devices has the writer used? Can you find evidence of similes, or metaphors? If so, what feeing or effect do they create?

The structure

- Do you notice anything particular about the layout or the structure? How are the words, lines and stanzas set out or separated?
- Why do you think the poet might have done this?

The sense of place and culture

- What place and culture does the poet connect her mother with?
- Does this add to the happy way Nichols views her past or not, do you think?

Glossary
Stanza: a separate section in a poem, usually a set number of lines

Focus for development: Analysing themes in 'Praise Song for my Mother'

A student has begun to write about 'Praise Song', focusing on some of the language used by the writer.

> The key theme of the writer's relationship with her mother is made clear in the first stanza. She comments that her mother was 'water' to her, and was 'deep and bold and fathoming.' This metaphor suggests that her mother gave her life, like water, and was also deep in her understanding ('fathom' can mean to 'work out the meaning of something').

This is a **Grade C response** because it

- uses a topic sentence to make the main point about the theme
- supports this by two quotations which are skilfully embedded
- explains what language device is being used (a metaphor) and what the lines might mean.

You would write in a similar way about the poem's structure. Here, the same student has commented on the writer's use of **repetition.**

> The repeated words 'replenishing replenishing', which means filling up again and again, make me think of the idea of the waves coming in and out, like on a Caribbean island.

- How has the student also linked the comment to the cultural background (where the poet originally comes from)?
- Are there other words or phrases from the poem that link to the same culture?

ASSESSMENT FOCUS

Write a paragraph about the next stanza, using this structure.

Sentence 1: Use a topic sentence to say whether the next stanza develops and builds on the same idea or takes it in a new direction.

Sentence 2: Use a quotation to support the point you are making.

Sentences 3/4: Explain your idea more fully.

Remember

- Focus on language devices and structure.
- Make each of your points clear, precise and supported by evidence.

215

Planning your comparison

Learning objective

- To respond to a poem on a similar theme, but with differences of style, approach and content.

Read this poem by James Berry.

Thoughts on my Father

You are boned clean now.
You are lost like dice and teeth.
Don't bother knock
I won't represent you.

A sound brain you were,
your body a mastery,
but no turning into any stepping stone
or handing anybody a key.

Simply, it hurts that needing
we offended you
and I judge you by lack.

Playing some well-shaped shadow
the sun alone moved,
you wouldn't be mixed with cash
or the world's cunning.

So perfectly exclusive,
you tantalised me.
You split our home in passions.
Every year we were more blunted.

I knew nowhere.
My eyes looked out from you
my first god.

Omnipotence breathed
come boy come
to hungrybelly revelations

Lift your hat to doom
boy, in the manner that roadside
weeds are indestructible.

Stubborn tides you echo.

I moved your sterile tones
from your voice.
I lifted your mole from
my back.

You scar me man,
but I must go over you again and again.
I must plunge my raging eyes
in all your steady enduring.

I must assemble material
of my own
for a new history.

ACTIVITY

Read the poem again.

- Make a note of ideas that come to mind from specific words, phrases or structures.
- Jot down anything about the place or culture described. Is it similar to the setting of Grace Nichols's poem on page 214?
- Interpret at least two of your selected words or phrases, like this:

Quotation	Explanation/interpretation	Effect
'my first god'	Metaphor suggests father was his son's idol, as if he worshipped him.	Strong praise, but use of 'first' suggests dad wasn't like god for ever. Sound is clear and simple – like the poet once was about his father.
'your body a mastery'	He was physically powerful or in control.	Admired his father's physical abilities?
'hungrybelly revelations'	Means that feeling hungry revealed the father was not good at providing for children.	Weird matching up of 'hungry' and 'belly' – sounds as if belly was a living thing! Also sounds like a child's words.

Discuss with a partner:

- How is structure very important in both poems, especially the endings?
- How do the **last three verses** of James Berry's poem suggest that the poet is 'moving on' despite the influence his father once had?

Focus for development: Making detailed comparisons

- Look over your notes and interpretations.
- Write a clear introductory paragraph saying what you think the key theme (or themes) of the poem is and link this in some way to the theme(s) of 'Praise Song for my Mother'. Include one key piece of evidence from both poems.
- You could start:

> 'Thoughts on my Father' explores the theme of..., as shown by...
> In the same way / However, 'Praise Song for my Mother' shows that Grace Nichols wanted to..., as we can see from...

Now deal with each poem in turn. Use this plan to draft your key ideas and select appropriate quotations.

'Thoughts on my Father'

Paragraph 1: Introduce the key theme(s).

Paragraphs 2–4: Analyse specific language examples (words/phrases like the ones in the grid) that show this, and the effect of these language choices. Think about the sound of the language where you can, as well as what is described.

Add one or two examples of how the structure supports the theme (for example, how the poem begins or ends, or how a specific word, phrase, line or verse is made to stand out). You could focus on the choice of tense – is it mostly present, past or future tense?

Include one example based on the setting/cultural background.

'Praise Song for my Mother'

Paragraph 5: Introduce the key theme(s).

Paragraphs 6–8: Analyse specific language examples (words/phrases like the ones for 'Thoughts') that show this – and the effect of these language choices. Again, think about the sound of the language where you can:

Add one or two examples of how the structure supports the theme (for example, how the poem begins or ends, or how a specific word, phrase, line or verse is made to stand out). You could focus on the choice of tense – mostly present, past or future?

Include one example based on the setting/cultural background.

Paragraph 9: End with a broad statement in which you link the two poems, drawing on their similarities and differences. Follow the **P**oint, **E**vidence, **E**xplanation, **D**evelopment structure.

Remember

- **Stay focused on your selected theme(s).**
- **Follow the structure of your plan.**
- **Comment on the culture and background if appropriate.**

Grade Booster

> *How is the theme of family conflict presented in any text(s) you have studied?*

Make sure you

- consider how the idea or theme is presented at the start of the text (including subtle hints and suggestions)
- look at how the theme or idea is developed by significant incidents, moments or situations, and how it may have changed by the end
- explore how the theme is presented through use of language, setting, movement, key detail, imagery and structure.

Evaluation – What have you learned?

With a partner, use the grade checklist below to evaluate your work on the Extended Assessment Task.

- I can show I clearly understand the main ideas and themes.
- I can explain these ideas and themes in clear and logical ways.
- I can understand how language features and structure work, and can support my ideas with relevant quotations.

- I can show some understanding and awareness of the main themes and ideas.
- I can support these ideas with quotations and evidence which are often relevant.
- I can make my own points but these are not developed in as much detail as they could be.

- I can show some understanding of the ways a theme has been presented.
- I can use quotations to support my ideas, but they are sometimes not really relevant and are often not explained.
- I can offer some basic explanations about what the writer has to say.

You may need to go back and look at the relevant pages from this section again.

Controlled Assessment Preparation

Introduction

In this section you will

- find out what is required of you in the Understanding Creative Texts Controlled Assessment task
- read, analyse and respond to three sample answers by different candidates
- plan and write your own answer to a sample question
- evaluate and assess your answer and the progress you have made.

Why is preparation like this important?

- If you know exactly what you need to do, you will feel more confident when you produce your own assessed response.
- Looking at sample answers by other students will help you see what you need to do to improve your own work.
- Planning and writing a full sample response after you have completed the chapter will give you a clear sense of what you have learned so far.

Key information

Unit 3 Section A is 'Understanding Creative Texts'.

- The controlled part of the task will last **3–4 hours**, and is worth **40 marks**.
- It is worth **20%** of your overall English GCSE mark.

What will the task involve?

- You have to complete **one** task, which will be made up of three smaller responses – one response for each text (or collection of texts) you have studied.
- Your responses will be based on **one or more** of the **Shakespeare plays** you have studied, **one or more** of the **English Literary Heritage** texts and one text or a collection of texts from **Exploring Cultures**.

What does the task consist of?

It is likely that your teacher will have focused you on a task related to either **Themes and ideas** or **Characterisation and voice**.

You will have to respond by writing three pieces with a recommended total of **1600 words**. This will be done in 'controlled conditions', possibly in your own classroom, over a period of up to four hours.

Here are some example questions based on the general task areas set by the exam board.

Characterisation	• Explore the way a central character is presented and developed in a text or texts you have studied. • Explore the ways writers develop and use contrast in characterisation in a text or texts you have studied.
Theme	• Explore the way family relationships are presented in a text or texts you have studied. • Explore the ways the theme of power is developed in a text or texts you have studied.

The Assessment

The assessment objective for this unit (AO2) states that you must:

- Read and understand texts, selecting material appropriate to purpose.
- Develop and sustain interpretations of writers' ideas and perspectives.
- Explain and evaluate how writers use linguistic, grammatical, structural and presentational features to achieve effects and engage and influence the reader.
- Understand texts in their social, cultural and historical contexts.

Targeting Grade C

Some of the key features of Grade C and Grade D responses are as follows:

Grade D candidates	See example on pages 221–2
• show some evidence of understanding key meanings in texts and some ability to look for deeper interpretations • write about writers' ideas, often clearly, generally supported by relevant quotations • display some knowledge of language features and how they support the effect created.	**(D)**

Grade C candidates	See example on pages 223–4 and 225–6
• show clear evidence of understanding key meanings in texts, with some ability to look for more significant or deeper interpretations • write clearly about writers' ideas, supported by relevant and appropriate evidence or quotation • display understanding of the effects created by language features used and support points with relevant quotations.	**(C)**

Exploring Sample Responses

ACTIVITY

Read the following extract from the first part of a student's response to this task.

> *How is a central character presented in a text you have studied?*
>
> *Consider how Shakespeare presents the character of Romeo in Act 1 Scene 1 and Act 1 Scene 5, and what this reveals about his development over the course of the play.*

As you read the response, think about whether it is closer to a Grade D or C, and why.

Consider the key elements a marker would look for:

- how clearly and effectively the writer has conveyed his/her ideas
- whether the author's themes and the student's ideas are shown
- how well the student comments on the language used
- how well the student supports the point he or she makes
- whether there is any personal interpretation of ideas.

Example 1: Characterisation in Shakespeare

Romeo changes as the play goes on. For a start when Romeo first appears he's dead moody because this girl is not interested in him. It says,

'Romeo shuts up his windows' (Act I Scene I).

This means he does not want to be seen by anyone and is moping around. Like when you won't speak to anyone when you're told off by your mum except this is about love and his feelings for a girl.

Then everything changes when he meets Juliet at the ball. He goes there with Mercutio and the others and when he sees her he is just completely stunned by her looks and how she acts. He says she's really beautiful: 'She doth teach the torches to burn bright' he says (Act I Scene 5).

He is there because his friend Mercutio told him to go although Romeo did have some bad feelings about it. But as it turned out he met Juliet, and they kiss and it is only afterwards that they find out who they are and remember that their families hate each other like it said at the start before the play.

But now Romeo is now changing. He forgets all about

221

Rosaline. He says 'did my heart love till now?' (Act 1 Scene 5). This shows things are all different and they've fallen in love.

This goes on too in the rest of the play like when Romeo sees Juliet on the balcony in Act 2 Scene 2 he faces death to see her as he is not meant to be there. It's Juliet's garden and this shows he is brave and fearless and his love is real. In the scene he promises to marry Juliet, which is a very big step for anyone. The evidence for this is the quote:

'the exchange of thy love's faithful vow for mine' he says.

Also, in the rest of the play he shows his love for Juliet because he doesn't want to fight with the Capulets but he has to. The thing is that you had to marry who you were told back then so it was tough for everyone even the parents. They want the best for their daughter and they don't know she's fallen for someone else. Romeo would be a good husband as his real feelings for their daughter show but they will never know.

Examiner feedback

The candidate makes some good points and focuses on Romeo, but there is too much retelling of events and not enough discussion of how Shakespeare presents him or analysis of the language. Some quotations are used but not always very well-selected: for example, 'shuts up his windows' would work better with the remainder ('locks fair daylight out') as it is the darkness – the being moody – that's important.

The candidate does provide a range of examples and comments on Romeo's character but a more formal approach and vocabulary, for example avoiding 'like' and 'dead moody', and using 'Prologue' rather than 'start of the play', would improve the response. References to imagery such as simile or metaphor would also help, especially in the selected scenes.

Finally, quotations could be embedded a little more fluently in the writing.

Suggested grade: D

ACTIVITY

- Rewrite the first two paragraphs. Include the longer quotation and try to embed it as part of the sentence.
- Try to make the personal references sound more formal. For example, take out direct references to 'your mum'!

Read the following extract from a response to this task.

> **Explore the ways writers develop and use contrast in characterisation in a text you have studied:**
>
> **How does Charles Dickens present the development of Scrooge during the course of A Christmas Carol?**

The following is the first part of a possible response. Look at the annotations. Could any of these comments be made about your own work?

Example 2: Characterisation in English Literary Heritage texts

The essay focus is introduced clearly →

Scrooge changes a lot over the course of the story. We see a real contrast between Scrooge at the start when he is **mean, cold and cruel**, and the end when the writer shows us a new, good side to him.

← Quite good to use these three adjectives to describe him

At the beginning, Scrooge is shown like this **through a simile**.

Good appropriate quotation and mention of simile →

Dickens says, he was **'hard and sharp as flint'** which makes him seem like a sharp stone which no one can break.

We also see him in his 'counting house' which shows that he is completely obsessed with money, like he can't get enough of it but it hasn't made him happy. Though at this point he doesn't seem to want to change.

← Further evidence in new paragraph

When his nephew Fred visits him to wish him happy Christmas

Explanation follows but more could be said about why this is funny →

all he can say is 'every idiot who goes about with "Merry Christmas" on his lips, should be boiled with his own pudding, and buried with a stake of holly through his heart.'

Dickens says that he speaks this line 'indignantly' which shows he is cross about how people like Christmas. **Actually this is also quite a funny line.**

Good new example but needs a quote; also chance here to add some historical context →

Dickens really stresses how nasty and bad Scrooge is when the charity people come to ask him for money for the poor. He tells them that there are poor-houses – which were a bit like

prisons – *for poor people **and anyway if some died then that*** — Quotation is a bit long and not embedded very fluently

was not a bad thing really as England had too much population!

Everything is built up to show his cruel and wicked money-grabbing personality. Even when it comes to little things like the fires in his office, because he controls everything and 'had a very small fire, but the clerk's fire was so very much smaller that it looked like one coal. But he couldn't replenish it, for Scrooge kept the coal-box in his own room.'

Again this emphasises his coldness – both in his actual life and in his heart.

Good summing up at this point →

Another key way that Dickens shows Scrooge's character at the start is through what he says. He keeps on saying *'Humbug!' which is his way of saying 'Rubbish!'* to any nice suggestion that people like Fred make. This is like a catch-phrase which Scrooge says all the time.

← Good to mention how Scrooge speaks but better to use the technical term: 'dialogue'

All this sets up the way that Scrooge will change so that we can see the contrast as he is visited by the three spirits.

Examiner feedback

This is a clear explanation of how Dickens presents the character of Scrooge and it sets up the idea of contrast well. The quotations selected are all appropriate, although they could perhaps be shorter on occasions and embedded a little more fluently. Generally, the points made are relevant if sometimes lacking in development; for example, the reference to humour could have been linked to a discussion of 'tone', a word which the candidate doesn't actually use. Another aspect which isn't mentioned here is that of exaggeration – the way Scrooge is described is fairly extreme! However, overall this is a solid first part of the response which mentions aspects of behaviour, speech and appearance.

Suggested grade: C

ACTIVITY

In what ways is this response an improvement on Example 1 on pages 221–2?
Go back to the feedback on the Grade D essay and compare:
- references to language and particular devices the writer uses
- the development of ideas
- the use of quotations.

Read the following extract from a response to this task.

> *Explore the way the idea of personal identity is presented in texts you have studied.*

This is the first part of a response to this task, relating it to the poems, 'Checking out me History' by John Agard and 'Thoughts on my Father' by James Berry (see page 216).

Use the annotations to help you decide what the writer has done well.

Example 3: Ideas in Exploring Cultures Poetry

Starting with a quotation draws reader in →

'I carving out me identity'

These words tell us that this is a powerful, personal poem as our 'identity' is vital to us all. They is the last line of 'Checking out me History' by John Agard, a poem about someone who doesn't like his own background being ignored. I am going to compare this with the poem 'Thoughts on my Father' by James Berry which takes a bit of a different view of the theme of identity because it is more about his father not his life.

But I will start with **John Agard and what he has to say**.

Makes a good point then supports it →

The first thing he does in the poem is that he links up identity and history. It says,

Bandage up me eye with me own history
Blind me to me own identity.

He uses this **metaphor** about 'dem' – possibly teachers or other adults – who have stopped him from seeing his own past and the alliteration of 'blind' and 'bandage' stresses the idea of damage.

— Refers to a device used by writer but doesn't quite develop the analysis far enough

A new paragraph introduces a new point →

After this the next verse bit tells us all about famous figures from British history (which is all white and English) and then presents Caribbean or African figures. These are people who Agard believes he should have been taught about. Examples of this are '1066 and all dat' which means the Norman invasion but nothing about the 'slave with vision' – Toussaint

l'Ouverture who beat Napoleon. Then he mentions Mary Seacole, a West Indian nurse in the Crimean War **who helped the British**. ← *Missed opportunity to mention irony here*

John Agard uses some powerful metaphors, 'a healing star' and a **'powerful sunrise' to describe her which makes her seem as important as Florence Nightingale, like she meant hope for lots of soldiers, like a light shining.**

Throughout the poem Agard is also saying that his own identity, which is to do with people from his own culture and background, has **been put down** by being told traditional stories and rhymes like Robin Hood or Old King Cole rather than about his own history.

Becomes a bit too chatty

Covers structure and tries to explain the effect

The poem's structure is also really important because he **keeps repeating the line 'Dem tell me'** (this means 'They tell me') which goes back to the point about teachers and adults, and it sounds like he has no time for them! The effect is that the repeated words are like drum-beats you can't forget.

It is **very interesting** that he has to tell us lots of details ← *Shows personal engagement* about his famous people like Toussaint, Nanny and Mary Seacole who are not familiar like Florence Nightingale. These are Caribbean heroes from his history. **The poem ends very** ← *New paragraph needed to end this first part of the response* **powerfully**. He says he is going to make his own identity now. He says he is 'carving' it out, like when you carve your name on a tree and it stays there and doesn't change. I think this may be an image from his childhood or growing up.

Examiner feedback

This candidate has engaged very well with the poem and the writer's theme but the work is a little confused and jumbled in places. The candidate mentions language use such as metaphor and mostly explains the effect, but on other occasions misses the chance to develop ideas (for example, not mentioning the irony of Seacole helping the British but now being forgotten by them). Occasionally, the language lapses into being a bit chatty and informal ('verse bit', 'like when you...'). All in all, this is a strong response which needs some refinement and perhaps more regular mention of the word 'idea' and the writer's presentation of it.

Suggested grade: C

EXTENDED PRACTICE TASK

Write about a character who has made a particular impression on you in a text or texts you have studied. You can choose to write about character(s) from:

- a Shakespeare play (e.g. Mercutio in *Romeo and Juliet*), an English Literary Heritage text or texts (e.g. Tiny Tim in *A Christmas Carol*)
- a character from an Exploring Cultures text or texts (e.g. Crooks in *Of Mice and Men*)

What made an impact on you, and how did the writer present the character?

If you only do five things...

1 Prepare carefully in advance of the task on your chosen texts – early preparation will be important.
2 Know the texts very well so that you don't waste time looking for references on the day.
3 Stick to the focus of the task. If you are writing about theme, keep coming back to the key word (for example, 'power' or 'conflict').
4 Make sure you keep referring to the *effect* of the choices writers make; don't just say what they did.
5 Strike a balance between comments on language choices (vocabulary, imagery), grammatical choices (tenses, sentence types) and structure (how and when information is revealed, ordered and patterned), and use appropriate technical terms (stanza, chapter, scene).

5 Unit 3B **Creative Writing**

What's it all about?

Writing creatively really enables you to show off your most imaginative ideas, original thinking and best writing techniques.

How will I be assessed?

- You will get **20% of your English marks** for your ability to write creative texts. You will have to complete two written pieces in a Controlled Assessment lasting up to **four hours**.
- You will be marked on your writing of **two** written responses taken from a **choice of three areas**. These are
  - *Moving Images:* watching moving image texts and developing writing from them
  - *Prompts and Re-creations:* using a text or prompt to develop writing
  - *Me. Myself. I.:* writing from personal experience

- The two pieces of writing will total up to **1400 words**. They needn't be the same length: the way you split the total will depend on the tasks.

What is being tested?

You are being examined on your ability to

- write for specific creative purposes
- communicate clearly, effectively and imaginatively
- organise information in a structured and inventive way
- use a range of paragraphs
- use a variety of sentence structures and styles
- use a range of linguistic features for impact and effect
- write with accuracy in punctuation, spelling and grammar.

Moving Images

Introduction

This section of Chapter 5 shows you how to

- explore the area of creative writing linked to 'Moving images'
- understand what a Controlled Assessment task in this area is asking you to do
- produce creative responses to a range of moving image texts
- practise and develop extended responses.

Why is learning about this area important?

- This is one of the three areas of creative writing, from which you will have to choose two tasks to respond to.
- The skills you develop here will feed into your other reading, writing, speaking and listening tasks and responses.

A **Grade D** candidate will

- show evidence of having tried to use the form and style to interest the reader
- include some use of detail in ideas, and begin to engage the reader
- use simple and compound sentences and some complex ones
- group sentences into paragraphs quite effectively.

D

A **Grade C** candidate will

- use the main conventions of creative texts consistently
- write clear and well-structured creative pieces making the meaning clear to the reader
- try consciously to achieve certain effects in his or her writing to interest the reader, for example through vocabulary choices
- use clear paragraphing and sentences, which are sometimes varied.

C

Prior learning

Before you begin this section, think about

- a book you have read which would make a good film
- a haunting or memorable scene from a film you have seen and how you would describe it in words.

> Why would it make a good film? Is it the story, setting, themes, characters – or what?

> What would you have to do to turn it into a successful piece of writing?

Moving images: generating ideas

Learning objective

- To explore the writing possibilities that can arise from a moving image text.

What is involved in generating ideas from moving image texts?

- You will be shown moving image texts (film sequences, video or DVD clips) from which you will be expected to compose your own extended creative text.
- You will respond by using what you have seen as a 'springboard' for your own creative writing. This means you won't just describe what you see on the screen but will develop elements of it using your own ideas.

Checklist for success

- You need to consider original and inventive approaches to the material.
- You need to use rich, varied language that engages the reader.
- You need to sustain your ideas, style and tone throughout your writing.

Focus for development: Building ideas

A student has chosen a memorable scene from a film to inspire his own piece of creative writing. He will take some of the powerful ideas from the original and add his own to them.

His choice is the opening sequence to *Great Expectations* (David Lean, 1946).

The student has made notes about particular ideas that stood out from the scene, and how these might be developed in his own story. Here are his notes as a spider diagram.

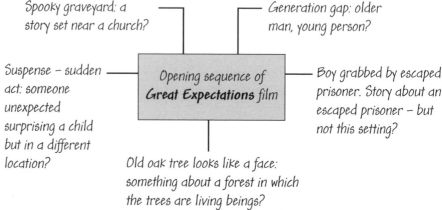

Spooky graveyard: a story set near a church?

Generation gap: older man, young person?

Suspense – sudden act: someone unexpected surprising a child but in a different location?

Opening sequence of **Great Expectations** film

Boy grabbed by escaped prisoner. Story about an escaped prisoner – but not this setting?

Old oak tree looks like a face: something about a forest in which the trees are living beings?

From the diagram, the student decided that the idea of 'someone unexpected surprising a child in a different location' would work well. Here are the set of notes he wrote for the **plot**.

- *A girl is on bus on her way home from school.*
- *She is approached by a down-and-out woman who demands money.*
- *When she looks closely, she is amazed to see the woman looks identical to her mother!*
- *Girl wonders what to do...*

Although this is only a short scene – or a very short story – it has the same ingredients as a longer one:

- **Introduction** – girl on bus
- **Complication** – down-and-out woman demands money
- **Key moment** – woman like her mother?
- **Conclusion** – girl does not follow up on the meeting; ending left open.

ACTIVITY

Choose one of the other ideas in the spider diagram.

Write a simple four-bullet plan, like the one here, noting down what would happen in your new version. You could use one of these ideas to set you on your way.

- *Poacher out in a forest at night*
- *Suddenly, he notices one of the trees which...*
- *Then...*
- *It ends by...*

The film you watch is just a springboard for your ideas. You don't have to stick to the story.

Remember

- **You don't have to write a full story – focus on a powerful scene or moment.**
- **Plan for a story with simple characters and a good setting.**

Making your writing visual!

Learning objective

- To learn how to make your writing easy for the reader to picture.

Checklist for success

- You need to make sure the reader can 'see' a picture when they read your work, so focus on objects, people and locations and use vivid detail.

ACTIVITY

Based on the *Great Expectations* scene on page 230, here is part of a **Grade D** response about a graveyard in which a runaway child is hiding from the police and the gang she has been forced to work for.

> The police officer ran after me as I ran away towards the graveyard. There were gravestones all over the place. I knew if I didn't reach the church I was finished. I would end up being sent back to work or even prison. I got closer and could now see the windows of the church up above me.

Next read this extract from a good **Grade C** response:

> The gravestones were like grey fangs coming out of the earth. I knew if I didn't reach the safety of the church, the man pursuing me would trap me like a rat and I would end up on the cold floor of a cell.

- Pick out at least two ways this is an improvement on the Grade D response.
- Now, add a further sentence to the second example, adding a more visual description of the windows (perhaps using a simile, comparing them to eyes).

ACTIVITY

Now consider how the imagery would change, if the tone was lighter and the plot less serious. What do you notice about the similes and metaphors here, compared with the gravestone ones?

> Running through the graveyard was like taking part in a strange race. I didn't have my glasses on, so it became an obstacle course full of unexpected hurdles in the shape of the gravestones. I banged my big toe at least twice. If Lee caught up with me, he would look at me with those eyes, like a sad puppy's, and I wouldn't have the heart to tell him it was over.

Focus for development: Using detail appropriately

By focusing on a specific object, person or sensation you can really enrich your writing. The best ways of doing this are to

- use **interesting** and **specific vocabulary**, for example 'oak' rather than 'tree'; 'torch' rather than 'light'
- use **similes** or **metaphors,** for example 'oak, with bark like an old man's skin'.

A student writes…

*How **exactly** do I add detail?*

Answer…

Often all you need to do is add extra description before or after a noun. For example, 'A **huge white-bellied** shark leapt out of the water, its teeth **like giant knives**'.

ACTIVITY

Look at how one student developed her ideas about being chased into the graveyard.

> **Part I**
>
> **Paragraph I** – *Girl runs into graveyard, describes spooky setting*
>
> **Paragraph 2** – *She hides behind gravestone as a police officer blocks entrance to church. He calls to another officer to help him. Luckily, the fog comes down and the girl creeps towards the back door of the church.*

Finish the two sentences below which focus on the senses of sound and sight. Choose the best image from the lists below or, even better, come up with your own.

The police-officers' voices were like … cutting through the night.

> the howls of wolves / loud sirens / soapy bubbles

I crept breathlessly through the … of fog.

> grey wall / protective blanket / choking barrier / cuddly duvet

ASSESSMENT FOCUS

Continue the girl's story.

- First, complete paragraph 2 from the previous activity. You will need to add at least one further sentence to the two above.
- Then imagine the runaway girl falls down and is caught by the police. Write the next two paragraphs as they catch her. Include a short explanation of why she is running away (for example, from a gang forcing her to beg or who run a sweat shop).

Remember

- **Write detailed descriptions, using imagery and effective vocabulary.**
- **Focus on specific objects, features, people or sensations.**

Writing for film

Learning objective

- To learn how to write short stories in a style that might be adapted for film.

A student writes…

Is it always good to start with a conversation?

Answer…

You could equally begin with a good description of a place or person or a character's thoughts.

What does writing for film mean?

You may be asked to write a sequence or a short story which has 'filmic' qualities or, in other words, would make a good basis for a film. This means writing that

- has a strong description of place
- uses powerful dialogue
- centres on a memorable character or characters (probably no more than two)
- makes the reader curious about what will happen next.

ACTIVITY

Read this student's opening to a short story.

> Jake stood by the open door with a sly look on his face.
> 'You comin' or not? We can be there in ten minutes.'
> I looked at the souped-up hatchback. It had black shark teeth design down one side. The engine was snarling like a baby tiger.
> 'Well? What you frightened of?'

Discuss with a partner:

- How has the writer of this opening paragraph made us think and ask questions?
- How has he painted a picture in our minds as well?

Improving a first draft

This was the opening paragraph to the story above, in its first draft.

> Jake was my brother. He was 17. He was always getting in trouble especially in his new car which was a hatchback. He always tried to get me to join in especially when he wanted to go down to the beach front where he could race his car. I didn't like going.

This is very correct, and tells us lots of information, rather than showing us it through events or dialogue. It might work as a second paragraph because at some stage we need to know who Jake is. The improved draft in the Activity box above is more like a Grade C because it makes us want to find out more.

Continue the conversation between Jake and the narrator. Try to include some of the factual information, but also add some visual description. Start like this:

I looked at Jake, my older brother. He was wearing...

When writing dialogue don't over-use 'said' words ('said', 'cried', 'asked'). If it's easy to tell who is speaking and to guess how they are feeling, these words often aren't needed.

Focus for development:
Writing better dialogue

You will have noticed that the dialogue on page 234 was quite basic. This is good. Don't try to over-write dialogue. Do use it to reveal information about the story, characters or the situation.

You must also make sure you know the rules for setting out speech. The first example below shows a range of problems in how dialogue is used and set out.

Bad dialogue

'I don't want to go down to the beach-front with you because you'll drive too fast' I explained. Jake wasn't very happy about all that and said, 'You're just stupid and there won't be any problems.'

'there will be cos the police will arrest you or there'll be a crash and we could get hurt,' I said to Jake giving my reasons why I didn't want to go. He didn't seem to care.

Add two more lines to the 'good' dialogue: one from the narrator and one from Jake. Write one line of description between them.

Speech marks only for the actual words spoken

Punctuation inside speech marks

Capital letter for first word spoken

New line / paragraph for each speaker

Good dialogue

'I don't want to go to the beach-front,' I explained.

Jake looked at me nastily.

'There'll be problems. With the Police. Or you'll crash.'

In the background, the car continued snarling.

'Suit yourself,' Jake said.

Short phrases sound more like real speech

Description between speech

'You? I didn't expect you to come.'

- Using this first line of dialogue, spend 10 minutes jotting down ideas about who the people might be and what the situation is.
- Then write the opening paragraphs of a story with two main characters. You could base it on the situation above (these could be Jake's words to his brother as he waits to race his car).

Remember

- **Keep the reader guessing, but include some information!**
- **Make your dialogue short and to the point (don't over-use names or 'said').**
- **Add visual description where you can.**

Grade Booster

Extended Assessment Task

Generate ideas, plan and write a response of about 700 words to this task.

> **Write a story that would work as a television drama or thriller, set in the near future.**

Make sure you

- use convincing dialogue
- hold back key information
- write vividly using a range of language devices and techniques
- don't waste time with unnecessary or dull details setting the scene
- plan your story structure carefully before you start writing.

Evaluation – What have you learned?

With a partner, use the grade checklist below to evaluate your work on the Extended Assessment Task.

- I can write a clear and well-structured creative piece which uses some language devices and structures for purpose and effect.
- I can use clear and sometimes varied paragraphs and sentences.

- I can write a creative piece which mainly matches the task I have been set and is generally accurate and clear, but sometimes undeveloped.
- I can demonstrate only a limited variety of vocabulary, and sentence or paragraph structures.

- I can write using creative ideas of my own and the story can be followed.
- I can use paragraphs to order my story but I don't use them creatively or in a varied way.
- I can use mostly clear sentences but they are not always as varied or interesting as they could be.

- I can come up with creative ideas but they are not ordered in a clear way.
- I can use paragraphs but they are often unclear or too long and need to be reorganised.
- I can write mostly accurate sentences but they are generally the same length and can be repetitive and dull.

You may need to go back and look at the relevant pages of this section again.

Recreations and Prompts

Introduction

This section of Chapter 5 shows you how to

- explore the area of creative writing inspired by a prompt (usually the opening or closing sentence of a story) or a stimulus text, such as a poem
- understand what a Controlled Assessment task in this area is asking you to do
- develop responses to a range of ideas or other texts
- practise and develop extended responses.

Why is learning about this area important?

- This is one of the three areas of creative writing from which you will choose two tasks to respond to.
- The skills you develop here will feed into your other reading, writing, speaking and listening tasks and responses.

A **Grade D** candidate will

- show evidence of having tried to use the form and style to interest the reader
- include some detailed ideas, and begin to engage the reader
- use simple and compound sentences and some complex ones
- group sentences into paragraphs quite effectively.

D

A **Grade C** candidate will

- use the main conventions of creative texts consistently
- write clear and well-structured creative pieces, with the meaning clear to the reader
- try consciously to achieve certain effects in his or her writing to interest the reader, for example through vocabulary choices
- use clear paragraphing and sentences, which are sometimes varied.

C

Prior learning

Before you begin this section, think about

- the opening lines of a poem and come up with a couple of ideas for stories based on these lines
- previous creative writing you have done – what you did well, and what needed more work.

> Who would tell your new story? The same person as is in the poem, or would it be told from a different viewpoint?

> Did you use a range of long and short sentences – for effect?

Generating ideas from a prompt

Learning objectives

- To generate ideas from a simple prompt.
- To structure a story from those ideas.

⭐ Examiner's tip

Your story could be any **fiction genre**, provided it works. For example, it might be **historical**, featuring a town where a medieval battle takes place, or **futuristic** – a building on a distant planet!

What does generating ideas from a prompt mean?

Some of the tasks you will be set will only give you a **short extract or sentence** to work from.

ACTIVITY

Read this prompt for a Controlled Assessment Task.

> **Write a creative piece that leads up to these final sentences:**
>
> *He stood at the top of the building looking down at the streets below, trying to make sense of everything that had happened. It would take some time.*

With a partner:

Mindmap **two or three story ideas** that arise from the few simple lines mentioned.

You need to be able to answer these questions:

- Who is this person? What do we know about him?
- Where is he? Why is he there? What happened to him?

ACTIVITY

Between you, choose the **best idea** and very simply sum up in **four stages** what happens in the story. Use a grid like this.

Stage 1 Grab the reader's attention with setting or action	A teenager explores a deserted hi-tech office block.
Stage 2 Development/complication	He/she discovers a middle-aged man hiding out there. He has faked his own death to escape from debts and home problems. The teenager promises help and fetches food and drink, returning with a friend.
Stage 3 Development/climax	Police see someone has broken in. They hunt them down. The two friends have to decide whether to give the man away or not.
Stage 4 Resolution/ending	They decide the right thing to do is to tell the police. But by the time they get to where the man is hiding, he has gone.

Focus for development: Building an ideas bank

- Now build an **ideas bank**. You could create folders or documents on the computer, or divide up a note-book.

Then, within each one, build up more detail. For example:

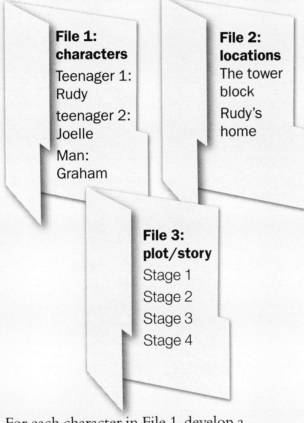

File 1: characters
Teenager 1: Rudy
teenager 2: Joelle
Man: Graham

File 2: locations
The tower block
Rudy's home

File 3: plot/story
Stage 1
Stage 2
Stage 3
Stage 4

For each character in File 1, develop a **description card,** like this.

Joelle
• 16 • Rudy's cousin • Tomboy, daring, more street-wise than him; red hair, slim, tall

- Either use the sample story or your own, and develop miniature **character cards** for your main characters. Add as much detail as you want – you don't have to use it all!
- You can also create **location cards,** for example 'inside tower block', 'Rudy's home', and add details.

These can be kept alongside your **plot details.**

ASSESSMENT FOCUS

Once you have the bare bones of your story, characters and location, you need to see how well it fits together. One way of doing this is to tell it as a story to a partner. You can improvise details as you go along, too.

- Tell your story in just a maximum of three minutes.
- Ask your partner to question you occasionally if anything is unclear, for example why did your character go to the tower block?

Remember

- First get your ideas down on paper or screen – this is very important.
- Don't even begin your story until you have planned some excellent characters, a good simple plot, and some atmospheric settings.

Structuring a story for effect and impact

Learning objective

- To make your story engaging through structure and variety.

Checklist for success

- You need to make sure your ideas and plot lines are clear enough to follow, but also keep readers engaged.
- You need to use a variety of sentences and paragraphs to make sure your reader wants to read on.

Below are two **openings** to the tower block story from pages 238–239.

Grade D response

> Rudy was 15 and school was closed due to the snow. He was bored and he didn't know where his cousin Joelle was. He was fed up hanging around the streets. However, he was fascinated by the modern tower block near his house. The company had gone bust but sometimes he thought he saw a light on the fifth floor.
>
> So that afternoon, he noticed that the snow must have affected the alarm system. When he pushed the security door at the back, no alarm went off. He went inside and found himself by the lift. It would be cool to go to the top and look out over the city. He didn't have anything else to do.

This is good because

- we are introduced to Rudy and find out quite a lot about him and Joelle
- the paragraphs are clear: one is about the situation; the other how Rudy gets in
- the story is hinted at: there is the mention of the light being on.

However, the sentences are dull (five begin with 'Rudy' or 'He') and very few visual details are included.

ACTIVITY

Discuss with a partner how this **Grade C response**

- conveys the same information
- engages the reader
- adds new information.

> The door opened and, to his surprise, no alarm went off. It must be the snow, he thought. Rudy shivered. There was no heating inside the block. Since the company had gone out of business the place had been empty, like a rectangular concrete shell. He had often noticed a flickering light on the fifth floor and now he was inside. It had been easy.
>
> He wondered where Joelle was. She would just go

> straight to the lift doors and ride up to the top floor and shout out across the city. He hesitated. Maybe this wasn't such a good idea.
>
> However, he didn't have anything else to do. School was cancelled and no one cared where he was if he was honest. He pressed the small silver 'up' button and waited.

Focus for development: Using paragraphs to make an impact

The information you reveal and how you reveal it is key. The extract above does this well:

Paragraph 1: (long, lots of detail) reveals setting, creates atmosphere, introduces main character, hints at story

Paragraph 2: (shorter) offers new information (about Joelle) and adds suspense (will Rudy leave?)

Paragraph 3: (very short) moves plot on (Rudy decides to explore) and adds further new information (hints no one from his family cares).

ACTIVITY

Plan two more paragraphs to show the **complication phase** of the story. They should introduce the meeting with the middle-aged man hiding out.

For each paragraph:

- First sketch a very simple idea of what is happening in it. For example, Paragraph 4: Rudy in someone's office looking out of the window; hears a noise?
- Then add some basic details about what happens, what is shown and how the plot is moved on.
- Think about how the paragraphs can contrast, too, for example Rudy quietly looking around turns to sudden action when he sees the man.

ASSESSMENT FOCUS

Now write the two paragraphs. Make sure you do the following:

- Make any dialogue carry important information about the story or characters. (See page 235 for more on dialogue.)
- Include visual details so that the story is not just action, for example 'an old computer desk on its side'.
- Move the story on in these two paragraphs and make sure they tell us more about the character(s) and plot.
- Begin each paragraph in a different way, not just with pronouns ('He','She') or names.

Remember

- Make sure each paragraph does a job, for example providing new information or creating a contrasting atmosphere.
- Try to show things happening by including descriptive detail where you can.

Adding variety and interest

Learning objective

- To use a variety of sentences and verbs in your creative writing to interest the reader.

What does adding variety and interest mean?

Good writing is more than just interesting imagery and flowery description: powerful verbs and a variety of sentences, for example, also keep the reader hooked.

Varying sentences

A range of sentences can bring suspense and keep you reading. This student has written a *Lord of the Rings* style short story in response to the task.

Grade C response

> The men from the Iron City were unaware of the eyes watching them from the tower. They crept forward. The leader took a step and his men followed him. Then another. Because of the danger, he signalled for his men to stop. No one moved. Not a hand stirred.

Look at the variety of sentences.

Simple sentence: They crept forward (one simple clause)

Compound sentence: The leader took a step **and** his men followed him (two joined equal clauses)

Complex sentence: **Because of the danger**, he gestured for his men to stop. (**sub-clause** and main clause)

(See pages 74–77 for more about using different sentence types.)

ACTIVITY

- Write the next paragraph. Show the men hesitate again as they approach the tower.
- Or write your own paragraph based on the ideas you are developing.
- Use a range of short and long sentences.

Focus for development: Using powerful and specific verbs

- You can add excitement by selecting your **verbs** carefully.
- Remember, too, to keep things **visual** so that the reader can picture what you are describing.

ACTIVITY

Improve this **Grade D response** by changing the highlighted verbs to ones with more impact.

> The leader **went** rapidly along the narrow alleys of the city, his dagger **held out** in front of him, **shining** in the dark. He **managed to** get over the rubble and rubbish in his way. His cloak waved **about a bit** in the wind.

ACTIVITY

You can also use carefully selected verbs, which may not be powerful or exciting, to give a good sense of a character. Look at this example.

> She **hovered** on the doorstep, waiting for someone to come to the door. Her eyes **flicked nervously** from the pot of dead flowers to the large bell, and she **fiddled anxiously** with the buttons of her woollen coat.

- Note down what the **verbs** and the **adverbs** (here, the words ending in 'ly') suggest about the character at the door.

Examiner's tip ★

Plan contrasting situations into the plot of your story. For example, a quiet conversation between two characters could be followed by a chase or pursuit. This will allow you to write in a range of styles.

ASSESSMENT FOCUS

Write a paragraph based on this prompt.

> *As she pulled the book off the shelf, something fell out and landed on the floor. She picked it up. It was a photograph…*

Continue from here, dealing with the situation as it develops: for example, the photo might contain dangerous information and the girl or woman has to hand it over to someone.

In your paragraph, use verbs and adverbs to

- show how the character is feeling
- create a visual impact for the reader.

Remember

- **Use a variety of sentences lengths and types.**
- **Include verbs and adverbs to convey character and atmosphere.**

Re-creations: changing the viewpoint of a text

What does re-creating a text mean?

When you re-create a text, you take an aspect of it and change it. For example, you might change its form or who tells the story. The story of a teenage boy recalling his first day doing a weekend job could be transformed by telling it from a different viewpoint.

ACTIVITY

Read this story extract and discuss with a partner:

- Who else from the extract could tell this story?
- Note down at least two other possibilities.
- Which, in your opinion, might lead to the most interesting story?

> **My first proper job**
>
> After my mum dropped me off, I waited outside the shop in the pouring rain. Inside I could see the manager chatting to one of the assistants. Why didn't they open up and let me in? I was nervous and soaking wet. I checked my mobile and even thought about texting them: 'can't you see me, you losers?'

ACTIVITY

Changing the perspective can create some really interesting ideas. Here is the same basic story with a quite different person telling it.

> I could see him hanging around outside the shop opposite. He was a good-looking boy, a bit like my grandson Nicky, but was clearly miserable. It was a shame I was stuck in the wheelchair in the flat. I could have made him a nice cup of tea. Poor lad. I think the shop sells some sort of computer-thingumees, but I've never been in, of course.

- What can you tell about this **narrator** (the person telling the story)?
- What is different about the tone of voice used?

⭐ Examiner's tip

A story can have more than one narrator. Try using two narrators, each speaking in every other paragraph. This works well if you give them very distinct voices.

Focus for development:
Changing a poem into a story

Another interesting way of re-creating a text is to take a few lines of a poem and retell it as a story from a different viewpoint. In this example, the poem's narrator describes how, as a child, she and her parents were involved in the rescue of a drowning girl from a lake.

We once watched a crowd
pull a drowned child from the lake.
Blue-lipped and dressed in water's long green silk
she lay for dead.

Then kneeling on the earth,
a heroine, her red head bowed,
her wartime cotton frock soaked,
my mother gave a stranger's child her breath.
The crowd stood silent,
drawn by the dread of it…

from 'Cold Knap Lake' by Gillian Clark

There are many interesting possibilities here. For example, the same experience could be retold as a story by someone who watched everything happen but did nothing.

> *I was walking the dog when it happened. I heard a cry, a splash, and the next thing I knew I was by the bank staring at this child struggling…*

ASSESSMENT FOCUS

- Using the skills you have learned about writing powerful stories (see pages 240–3), write the opening two paragraphs of this story from any viewpoint you choose.
- Make sure you only include things that the narrator sees or experiences. For example, if either the mother or daughter is your narrator, remember she doesn't see the girl fall into the lake.
- (You can read the whole poem in the AQA anthology, *Moon on the Tides*.)

ACTIVITY

- Write down two more possible narrators.
- What else would you need to do to turn this poem into a story? (What is different about how a poem is told and set out?)
- Is there any other information in the poem you could use? For example, when does it seem to be set? How is the drowning girl described?

Remember

- **Choose an interesting perspective.**
- **Use ideas and details from the original poem.**
- **Have a clear idea of the structure of your short story.**

245

Grade Booster

Extended Assessment Task

Generate ideas, plan and write a response of about 700 words to this task.

> **Write a creative piece that leads up to these final two sentences:**
> *The room was completely empty. Not a trace remained of anyone ever having been there.*

Start by generating ideas using a format you find useful, such as a spider diagram like the one on page 230.

Then build a plan for your story, dividing it up according to the key events and stages, as you did on pages 238.

Evaluation – What have you learned?

With a partner, use the grade checklist below to evaluate your work on the Extended Assessment Task.

- I can write a clear and well-structured piece of original or re-creative writing, which uses some language devices and structures for purpose and effect.
- I can use clear and sometimes varied paragraphs and sentences.

- I can write a piece of original or re-creative writing which mainly matches the task I have been set and is generally accurate and clear, but sometimes undeveloped.
- I can use only a limited variety of vocabulary and sentence and paragraph structures.

- I can write using creative ideas of my own and the story can be followed.
- I can use paragraphs to order my story but don't use them creatively or in a varied way.
- I can use sentences that are mostly clear but are not as varied or interesting as they could be.

- I can generate creative ideas but they are not ordered in a clear way.
- I can use paragraphs but they are often unclear or too long and need to be reorganised.
- I can write mostly accurate sentences but they are generally the same length and can be repetitive and dull.

You may need to go back and look at the relevant pages of this section again.

Me. Myself. I.

Introduction

This section of Chapter 5 shows you how to

- explore the area of creative writing linked to 'Me. Myself. I.' – writing about personal experiences
- understand what a Controlled Assessment task in this area is asking you to do
- develop writing from experiences you have had, or your memories of places and people.

Why is learning about this area important?

- This is one of the three areas of creative writing from which you will choose two tasks to respond to.
- The skills you develop here will feed into your other reading, writing and speaking and listening tasks and responses.

A **Grade D** candidate will

- come up with ideas but will not develop them sufficiently
- make an attempt to use key conventions but not always successfully
- use some variety in sentences, paragraphs and vocabulary but not always for a deliberate effect on the reader.

D

A **Grade C** candidate will

- convey personal feelings and impressions clearly and in a structured way
- consistently use the main conventions of creative texts suited to writing about personal experiences
- try consciously to achieve certain effects in his or her writing to interest the reader, for example through vocabulary choices
- use clear paragraphs and sentences, which are sometimes varied.

C

Prior learning

Before you begin this section, think about

- your memories of your life five and ten years ago, focusing in particular on places, people or events that stand out
- autobiographies or accounts by people (famous or not) about events from their lives

Where were you living? What was your house or flat like at the time? Who were the most important people in your life?

Try to find some and read them, if you are not familiar with any. Why/How did they make experiences interesting to other readers?

Writing about personal experiences

What does writing about personal experiences mean?

It means writing about events, people and places that have featured strongly in your life.

ACTIVITY

In a small group, take turns to tell out loud a short anecdote from your life. You must not speak for more than four minutes. It could be

- a funny or serious incident that happened to you, or which you witnessed
- something that changed how you felt about the world or other people
- a memorable meeting with someone.

When you have finished, think about your anecdote and the others you listened to. Were they all as good? Why / Why not? What made the better ones interesting? Was it what happened in the story? Or the way it was told?

ACTIVITY

- Read the autobiographical extracts on page 92 by Kathy Lette and page 14 by D H Lawrence.
- Why did these writers choose to write about these particular experiences?
- How do they bring them to life and make the experiences interesting to the reader?

ACTIVITY

Using a spider diagram, create a map of all the elements of your anecdote.

Then add the details that would make it a 'proper' story. If you wish, **embellish** them (add some details, which you can make up), like this:

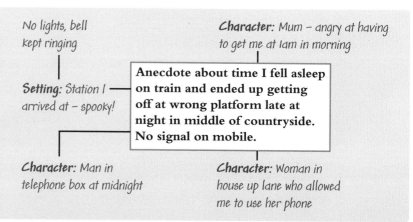

No lights, bell kept ringing

Setting: Station I arrived at – spooky!

Character: Man in telephone box at midnight

Character: Mum – angry at having to get me at 1am in morning

Anecdote about time I fell asleep on train and ended up getting off at wrong platform late at night in middle of countryside. No signal on mobile.

Character: Woman in house up lane who allowed me to use her phone

Focus for development: Losing the plot

One problem with personal stories is that you can get lost in telling the story. Events end up dominating and there's no real 'colour' to what you recount.

Here is an example from a student writing about a memorable event from his childhood.

Grade D response

> The campsite we stayed on was awful. It had no facilities and it rained nearly every day. However, it was near a river and we spent most of the time trying to cross it by building a stone bridge. This took up nearly all the holiday and it was only on the last day that we finished it. By then the river was really high. It was quite dangerous but one by one we crossed, until it was my turn.

ACTIVITY

With a partner, make some quick notes:

- How well can you picture the situation in your mind's eye? Has the writer provided enough visual detail?
- What do we find out about the other people involved?

Improve the example above by writing a paragraph with detail about the effect of the rain on the site. Start like this.

> The effect of the rain on the campsite was catastrophic. My parents' tent...

ASSESSMENT FOCUS

- Now, either take your anecdote from earlier, or choose your own memorable event from your childhood.
- Use a spider diagram to map out the key elements.

Then, for each element, write two paragraphs describing the people and the places.

Remember

- Personal anecdotes only make interesting stories if they are developed with detail.
- Focus on characterisation and place, as in a fictional story.

Writing about memorable people

What does writing about memorable people involve?

You may be asked to write about a person (or people) who made an impression on you. It could be someone you know well or have met only once in your life. Through your story or account, you will need to explain what is special about them.

Read this opening to a piece of writing by the BBC reporter, Fergal Keane, about meeting a young boy who survived the Rwandan massacres.

Glossary
genocide: killing of a large number of people from the same ethnic group or country
evaded: escaped

Like nearly every other survivor of the genocide I have met, Placide always looked away when answering questions about what had happened to him. He did not look into my face, but rather into some unreachable distance, in whose limitless spaces he seemed lost. Yes, he could tell me his story and he could remember names, dates, places and incidents. But he would not meet my eyes and so that most fundamental of human contacts evaded me through the long hour I spent with him. Later, I would find out why. But only after I had made a very foolish and hurtful mistake.

A Boy Called 'Grenade'

ACTIVITY

Discuss with a partner:

- What particular feature of Placide's behaviour does Fergal Keane choose to tell the reader about?
- Which words or phrases describe the powerful effect this has on Keane?
- In what other way does he draw the reader into his account? (Think about what he *doesn't* tell us.)

Now, write a paragraph about someone you know well, concentrating on one feature alone. (It could be how they move, dress, speak or a particular expression.)

Focus for development:
Revealing Information

With personal writing, you *know* who you are talking about, but the reader does not. Sometimes, it can be very effective to hold back information to make them want to find out more.

Read this extract from a **student** response.

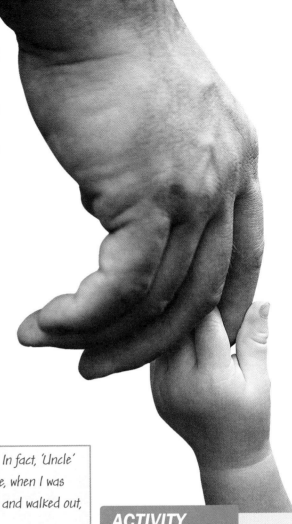

> When I was a baby it was my Uncle Joe who took me in when my father walked out. He became like a father to me, and I have him to thank for where I am today.

Now compare it with this version.

> I have known Uncle Joe all my life – literally. In fact, 'Uncle' Joe isn't really what I should call him. You see, when I was just six months old my father put on his coat and walked out, never to come back.

Both tell the same story, but the second makes the reader wait before it reveals how Joe helped.

ASSESSMENT FOCUS

Here are three possible forms that you might choose for your personal writing.

A A description of the person, looking back to when you first met them, when, where and how (like the Fergal Keane example).

B A story in which your memorable person appears and becomes the most important element.

C A letter to your friend introducing them to this person whom they are going to meet.

Choose the form that best suits the person you wish to describe and write a short plan of how you will structure your response.

ACTIVITY

Write an opening paragraph about someone you know well. Try holding back the most important thing about the person until near the end – even if it is someone like your brother or sister.

Remember

- Focus on one or two specific details or features of this person to make your description personal and real.
- Hold the reader's interest by using different ways of revealing information.
- Use what you know about the features of the form you have chosen.

Refining personal writing

Learning objectives

- To improve the way your writing is structured.
- To use symbols to interest the reader.

Examiner's tip

Look back at the poem 'Cold Knap Lake' on page 245, as an example of an older narrator reflecting on childhood memories.

What does this involve?

When you refine your writing, you use particular techniques to take it to the highest level.

Checklist for success

- You need to use contrast in your writing. For example, this might be between the immediate experience and remembering that experience.
- You need to use writing techniques like metaphors to add mystery or impact.
- You need to link paragraphs fluently with connectives.

When writing about personal or memorable experiences, you can contrast the experience itself (exciting!) with the memory of it (thoughtful). For example:

> We were ushered into the small room, and there he was – my favourite singer, my favourite person, my idol. **He took off his dark shades and I almost fainted!**
> 'What's your name, honey?' he asked.
> **Looking back**, I realise I had stars in my eyes. **I had been** blinded by the soppy records, the posters, the stories in the gossip magazines. **How could I have ever liked him?**

In the moment!

Use of tense shows things have changed

Remembering the past

Rhetorical question shows she has grown up!

ACTIVITY

Write two paragraphs in which you reflect back on a person you met or an experience which you now feel differently about, for whatever reason.

Paragraph 1: Recall the moment when you saw this person, or experienced something. For example, 'It was a summer's night when **he made fun of me…**'

Paragraph 2: Use linking connectives or different tenses to contrast your feelings now as you reflect on what happened. For example, '**However**, I now see that I **had been** following my mates…'

Focus for development: Using symbols

Often, when writers reflect on past experiences, certain items, objects or locations take on symbolic importance.

In this extract from a poem, the poet Christopher Harris recalls a flat he used to visit as a child.

> I go past his flat now and then.
> My grandad's.
> The windows look the same.
> Like old picture frames,
> Slowly rusting away.
> He's not there now, but I still stare.
> Back into my childhood.
>
> *from 'Grandad's flat'*

ACTIVITY

With a partner, make some quick notes:

- Why do you think the poet uses the symbol of the windows being 'like old picture frames'? What does he see through them?
- Is there any significance to the windows 'rusting'?

ASSESSMENT FOCUS

Write a paragraph or two about an important object or item from your past. Decide what it represents but do not spell this out in your writing. Let the reader work that out. You could describe

- the school gates of your primary or secondary school
- your favourite childhood book
- your first bike
- an item in your garden or flat or house.

For example:

> The huge iron gates (they seemed huge to me) opened up a new world; a frightening and exciting one ...

Remember

- Link a range of ideas (feelings, connections) to the memorable item or object.
- Contrast feelings using connected paragraphs.

Grade Booster

Extended Assessment Task

Using the ideas and the skills you have learned from this chapter, write a 700-word response to this task.

> *Write about a place that is memorable or has made an impact on your life for whatever reason. You can choose the form you write in that best suits what you have to say.*

Make sure you

- write vividly, bringing the place to life through wide and varied vocabulary, sentences and paragraphs
- show your past feelings and your feelings now
- keep the reader engaged by holding back information
- refine your writing through the use of symbols and metaphors.

Evaluation – What have you learned?

With a partner, use the grade checklist below to evaluate your work on the Extended Assessment Task.

- I can write a clear and well-structured creative piece based on my experiences, which uses some language devices and structures for purpose and effect.
- I can use clear, sometimes varied paragraphs and sentences.

- I can write a creative piece which mainly matches the personal writing task set and is generally accurate and clear, but is sometimes undeveloped.
- I can paragraphs and sentences, but they are not very varied, and neither is my vocabulary.

- I can write a creative piece of personal writing which answers the task set, but is not always clear in its structure or ideas.
- I can use sentences and paragraphs but with little variety.

- I can write a creative piece of personal writing but it is disorganised and does not set out my ideas clearly.
- I can write in paragraphs but they are not used properly, and my sentences are sometimes incomplete or difficult to follow.

You may need to go back and look at the relevant pages of this section again.

Controlled Assessment Preparation

In this section you will

- find out the exact facts about, and requirements of, the written element of the Controlled Assessment task: Producing Creative Texts
- read, analyse and respond to three sample answers by different candidates
- plan and write your own answer to a sample question
- evaluate and assess your answer and the progress you have made.

Why is preparation like this important?

- If you know exactly what you need to do, you will feel more confident when you do the real task.
- Looking at sample answers by other students will help you see what you need to do to improve your own work.
- Planning and writing a full sample written response after you have completed the whole chapter will give you a clear sense of what you have learned so far.

Key information

Unit 3 Section B is 'Producing Creative Texts'.

- The controlled part of the task will last **three or four hours**, and is worth **40 marks**.
- It is worth **20%** of your overall English GCSE mark.

What will the task involve?

- You have to complete **two** written tasks.
- The recommended **number of words** for the two pieces is **1400 in total**.

What does the task consist of?

You will complete two different tasks, which will have been chosen from two out of three possible areas:

- **Moving images** (writing related to moving images such as film)
- **Re-creations and prompts** (using a text or prompt to develop writing)
- **Me. Myself. I.** (writing from personal experience)

The two responses do not need to be of equal length so, for example, you might write 800 words re-creating a poem as a short story, and 600 words writing about someone who has made an impression on you. These tasks will be prepared in advance and then written in 'controlled conditions', possibly in your own classroom or the school hall over a period of up to four hours.

Here are some example tasks based on the general topic areas set by the exam board.

Moving images	Watch the first 5 to 10 minutes of a film. Using what you have seen as your inspiration, write a creative piece which aims to capture a similar atmosphere.
Re-creations and prompts	Look at the poems from the Literary Heritage section of the Anthology. Choose a poem and use it as a starting point for your own story, but write it from a different perspective from the original.
Me. Myself. I.	Write about a place that is important to you. It can be a natural space, a building, an area – your choice. The place should be the title of your writing.

The Assessment

The assessment objectives for this unit (AO3) state that you must:

- Write clearly, effectively and imaginatively, using and adapting forms and selecting vocabulary appropriate to task and purpose in ways that engage the reader.
- Organise information and ideas into structured and sequenced sentences, paragraphs and whole texts, using a variety of linguistic and structural features to support cohesion and overall coherence.
- Use a range of sentence structures for clarity, purpose and effect, with accurate punctuation and spelling.

Targeting Grade C

Some of the key differences between a Grade C and Grade D responses are as follows:

Grade C candidates	See example on pages 259–60 and 261–2
<ul><li>use a range of sentences and a varied vocabulary to maintain the reader's interest</li><li>write in clear paragraphs that link well; punctuate and spell accurately in general</li><li>demonstrate clear understanding of form and genre</li><li>develop subject matter appropriately to sustain the reader's interest</li><li>use a range of language features, such as imagery, in an attempt to have a conscious effect on the reader.</li></ul>	©C

Grade D candidates	See example on pages 257–8
<ul><li>attempt a range of sentences and use a wider vocabulary that is not always appropriately selected</li><li>use paragraphs with some sense of overall structure</li><li>use mostly accurate basic punctuation and spelling</li><li>show some basic understanding of form and genre</li><li>make some attempt to develop ideas, not always sustained or followed through</li><li>begin to use a range of language features, such as imagery.</li></ul>	D

Exploring Sample Responses

Read the extract below from a response to this 'Moving images' task

> *Watch the first 5 to10 minutes of a film. Using what you have seen as your inspiration, write a creative piece which aims to capture a similar atmosphere.*

As you read it, think about whether it is closer to a C or D grade, and why.

Consider these key elements a marker would look for:

* how well the writer has engaged the reader by creating atmosphere through his or her choice of vocabulary, language devices and other decisions about content
* a clear understanding of what makes a creative story work in terms of structure, developing ideas and detail
* accurate and, where appropriate, creative use of punctuation, sentences and paragraphing.

Example 1: Moving images
Moving image text: *Great Expectations* (1946)

Pippa Hawkins had a brother. His name was Joshua. He disappeared five years ago. She didn't know where he was. He was fishing when he disappeared and no one found his body.

So she walked by the sea always looking for him in case she got some clue or something about where he was. Cos she didn't believe he was dead because how could that happen just like that? People didn't just disappear well no one she knew anyway.

Sometimes in her house things went missing like this ring he once gave her. She lost it but she was sure she didn't lose it. It was more that she thought this ghost or something was in the house nicking stuff and she thought it might be him like those programmes on the telly when there are poltergeists that move stuff and it sends shivers down your spine, well mine anyway.

There was this time when there was the window open too and she swore someone has been in her

ctd.

room. 'No you're seeing things,' her parents said but she wasn't!!

Suddenly this person grabbed her as she was by the sea. It was completely terrifying, like a monster who had grabbed her it was so strong. She felt a pain like an electric shock in her arm. But it wasn't a monster. In fact there was a tall thin person standing right there. He had his face covered in a scarf.

'Don't say anything!' he whispered in a horrible way.

'I won't say anything,' she replied.

'Do as I say and you won't be harmed,' he said.

Then he took off the scarf. Wow! It was her brother. This was really weird. He looked older but it was definitely him. She knew her bro but she felt sick inside. Perhaps it was a ghost? But she touched him and he was real.

'Joshua. Is it really you?' she asked him.

Joshua held her by the hand.

'Yes,' he said worriedly. 'I'm dead sorry I frightened you but I was worried you would cry out and they would catch me.'

'Who would catch you?' she asked him curiously.

'It's a long story,' he replied. 'I'll tell you all about it OK?'

Examiner feedback

The candidate tells the reader far too much when he or she could have shown a lot more. Rather than give all the information about the brother at the start, this could have been held back. The style is also too informal in places ('cos', 'or something', 'dead', 'stuff', 'bro') and sometimes the 'voice' of the writer becomes too personal ('well, mine anyway'). There is some use of comparisons and the story does have an exciting moment, but much more detail on setting and atmosphere is needed, as is greater variety of sentences. Also, the slight style clumsiness, some errors of tense and punctuation ('She lost it but she was sure she didn't lose it') and the lack of linked paragraphs make the piece read unevenly.

Suggested grade: D

ACTIVITY

Rewrite the response above. Focus on the following:
- improving the general description – give more detail, use imagery and any other language techniques you think are appropriate
- removing informal chatty words or phrases
- improving sentences by adding more variety – some longer, some shorter – for effect.

Read the extract below from a student's response to this task.

> **Look at the poems from the English Literary Heritage section of the Anthology. Choose a poem and use it as a starting point for your own story, but write it from a different viewpoint from the original poem.**

As you read, look at the annotations around the text. Note down any ideas you have about what the writer does well.

Example 2: Re-creations and prompts
Poem choice: 'My Last Duchess'

Opening tells information rather than shows →

When I married the Duke I did not know what kind of man he was. He seemed kind and although much older than me he was really delighted that I would take on his famous family name.

The trouble began when we used local people to help pick the fruit from the orchards we owned outside the castle. I was bored. The Duke left me and travelled for days and all I had to **occupy** me was reading or playing the grand piano. So, one sunny afternoon in late September I **strolled** in the orchard as the workers gathered the fallen golden apples.

— Good range of vocabulary

Good short sentence for surprise →

Then I saw him. A handsome young man who was kneeling by a large, wicker basket picking the apples from the ground.

He looked up, and nodded his head.

Fits the style and tone of the story →

'**Good afternoon, your ladyship**,' he said.

I blushed **like mad**, and couldn't speak. He was about the same age as me, much younger than my husband. I turned and hurried off without a word.

A little chatty and informal – doesn't match story

My husband, the Duke, was a jealous man so I was worried that if I showed my feelings openly everyone in the village would gossip. Then my husband would find out.

ctd.

259

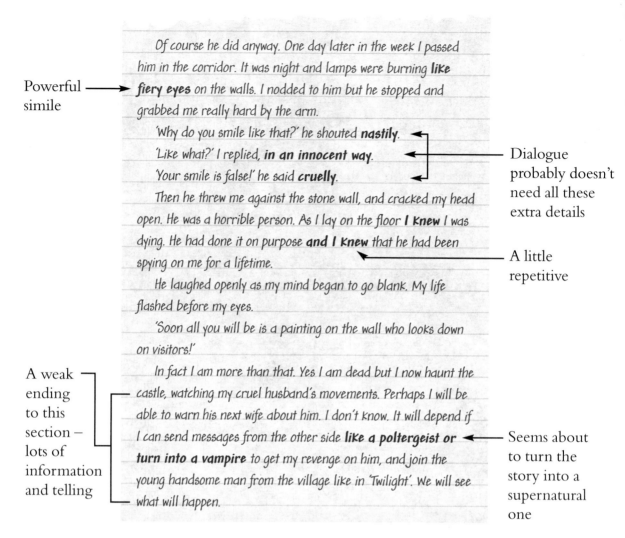

Powerful simile →

*Of course he did anyway. One day later in the week I passed him in the corridor. It was night and lamps were burning **like fiery eyes** on the walls. I nodded to him but he stopped and grabbed me really hard by the arm.*

*'Why do you smile like that?' he shouted **nastily**.*

*'Like what?' I replied, **in an innocent** way.*

*'Your smile is false!' he said **cruelly**.*

← **Dialogue probably doesn't need all these extra details**

*Then he threw me against the stone wall, and cracked my head open. He was a horrible person. As I lay on the floor **I knew** I was dying. He had done it on purpose **and I knew** that he had been spying on me for a lifetime.*

← **A little repetitive**

He laughed openly as my mind began to go blank. My life flashed before my eyes.

'Soon all you will be is a painting on the wall who looks down on visitors!'

A weak ending to this section – lots of information and telling

*In fact I am more than that. Yes I am dead but I now haunt the castle, watching my cruel husband's movements. Perhaps I will be able to warn his next wife about him. I don't know. It will depend if I can send messages from the other side **like a poltergeist or turn into a vampire** to get my revenge on him, and join the young handsome man from the village like in 'Twilight'. We will see what will happen.*

← **Seems about to turn the story into a supernatural one**

Examiner feedback

This is a clear and well-thought out response which takes the viewpoint of the murdered Duchess from the poem and tells her story. In general, the language fits the style of the piece. The story engages us as readers although the structure could have been better – the opening and ending are both a little weak, telling us rather than showing us what happens – but the way the characters are described is excellent. There are some good uses of language: the 'fiery eyes' of the lamps, the varied vocabulary and the range of short and long sentences for effect. Overall, an atmospheric piece of writing whose structure needs further work.

Suggested grade: low C

ACTIVITY

Re-write the last paragraph of the response, removing the references to vampires and poltergeists. You could describe

- how you will move around the castle
- the places and rooms you will watch over
- the next young woman whom the Duke pursues. Do you try and warn her about him?

Read the following student response to this task.

> **Write about a place that is important to you. It can be a natural space, a building, an area – your choice. The place should be the title of your writing.**

As you read, look at the annotations around the text. Note down any ideas you have about what the writer does well.

Example 3: Me. Myself. I.

The Colonnade

Good start to describe setting →

Made of solid concrete, the colonnade was a soul-less place in winter with its café closed, and the deck-chairs stacked away behind closed doors. Usually on a winter's day only a few brave walkers with their dogs went along the promenade.

But for us, on summer evenings, it was the place to be. The place where we met, laughed, joked – like a second home **I spose**. ← Too informal

Good use of question to engage reader →

Why was it so special to me back then? Well, I didn't have my own room at home, and had to share with my little brother so I really wanted a place where I could meet my friends. The colonnade was ideal. On summers' nights we would nick the deck-chairs and put them in a circle, and just listen to music. The beach was only a few feet away, so often we'd muck around in the still cold sea (it was England!).

Good use of simile

One time, Simon (my best friend) and I dared each other to swim to the nearest buoy. The waves were **pounding like boxers** on the shoreline, and there was lots of stormy weather on the way I reckon.   ctd.

261

> We were both strong swimmers, but the current was even stronger **like** ← Another
> **a magnet** and halfway there we gave up and turned back. Both of us felt   good image
> the same moment of panic. Our friends were too far away to hear us call,
> and the lifeguards had all gone home. We encouraged each other as the
> waves **churned** around us and the storm began. Thank god, we made it
> to the shore. We lay on our backs staring at the sky panting and laughing.
> But to tell the truth we had been frightened **a lot. We will never do it** ← Tense is
> **again.**   wrong here
>
> Simon has moved away now. His dad got some job up north so I don't
> see him, though we keep in contact through Facebook and text each other
> from time to time.
>
> Funnily enough, I don't go the Colonnade any more. It's like I have
> outgrown it. There are other, younger teenagers there now – I even saw
> my younger brother with his friends. The council have also opened the
> café all year round and repainted the concrete. Now it's all sparkling and
> trendy, and at night-time, more people walk along the promenade, not
> just men with their dogs!
>
> **To me it will never be the same again.** There were probably
> moments when we sat around bored and with nothing to say to each
> other. But I only remember the good times.
>
> Yesterday I walked down to the beach with our dog. But I don't take
> him near the colonnade. When we get to the front by the big nursing home
> I go in the opposite direction. It's like I do and I don't want to remember
> which is **kind of weird** but I wonder if my brother will have the same
> memories as me as he gets older?

Vocabulary choice is precise (annotation pointing to *churned*)

Weak expression (annotation pointing to *a lot*)

Structurally good end as writer reflects on the meaning of the experience (annotation pointing to *To me it will never be the same again*)

A bit informal (annotation pointing to *kind of weird*)

Examiner feedback

This is a good response which paints a detailed picture of an important place for the writer. There is detailed and varied vocabulary and some good imagery ('like a magnet') and the sentences are varied for effect ('We never did it again').

The change in the way the writer sees the place – as it was when he went there, and how he sees it now – is also conveyed well and we get a real sense of the writer's personal feelings when he talks about his younger brother and his friend moving away. These little details engage the reader.

Finally, the structure is excellent. Perhaps at one point he gets a little confused with his use of tenses, mixing up his memories of the swim with the actual moment, but the ending is very well written and links to the start.

Suggested grade: C

EXTENDED PRACTICE TASK

Re-creations and prompts

The other day I walked past the house for the first time since that summer. On the outside it looked the same, but I knew it was empty, and why they had left.

Use this as the starting point for a story of your own.

If you only do five things...

1 Read a range of creative texts, especially short stories, and note the ways that the best writers interest and engage you.

2 Where appropriate, plan for original ideas and different perspectives on the task set: this will make the reader sit up and take notice. Also, develop detailed ideas so that any ideas or scenes you describe can be taken further.

3 Draw on what you know about the conventions of story-telling, but be flexible in order to make an impact on the reader, for example by holding back information to keep the reader's interest or build suspense.

4 Use a wide range of vocabulary, sentences and paragraph types and don't forget to check the accuracy of your spelling and punctuation.

5 Use devices such as similes and metaphors to make your writing come alive.

ACKNOWLEDGEMENTS

The publishers gratefully acknowledge the permission granted to reproduce the copyright material in this book. While every effort has been made to trace and contact copyright holders, where this has not been possible the publishers will be pleased to make the necessary arrangements at the first opportunity.

Chapter 1 p7 'Nobody's Safe' article from *Reveal Magazine* 2009 published by Nat Mags; p8 Mykonos extract from *The Greek Islands: Eyewitness Travel Guide* published by Dorling Kindersley; p9 'After the rain, here comes The Sun' *The Sun*, 25 November, 2009 © NI Syndications. Reprinted with permission; p10 'Bolt 100m Record is beaten by a cheetah' *Metro*, 11th September, 2009. Reprinted with permission of Solo Syndication; p11 Potato Lovers Hate Waste advert. Reprinted with kind permission of WRAP www.wrap.org.uk; p12 screenshot from Club 18-30 website. Reprinted with kind permission of Thomas Cook Group PLC; p13 extract from a leaflet for Best Western Wroxton House Hotel, Banbury, Oxfordshire. Reprinted with kind permission; p15 extract from 'Roman Pavlyuchenko and Jermain Defoe leave it late to break Burnley hearts' by Henry Winter, 21 January, 2009 www.telegraph.co.uk. Reprinted with permission; p17 Dolland & Aitchison leaflet (this leaflet is out of date). Reproduced with kind permission of Boots Opticians; p18 short extracts from *Don'ts For Husbands* by Blanche Ebbutt, A & C Black 2007. Reprinted with permission; p19 article by Linda Robson from *Bella Magazine* 2009 published by Bauer; p20 'Arctic Gets Hotter' from the *Daily Mirror*, 5th September, 2009 pg 31. Reprinted with permission of Mirrorpix; p25 The Herta magazine ad is reproduced with the kind permission of Societe des Produits Nestle S. A.; p26 extract courtesy of *The Times*, 29 July 2009 © NI Syndications; p29-30 article from *Wakefield Express* 2009; p33 article by Richard White from *The Sun* Nov 2009; p34-35 extract and book cover image from *The Bookseller of Kabul* by Asne Seierstad published by Virago, part of Little Brown; p37 'Have you got money flu?' *Cosmopolitan*, January 2008. Reprinted with permission of The National Magazine Company; p39 'Shoptalk, Glamazon? I think not' *Mirror*, 25th November, 2009. Reprinted with permission; p40 cover of Leeds United Programme 2009 published by Leeds United; p41 Cover of *Sky Sports Magazine* October 2009. Reprinted with permission; p44 SPC Nature's Finest advert. Reprinted with permission of SPC Ardmona Operations Limited, Australia; p47 short extract from 'The dog that nearly drowned' from THE LONG HARD ROAD by Ron Hill, Ron Hill Sports Ltd 1981. Copyright © Ron Hill. Reprinted with kind permission of the author; p48 article from Walk on the Wild Side by James Parry from *Daily Express* 2009; p49 Rainforest SOS advert. Reprinted with permission of The Prince's Rainforests Project; **Chapter 2** p76 reproduced from charity leaflet with the permission of Save the Children UK © All rights reserved; p77 charity leaflet courtesy of Age Concern; p92 short extracts from 'To Groom or not to groom' by Kathy Lette, *Good Housekeeping*, August 2009. This was written by Kathy Lette, author of ten best-selling novels. Reprinted with permission; **Chapter 4** p193 'The Monkey's Paw' by WW Jacobs courtesy of Society of Authors; pp 204, 205 extracts from *Of Mice and Men* by John Steinbeck published by Penguin Books 2000 Copyright © John Steinbeck 1937, 1965. Reprinted with permission of Penguin Books and Curtis Brown Limited; p214 'Praise Song for my mother' by Grace Nichols from *The Fat Black Woman's Poems* published by Virago part of Curtis Brown; p216 'Thoughts on my father' by James Berry published by Fractured Circles; **Chapter 5** p245 'Cold Knap Lake' by Gillian Clarke courtesy of Gillian Clarke; p250 A Boy called 'Grenade' by Fergal Keane from *Letters Home* published by Penguin 1999.

The publishers would like to thanks the following for permission to reproduce pictures in these pages:

Advertising Archive: p35; **Alamy:** pp62, 64, 67, 107, 110, 118, 127, 139, 150a, 150b, 162, 167a, 167b, 173, 183, 207, 211, 228, 236, 245; **Alton Towers Resort:** p115; **BBC:** p152b; **Bridgeman Art Library:** pp178 'London', plate 38 from 'Songs of Experience', 1794 (colour printed etching with w/c), Blake, William (1757-1827) / Yale Center for British Art, Paul Mellon Collection, USA / The Bridgeman Art Library, 179 Portrait of William Blake (1757-1827) Leaning Forward, 1820 (pencil on paper), Linnell, John (1792-1882) / Fitzwilliam Museum, University of Cambridge, UK / The Bridgeman Art Library; **Cavendish Press:** p43b; **Corbis:** pp19, 75, 79; **Getty Images:** pp23, 43a, 55, 112, 113, 114, 116, 120, 123, 132, 141, 145, 157; **iStockphoto:** pp10, 12, 13, 37, 38, 44, 69a, 69b, 72a, 72b, 74, 76, 77, 78, 82, 85, 86, 87a, 87b, 90, 92, 93, 95a, 95b, 97a, 97b, 98, 100, 101, 108, 124, 125a, 125b, 134, 136, 140, 148b, 148c, 151a, 151b, 170a, 170b, 192, 195, 199, 200, 209, 214, 230, 238, 239, 243; **Mary Evan's Picture Library: pp**21, 180; **Movie Store Collection**: p160; **North News and Pictures**: p7cl; **News Team International**: p7tr; **PA Photos**: p7br; **Photolibrary**: pp2, 66, 83, 91; **Rex Features:** pp14, 26 (Kelly Hancock/UCF), 50 (Ray Tang), 89, 118 (CSU/Arhcv/Everett), 122 (Steve Hill), 130, 144 (c.20thC.Fox/Everett), 147a, 147b (c.20thC.Fox/Everett), 148 (Alastair Muir), 152 (Brian J. Ritchie), 158 (Giuliano Bevilacqua), 164, 169 (Courtesy Everett Collection), 182 (c.W.Disney/Everett Collection), 184 (ITV), 186 (ITV), 190 (Courtesy Everett Collection), 216a (ITV), 216b (ITV); **Ronald Grant Archive**: p194; **Shutterstock**: pp8, 219, 224, 226, 231, 237, 247.